THE ALBIGEN PAPERS

RICHARD ROSE

The
Albigen Papers

This book is published by the Pyramid Press under the auspices of the TAT Foundation.

The Albigen Papers. Copyright 1973 by Richard Rose. Printed in the United States of America. All rights reserved. No part of this book may be reproduced or used in any manner whatsoever without written permission, except in the case of brief quotations embodied in critical articles and reviews. For information, address The Pyramid Press, 1686 Marshall Street, Benwood, West Virginia 26031.

Library of Congress Catalog Card Number: 75-2784.

Original Edition published in 1973, second edition 1975, third edition 1978.

Acknowledgements

Without the help of many others, this book would never have happened.

Robert Cergol
August Turak
Jeanne Mascara
Lynda Cronin
Dan Russel, Art work

Members of the TAT Society

Contents

       Foreword   9
       Introduction   11

FIRST PAPER
Social Illusions

Universal Practice of Deception—The Legal Fraud—Semantics   13

SECOND PAPER
Psychology and the Truth

Psychological Evaluation—A Look at the Mind—The Mind: Some Observations—Romance and Terminal Cases   35

THIRD PAPER
The Veil of Maya

Theological Evaluation—Search for God—Life After Death   63

FOURTH PAPER
On Gurus and Unique Systems

Cults—Yoga—Magic—The Kabbalah—Gurdjief and Ouspensky   99

FIFTH PAPER
Obstacles to Transcendental Efforts

Argument for Transcendental Research—The Curse of Intellectualism—The Self as an Obstacle—Oblique Dogmatic Systems—The Trap of Conditioning—States of Perception—States of Mind—Summary of Blocks—List of Obstacles   137

SIXTH PAPER
The First Steps

The Self—Progression—Friendship and the Search   179

SEVENTH PAPER
Discernment
Laws—Milk From Thorns								193

EIGHTH PAPER
Maximum Reversal System
Three Steps in Using the Maximum Reversal Technique—More Attempts at Verbalization				215

The Three Books of the Absolute
An Account of an Experience							229

*This book is dedicated to the Group,
A gathering of mostly young people
who with their Faith, will bring Hope
to many more.*

Foreword

There are probably two groups of people who will pick up *The Albigen Papers*. One group will consist of those relatively unacquainted with the nuances of spiritual work. To these people, curiosity, or the feeling that something is missing from their lives, will be their prime motivation. In short, the question these people are asking Mr. Rose is, Why? Why is spiritual work a reasonable solution to my philosophical and personal problems? What do spiritual endeavors have that science, psychology, and religion lack? Why should I put time and energy into something that is nebulous, paradoxical, and denounced by "authority" as being, at best, superstition?

The second group of readers belongs to a different mode of inquiry. To these people the questions of "Why?" have been answered by a careful process utilizing the functions of reason and intuition. These are the people who have been tantalized and inspired by the writers of esoteric works. They have read the accounts of enlightenment, and deep within themselves they feel the need to tread the same path. But close on the heels of inspiration are the seeds of despair. For as book after book has been read and put aside the inquirer soon learns that instructions on how to seek are much less common than the urging to seek. In this way a definite question is formed. The question is "How?" How can I order my life for the optimal spiritual gain? How do I find a group where real work is going on? What are the yardsticks for judging systems, teachers, and the like? How do I begin to become?

It is within the context of the answers to the reader's questions that the uniqueness and immense scope of *The Albigen Papers* are brought into proportion. For Richard Rose has spent his life in the search for Reality, and the difficulty he had in finding meaningful answers and guidance is still fresh in his mind. He too, had to wade through the mountain of conflicting opinions and confusion, that has been passed off as esoteric wisdom down through the ages. In writing this book, he has sincerely tried to abridge years of painstaking esoteric research; and through intuition and common sense, Mr. Rose tries to lay out for his reader the kernel of his experience. In doing so, he gives the reader some of the directives, warnings and admonitions that he himself never had. Through all of this he clearly manages to keep track of the reader's head and the twin questions of "How?" and "Why?"

The first half of the book is directed at the mind of the person who asks "Why?" In this section Rose ably strips from life the illusory garnish that keeps people slaving away in useless and vain attempts to prove their own egocentric importance. In a limited number of words Mr. Rose points out the inadequacies of the sacred cows of the modern world, and in so doing, manages to hold out the hope of something more through a determined course of self-analysis. This is the great positive overtone, that takes what might have been a mere critique, and instead provides the groundwork for a system of retreat from error that is the thesis of the second half of the book.

The second half of the book has a narrower, but in many ways more urgent scope. It is here that we truly begin to reap the harvest of Rose's lifelong search—first for the Truth, and then for ways and means of transmitting the Truth. Here are the answers to the sincere seekers of method—those who ask "How?" Again we see the ability of Rose to pass over the insignificant and catchy aspects of spiritual work, and instead to concentrate his attention on the pragmatic details of a highly abstract and individual subject. As for proof, Rose candidly points out that this system "worked for me, and in my lifetime."

Yet it seems to me that I have missed, probably, the strongest point of the book. Richard Rose manages to bring a sense of personal advice into the pages of *The Albigen Papers* not often evinced by writers of our day. There is a sincerity and ingenuousness about the book that produces in our minds a picture of the man himself and his dedication to his work.

Finally, Rose, in the last section of the book entitled *The Three Books of the Absolute*, tries to transmit to the reader a literary and intuitive sense of the complete spiritual experience Rose had at the age of thirty-two. Nowhere else have I found such a personalized spiritual experience rendered so effectively.

Richard Rose's book, then, emerges not only as a blueprint for a spiritual search, but rather as a complete picture of a man, his life, and his experience.

August F. Turak

Introduction

The aim of this book is to approach reality. As for reality, I do not define it in the usual materialistic sense. And, of course, I hope for a cumulative appreciation of reality as we travel from one chapter to another. I entertain the premise that all premises are vanity, and yet hope for some evolution through the vanity of words.

In other words, to start off with the premise that man is that which he thinks he is, would be to begin with incomplete knowledge, and to pursue a course of thinking that would not bring any degree of enlightenment, but instead would encourage us down the greasy path of wishful thinking.

We cannot launch ourselves into the world of the mind from a platform of fairy tale make-believe, unless we wish to land in Alice's wonderland. Too many of us for instance, are glib with God-definitions, and yet we know little or nothing on the subject, let alone, a precise definition. It might be a good idea to begin with a topic not so far removed, namely our self. And if we wish to know ourselves, we should not be prepared to settle for a definition that only involves evident mechanical parts, such as arms, legs, senses, et cetera. And the structure of our thinking must not be weakened by sophistry, wishful thinking, fear, or fatigue.

Let us take for observation, not some conceptualization for which our mind has no hope of solution or understanding, but let us take observation itself and analyze it. Let us look at the looker—and his observation processes.

Let us avoid undefined terms. Let us work with the idea that things can be said simply, and yet with some sort of system, methodicity, and common sense. This business of self-study is not new, so let us look at a few blueprints, to see if there is any message in their inconsistencies, inconsistencies both within the blueprints themselves, and in relation to the other blueprints of authority.

Let us find ways and means for checking our computers, while our computers are checking the grand project. We must learn to look for short-circuits, blocks, component-exhaustion, power-shunts, and the "haywire" mental bedlam that happens when foreign entities try to nest in the delicate wires.

It is true that this book covers a wide spectrum and that the first chapters have more obvious implications than the ensuing ones. The obviousness of the truth of the later chapters, may be better recognized, if the first four chapters are understood.

The first half of the book is projected as a sort of clearing out of the underbrush before planting. And this first half, being a sort of corrosive analysis, may be interpreted as destructive criticism alone. However, the main purpose of this book should reach a compensatory stage in the second half of the book, in dealing with *cosmic consciousness* as the ultimate reality.

There is an excessive amount of modesty emanating from most authors who write on the subject of *cosmic consciousness* or *satori*. I think that most of this modesty is just another attempt to be mysterious about a subject which may invite challenges about the author's knowledgeability. In short, it has been the custom of many writers on occult or transcendental matters who had only hearsay knowledge of those subjects, to infer that they dare not tell all.

There is no curse on the proferring of wisdom, or in the transmission of directions to states of being. There is, of course, a sort of automatic door which all readers close upon themselves, depending upon the degree of their capacity in that given direction.

I have repeatedly encountered the catch words that say, in effect, that a man who knows does not speak, and that he who speaks does not know. This dictum can be ignored. It can be lumped with the many slogans employed to conceal a speaker's ignorance or motives. It is a good screen for camouflaging a book that tells little but a mysterious story.

There was a time, prior to the turn of the century, when you dared not divulge an interest in even such harmless things as ESP or hypnosis, under threat of the rack or stake. Secrecy and symbolism were used to avoid trouble. And they are still used under the pretence of danger. I have met several other men who have experienced *cosmic consciousness,* and none wrote books about it, mainly because it is a difficult subject to encompass justly—especially when you have witnessed, not only the vanity of words, but also the vanity of life.

On the other hand, we do know that from Buddha downward to the present time, there are men who did talk about their knowledge of *satori,* or it would not have been transmitted. It is my belief that *satori-systems* flourished only in the monasteries in previous centuries, because monasteries were possible. In the western world, most of the monks are leaving the monasteries, and are going forth to mingle their perspiration with functional politics, in a vain new, animal-man and man-god religion. There are no quiet places left, it seems, for finding the peaceful breath of reality. And with this fear in mind, it is better that something be written. The chances for making personal contacts for spiritual purposes are inversely proportional to the density and madness of the population.

FIRST PAPER
Social Illusions

All of us are able to note discrepancies more quickly in our neighbor than in ourselves. And yet we listen to our leaders, whether they are politicians, social lions, psychologists, sociologists or ministers as they point out the discrepancies in their opponents . . . and we accept them, without bothering to look for discrepancies in the language of those same leaders. We are impelled by egotism to have great confidence in our ability to have picked the side of Truth, without noticing that millions of other people of opposite belief have equal conviction.

Sometimes, we are carried away to the point of murder. Or we are killed with our own cliches. We become so bloated with egotism that we puff up and float away into never-never-land, and not even our loved ones can rescue us. We denounce drug-addiction, and yet we are all addicted, and equally as dangerous as the drug-addict.

Let us, in this work, look at ourselves. Is it possible to understand the self? We wish to know. Not factual data. We wish, at this point, to experience the true state of being of the universe, and man's actual relationship to it. We wish to know man. We start with ourselves, and learn that we must find that part of man which is real, and that which is not. We are trying to find reality. And these things are difficult for robots, and even more difficult is it for robots to accept from any other robot, the alarming message that they are robots, and that such an informer might, by some chance, take over and run the robot's computer.

We must employ a bit of tightrope walking, hairsplitting and shadow watching. We begin this adventure by focusing the attention—by thinking. We notice the bigotry of science, yet we must attempt to be scientific or logical in our approach to the matter. However, we are absolved, if further along the path we discover that in order to appreciate or realize reality we must transcend logic. We are absolved, if for no other reason, than for facilitating this, the first step away from ignorance. We may never be guaranteed to experience the Absolute, but at least may be gratified by being able to abandon fragments of illusions in thinking, and gain hope of greater release from a state of conceit profitting for us a mountain of nothingness. Or still better, we may gain confidence enough to climb another mountain, and profit from the expanding reality we find at thin air, and pure air levels.

We must ride the wild horns of the paradox, all the way. Since this experiential world is one of polarity, no frontal assault on Truth is possible for us.

This book may seem largely controversial. The main theme to be remembered here, is that we shall approach Truth by retreating from untruth. By truth, I mean, that which is most likely among different attitudes or evidences. By untruth I mean the least likely. By Truth, which I capitalize for emphasis on the difference, I mean—the absolute state of being. For instance, let us say that when we describe coal as being black, we speak the truth. It is, however, only relative truth, as are all things appraised by the bicameral, sensory brain. Another fellow may come along and indicate that we suffer from retinal illusion, and convince us that coal is not black but colorless. We then ask ourselves, if our eyes, our most important contact with the world, deceive us—is it not then possible that more of the objective world than we wish to admit, is adjusted to our comprehensive faculty by nature, rather than exactly understood by the mind.

We become adjusted and we think that we walk in wisdom. Adjustment may be extolled for temporal contentment, but the contented cows in the dairy are allowed their contentment only as long as their vegetative machinery holds up. Their real purpose may be the dairyman's comfort or food. Therefore we must take a second look at many of the philosophical and psychological works which we instinctively accept as being logical and truthful.

It is important to have harmonious relations with our fellow-man. Conventionality has its place. However, when looking into the nature of things, we should not allow a system of social conduct to become the yardstick for all our thinking. For instance, the psychiatrist is supposed to be a doctor of the psyche who employs all the scientific data to date about the mind, to cure the mind of its ills, or to aid the mind. He is, in reality, something of a veterinarian, interested mostly in the habits of vegetating humans, and in the adjustment of those humans to the rules of the local dairy-herd. Religion finds itself adjusting to the mood of the times, instead of adjusting man to the Truth. The psychiatrist's therapy is not aimed at making man a better man, but a better running robot. They try to check the circuits in the computer so that the robot will do its work better, but not be a thinker of more clarity.

Are we only insignificant cows in a dairyman's herd? Are we still citizens of Babel, foolishly building a pyramid of words and sciences in the vain belief that we can transcend the earth with our own computers? Or is it possible that man's hunger for definition and individuality may some day be recognized? When we see our most determined efforts toward Truth being turned against us, we may even suspect that we are being watched by the dairyman, so that we may not rebel against our stanchions. Psychology and transcendentalism came into being, because man felt that religion had already been pretzled hopelessly contrary to the enlightenment of man. The transcendentalist followed the devotee, but he too became quickly infected with venality and divergence. Psychology was the first movement that undertook to understand man by observing the seemingly unobservable mind of man. It started in the right direction—the essence of man—but it too has succumbed to a sort of venality, and to a vanity of a priestcraft tolerated by the herd-government.

The Soviet psychiatrist will not advise you similarly to the American psychiatrist. Therefore, truth has a geographical condition. Man has been a pathetic creature, down through the ages. Each mass-effort, and each individual effort, to break the barriers of ignorance, has been thwarted... so that it seems as if heaven is plotting against him. Paradoxically, it may not be so. Perhaps we are overlooking something. Our desire for Truth need not deny us the possibility of individuality and immortality. We should try everything and anything, study every cult and cultist—look under every rock, if necessary. God may be under the next one, truly.

How many of us are there, who profess that we would desire to know the Truth, whether or not that knowing be tangible or absolute, yet who would shrink timidly (before the journey into Truth is half begun) before the nakedness of some previously unnoticed disclosures about the relative world. Too many of us are like the spinster who refused to disrobe because she considered a naked body to be sinful.

Let us pause and ask ourselves what we are. Are we truly the semi-divine creatures that we might imagine ourselves to be? Or are we beasts, according to our own definitions and standards? An article was published recently by an expert on jungle life which indicated that we were in some ways, worse than beasts. He pointed out, that of all the animals, we were the most internecine. The jungle animal may snarl and strike out in competition, but after a little sparring about, the weaker of the two retreats and leaves the prize to the stronger. The weaker is not foolhardy, nor is the stronger one revengeful. There are very few fights to the death among animals of the same kind.

Most of mankind's conviction about human divinity comes from man's looking downward, not upward. He endows himself with superlatives because he witnesses other inferior beings. However, man's ideas of divinity are somehow tied to morality, and most animals (excepting those who have lived too close to man, and those who resemble man) have better morals than humans. In a sort of hypocritical dignity man enacts legislation, affirming the immorality of non-pregnating sex practices. Yet statisticians such as Kinsey and Stoeckel tell us that the majority of all humans ignore this legislation, some secretly, some openly.

Who is it that casts this image that man is innately and irrevocably divine? Where lie the roots of this farcical pretence into which man thrusts his children generation after generation, century after century, and which is accepted so blindly that it has become highly offensive not to embrace the farce in its entirety? The implement that nature uses to bring about this perennial dream of divinity is the human ego. The pretence of divinity is fruitful for the young females who affect innocence, virtue, and beauty, or what-have-you. All are prompted to pose. Then somewhere along the line, with mutual back-scratching agreed upon, the play-acting becomes law. Language expedited the making of a complex drama from what was perhaps previously only a dull biological existence.

Little did the aborigine, who first adorned himself or herself with a feather or bone, realize the revolution that he caused. Nor is man in general, yet aware that our billion dollar cosmetic industry is the result of acts committed by primitive ancestors who found a thrill in pretence. We look further and wonder how much excessive toil and bloodshed resulted from the encouragement of this same love of pretence in other fields.

Feathers from the rear of a bird gave dignity to the brow of a chief, who in turn made a back-scratching deal with a witch-doctor. . . and thus perhaps our complex society was started.

At heart, each man is a killer, a thief, and a rapist. Yet he shows his teeth in a smile. He has learned to steal artfully, and his frustrations at being unable to express himself with true masculine aggressiveness has resulted in a creature (according to Kinsey) that is inverted, perverted and bestial. And as a result, his women have become—in their hunger for genuine male relationship—lesbians, fetish-lovers, and nymphomaniacs.

And where did all of this start? It started with the game of make-believe. Three daubs of blue and a bone in the nose makes one a member of the local medical association. And society was taxed to support him. Then came titles for the chief, for his son, for his queen, and for his favorite flunkies. Each found a feather-arrangement peculiar to his station. Then came the rituals that swelled the chests and egos, and impressed the slaves. Prostration before the chief, and a salute for his generals. Next came deification. The chief could do no wrong. The witch-doctor also became infallible, and we trust that the natives enjoyed the game as much as we do today.

Perhaps there came a day when the natives became restless, and tired of the game. Like children playing "house", too many were given insignificant roles, and their little egos hungered for some of the inflation. The chiefs saw that this would be a job for the generals if the witch-doctors could not handle it. But the witch-doctors responded to the occasion. They made everybody important by discovering the gods. The gods took some of the significance from the chiefs, which gave them a bloodless revenge. The gods, in turn, through the mouth of the witch-doctors, told them to obey the chief. Thus the generals no longer bore the name of executioner, but of a noble hunter. The innate urge to let blood was vented only on strangers. This further insured the sleep of the chief and of his generals, when they were at home.

The first gods were pulled fresh from the hat, with little imagination. The sun remained as a god for many centuries, because the theologians were accepted as specialists, and they were dealing with simple people. When contributions slackened, they discovered new gods. And when language found an alphabet, the need for pattern thinking arose. Now new gods arose with more meaningful names. One of the early abstract gods was Jod. This was a personification of the male regenerative principle. Theology evolved and was improved. However, the improvement was dictated by pressuring kings and high priests. In time the village chief had grown a gold crown, and the witch-doctor had traded his nose-bone for a tiara or mitre. The natives, now no longer amused or intimidated by god-stories, were now given individual godhood. The witch-doctor decided that each had a little piece from God, and it was called a soul.

The natives, once again were thoroughly frightened. But many of the chiefs or kings were convinced that their souls were more important than their gold, and the shamans in the long robes wound up with much pillage. Incidentally, a study of witch-doctors in Africa, medicine-men among the American Indians, and the shamans of Mongolia, uncovered evidence that all of them had a common denominator—they were mostly homosexual. There is no intention here to evaluate this, as to whether homosexuality abets psychic prowess, or whether witch-doctoring became the only haven for misfits. It is noteworthy, for the researcher to observe the tendency among high priests to wear long robes, and while pretending this to be a mark of modesty, to decorate these robes with sequins, gold braid, embroidery, and even jewels.

Again, I wish to insist that this is not an attack upon churches, but upon the ignorance and vanity of man. This by no means implies that man does not have a soul, but indicates rather the gradual evolvement of the soul idea. A very good reference on the matter is Frazer's *Golden Bough*.

We now return to the sequence of evolutionary steps in religion. That which we now call civilization, was emerging. The function of the witch-doctor became split. The next to appear on the scene were the high priest and the physician. The world of make-believe was growing. The men of specialty, naturally studied their parts, and a few of the actors became interested enough in their parts to quit acting and devote their time to study. Still, to this day, most men of specialty are mostly actors.

During that period of European history when the high priests over-awed the kings, when the divinity of man was most loudly proclaimed, and when man was exhorted to reflect the kindly and loving nature of God in man's relations to his fellow-man—then did the worst savagery of man break forth. And the high priests led the blood-bath, like their ancestral witch-doctors. The urge to kill is strongest in the animal that has the least to fear. The high priests were now the strongest. Their heads were so bloated with convictions of their own celestiality that they never dreamed that they would automatically revert to jungle-instincts. They found excuses to kill their own people who did not pay tribute to their churches. Then they allowed their celibate imaginations to devise instruments of torture. They burned women and children at the stake. A frustrated and impotent priesthood found satisfaction in impaling the helpless. Next, another theological trend began, away from the abstract realms of Aquinas and other manufacturers of invisible cloth. The trend was headed for materialistic thinking—toward science, metaphysics and occultism. Perhaps the high priests in the old dogmatic eras thought that they were preaching the truth, or creating truth through faith, but theirs was really a period of forgetting. . . forgetting their animal nature and the ever-present egos that invariably colored their dogma. Their efforts to impose a dream may have sprung from noble intentions. However, the natives can be roused from an imposed dream, if the dream becomes a nightmare.

Now our civilization is becoming increasingly complex, our make-believe has myriad ramifications. Our theologies have become more subtle, but they still compromise with the powers that control the populace, and religion had retreated, becoming now little more than a social emollient. We no longer put bones in our noses, although the female still wears rings in her ears and feathers in her hat. And we still have a massive form of mutual back-scratching in this system of make-believe. And it grows more absurd, daily. We now have church groups which are organizing and lobbying, not for control, but for a piece of the action—for recognition as being functionally important to the state. Churches (and police fraternities) campaign, not to disseminate the truth, but to ban certain movies that detract from their image and dignity.

Each profession paints a nice picture of itself, but it would be illuminating to see figures on percentages of crimes committed by policemen, to find the percentage of mentally unstable people among the ranks of psychologists and psychiatrists, and to find the percentage of thieves and alcoholics among the members of the legal profession.

It may shock us to be reminded that a uniformed, cold-blooded killer is recognized as a brave man. Yet how much braver is the lone, fratricidal killer, who has neither the protection of his government or his friends, and is comforted only by his solitary conviction as he goes about his killing. It will shock us to know that women, once they have decided to kill, are more vicious than men. And children, trying to be honest, will even kill their parents. Society utilizes children, as soon as they are able to bear arms, knowing about their immunity to fear and adult inhibitions.

When we walk down a busy street, let us look about us. We see charming people, seemingly. Actually, we are inspired by people posing. The beautiful starlet, on the stage or street may seem to be the epitome of tenderness, gentility and innocence. But give her a few hundred thousand dollars and her masculinity will transcend her feminine nature. She will buy and sell husbands, she will abort unwanted children, and often die in the process. And her lust will eventually find the headlines of every paper in the world. The quickest catalyst for changing the intended nature of woman, whether she be a housewife or a queen, is power. She is innately hostile, having this mechanism built in to protet her young. It is not uncommon to sink teeth into the male mate. Of course this is a trait of all mammals, whose instinct is to protect the litter, even from the male. The human female is more prone to neglect or destroy the litter, than the animal, because she is more prone to vanity. She finds her maternal instincts confused by vanity.

Let us take another look at the street. We see fancy food-stores that sell ersatz foodstuffs. We see libraries that pose as truth-factories, but wherein controversial books are banned to the researcher. We see automobile display-rooms where vehicles are sold for the curve of their fenders, but not for the worth of their motors or gears. We find acres of floor space for haberdashery and women's apparel, but we may search for a week to find a sensible clothing item. Sturdy building facades have been replaced by enameled tin, glass and plastic. Frustrated maternal and paternal instincts are evidenced by the many solicitous adults seen curbing their dogs. The corner peddler of nostrums is gone, replaced by loudspeakers and neon lights on the drug store. The brokerage houses go about their business with a fearful dignity, posing paper empires as monolithic structures—which in reality are eroded by simple rumor, buffeted easily by winds of chance, and can be sent tumbling by psychological factors not fairly understood by even the most masterful wizards of brokerage alchemy. We see furniture and appliance stores whose business-life is inversely proportional to the life of their products.

We now go to the professional people. A professional man is noted for his reluctance to speak. He proudly indicates this to be a mark of wisdom, but we know well that he does not dare to open his mouth before too many people, until he has become skilled in saying nothing with many words. Even the specialists are inadequate, and they also substitute the act (the farce) for actuality.

But we say, still, that people are basically good, and that there is progress from all of this ego-prompted civilization. And in between our most savage and internecine wars we advance in culture and improve our living conditions. And man also continues to lose sight of himself. People like to be told that they are good. It flatters their egos to be seen in church. It makes them feel very tall to stoop with a nickel toward the beggar's hat, or to write a check for a charity if the amount is deductible. Talleyrand once stated that words were invented to disguise or conceal meaning. So our acts are often carefully planned to build a certain public picture for the actor.

The lover charms the mate before beating her. The salesman is charming to an almost hypnotic degree while promoting a nearly worthless product. How often must Pollyanna be ravished before she settles for common sense, and abandons her make-belief? When are we strong enough or tired enough to see the nonsense of it all? And when will we be determined enough to try to sort some truth from the jumble of evidence available?

Do not think that only a small percentage of men are motivated by primitive drives. And do not think while admitting most men to be primitive, that you are not—just because you dropped a nickel in the collection basket, or because you were the actor carrying the basket. Our kindness is a mask, and our smile is not too much more meaningful than a similar gesture by an opossum or hyena. It means, stand still, and do not struggle while I bite you, or put the bite on you.

We are cowards, and that which we witness about us is a dynasty of fear in a playhouse of desire. Yesterday, and in ancient times, the man who manifested indifference to desire was extolled as a sage. Today, our society legislates that a man must have certain desires or find himself penalized. You may not be allowed to live in a simple unpainted house, nor in a shack across the track. The law will put leavening in your bread regardless of your choice. You must come up to the vanity of your neighbor or be condemned. Your vehicle must look a certain way, and function a certain way, or it will not be allowed on the streets. Unless you have a stipulated minumum of cash in your pockets you will be jailed, and the crime will be vagrancy.

Our general cowardice manages to keep us from biting one another. In other words, we muzzle ourselves, and pick those with the sharpest teeth to go unmuzzled, naming them as our protectors, prelates and representatives. And, as in the jungle, those with the sharp teeth pick off the weak and the slow of wit. We have deified our wonderland, and legislated that all must believe in it to the letter. Only those in charge of dream-planning may alter the dream, and they may alter it only a tiny fraction. Philosophy is allowed, and you are permitted to toy with ideas a bit, but make sure that it enhances the "party-line" of your area—be the dissertation one of religion or sociology.

Few will say, "I doubt that." It might be fatal to do so. You must be shrewd, inverted, indirect, and rely on language mechanisms of satire, wit, and the use of parable and fable. This you can learn from any peddler. And never imply that you do not have freedom of speech. This will label you, and some of the labels will frighten you into silence.

And now, knowing the risk, let us evaluate the questions that disturb both the wise and the stupid. What is man? Is he merely a compound of chemicals and corruption? Is he cast here for a reason, or is he a complicated accident? Does he have an inner mechanism more important than the body, which in turn is a teleological by-product of the growth of the inner mechanism? Is there a God? Is He available, or is He evasive?

What is the nature of God? And about heaven. . . is it important to know first about heaven, or first, about God? Or is it not better to know first about man? These things are important for us to know. Is there really a divine essence, available to those who seek and are sincere? Or are we but miserable children, carrying too far, a tale about a fairy godmother told by ancient parents as a soporific? Or is there balm in Gilead, and a magic wand that makes the corn grow, that parts the sea, enables us to kill our enemies, wards off sickness, and forgives us for the errors of the creator? Does God approve the sin-game?

Why do we presume that God is good, according to our standards? What do we do, to show a profit for Him? Is God a personal being, or will He forever remain impersonal and non-dimensional? Belabored as we are by our competitive vegetative existence, will it ever be possible to formulate a real theological research? What varieties of approach are there to the problem of identifying ourself in relation to the universe, and with the ultimate or Absolute? Some say that if you will seek, you will find. Others say, "Be still. God will choose you. . . you can do nothing."

It is easy to see that sorting the chaff from the grain becomes a monumental task. And yet, what is there left to do for those of us who have tired of the apparent nonsense which perhaps we once appreciated as the game of life? Of course, a very important point arises here. If we cannot see the many instances in everyday life whereby we are fooled— how can we pierce the infinite with this exceedingly finite mind? Still regardless of the odds, the human mind has a basic curiosity about itself, and a hunger for a continuance of life, that is, if present in animals, not as well verbalized by them as it is by humans. The landscape is studded with steeples. The preachers therein may be mostly freeloaders, and ninety percent of the parishes may be lazy religious hopefuls who lean entirely on their preacher to insure immortality for themselves (even as they confidently rely on the plumber to keep their spigots running), yet, man maintains by the steeples an ever-present reminder that vegetable-man is not satisfied with himself.

If there is a Supreme Conscious Personality which observes the diggings of man down through the ages, He must be well amused by the pathetic efforts and methods of man. We ourselves smile, at the aborigines shuddering at a bolt of lightning, and perhaps at the sacrificing of humans to appease the forces of nature. On the other hand, we may be quick to take up the hatchet against anyone who smiles at our peculiar form of worship—of fear and hope.

Scientifically we have evolved, but we have not figured out the puzzle. We no longer augur the intestines of animals, to find the propitious moment. . . but we still burn incense to appease the gods, and our augury has only evolved into such forms as astrology and the *I Ching*. There is still an attempt to understand ourselves through philosophy and religion. However, philosophy is like a tongue that spits in our own eye. And where once we had a few religions with many prophets, we have many cults and no prophets.

Is it possible to outline a system of search for mankind, that has magnified and multiplied its superstitions, and shortened the hours that might be spent in research, by building a frankenstein civilization so full of waste and nonsense that the exigencies of physical existence take up all of his time? It seems that with each new decade, the chances for man to have an energetic spiritual aim are less and less.

Where, in our mammoth libraries, will we start? How many lifetimes will it take to digest all the theories, beliefs, dogmas and sacred writings, if we are going to proceed in a scientific manner? What an army of tabulators will we employ if we are going to categorize phenomena that relate to our quest. If we are going to take the word of certain mystics, and approach the problem through faith—how shall we choose the sect to which we will surrender? What questions should precede such surrender?

Are there steps of preparation for wisdom? Shall we train ourselves to be as meek oxen. . . who are worked hard and then eaten? Shall we curry favor with those who pretend to know? Or shall we be sly, ignoring all ethics and rules, and with studied trickery, outwit the gods who would keep us enthralled? This may sound like sheer nonsense unless we have heard of Crowley, Gurdjieff, and some of the thaumaturgists.

We must not fail to mention the hucksters of celestial real estate. Sometimes those who most loudly extol the truth, commercialize ignorance. Those who preach humility for others, have the arrogance to glibly describe in meticulous detail any supernatural dimension, and at the same time to deny (when cornered) that finite men will ever really know anything about supernatural matters.

We may feel kindly toward the humble, and humility should be commendable for us if we are predisposed toward fatalism. If not, we shall be meek enough when the mortician has finished with us. If we are not submissive toward our condition of ignorance, or do not feel complete, then we must proceed as though we expected to achieve as a result of labor and effort. We must have the courage to strike out on unconventional paths, or have the patience to follow a well-beaten path to check out its reliability. In this business of life and death, we should manifest a life-or-death tenacity. We must be flexible in knowing when to listen, when to be sly, when to communicate to our fellows, and when to remain silent.

And in conformity with our dual existence, and our bifocusing senses, let us maintain a double approach at all times. We can expect confusion and dismay, but we can lessen our confusion by eliminating the most absurd and the least likely. The frontal attack on ignorance has failed, because we struck out for Truth, not knowing its direction, nor its appearance. Thus we would not know it if we saw it. Flexibility will here call for a reversal of tactics. Let us retreat from untruth. And while doing this, let us maintain objective observation, experimentation, and analysis for common denominators. These common denominators should be sought in the comparison of religions as well as in the examination of psychic phenomena.

There are several other questions which will demand answers, sooner or later. Is man hoodwinked by man, or by the gods? When does a robot become a self-conscious unit of life? Did God decide to keep us in ignorance, and manage to by simply instilling in us a complexity of fears and desires, and a grandiose ego?

In the realization that human frustration and fatigue makes for make-believe, we come to still another possibility. It is possible that make-believe is either an intuition of things to come, or is a factor in the creation of events. We find the Flash Gordon of two decades ago becomes the John Glenn of today, and this metamorphosis occurs in the destiny of other dreams and desires. Is it possible, that if humanity believed in God steadfastly—there would come a time when God would gratefully appear?

UNIVERSAL PRACTICE OF DECEPTION

We begin life with an eagerness to be deceived. There is a delight in magic and fairy tales. The baby has an utter conviction that its mother is infallible. It can conceive of no greater security than to have its nose buried in its mother's breasts, encircled by her arms. This is the conviction of instinct. . . not of logic yet, nor even of intuition.

As we grow older, we do not of a necessity lose our fetters, and suddenly become mature. We transfer one slavery for another. We build mighty rationalizations that are aimed to prove that we are *doing* or *thinking*. And yet, in most cases, all we do is translate the instinctive drive for foetal security into other symbols. When we get a little older, Santa Claus will usurp the maternal chair a little. He will be good to us if we are good, and he will punish us if we are bad. He and his little elves can see all, know all, etc.

Then as we grow older, there are other substitutes. For some it will be God, and for others, law. And for some men it will be simply another person who reminds them of the mother. . . a wife. And through all these transfers, the idea of authority permeates, and the idea of infallibility. There is magic in being awed, thunderstruck, loved and punished by that which is all-mighty and irresistible.

And so I come to this question. Is it ever possible to conceive of a grand architect or first cause without coloring it with emotions that emanate from prenatal or post-natal instincts and desires? Must desire, in other words, answer all our questions? And is any reasoning that bears any taint of desire or rationalization really valid? And if not, is any reasoning about God valid at all, until we have more valid information about our own real essence?

We concoct a heaven for the delights of our desires, and invent a hell for the wicked—who are those who would prevent us from having our dream. Of course we do not realize that we are also the wicked, and must endure the hell that we have created for ourselves.

We like to pretend maturity. We scoff at the immaturity of those who believe in another Santa Claus. We feel a certain stature in denouncing all that is not conventional. And we do not hesitate to denounce, even though we know that individual interpretations of conventionality are so varied that they cause chasms of misunderstanding between us and our next door neighbors.

Those of us who wish to stop and think about ultimate directions, are jostled by the herd, and repeatedly goaded by the exigencies of living. So that we wonder if it will ever be possible for other than a very few individuals to pause in this herd-stampede long enough to meditate. And among those who have been able to pause for a few hours, there is always present an insurmountable wall of illusion, greeting the searcher at every turn. And we must function in the herd, and from it take our sustenance, security and family survival. I think that nearly everyone who has tried to manipulate the Gordian knot of self-definition, has been aware of the near-impossibility of keeping the feet on two paths at once, while keeping the two paths separate at the same time.

The two paths consist of the world of pseudo-reality, and the world of ultimate reality. They cannot be mixed, and yet the illusions of the world of pseudo-reality, or the layman's world of materialism, definitely have a disastrous effect upon the efforts of a person trying to find the ultimate reality. A person who has an eye open for honest answers, cannot help being irritated by the tangles and cobwebs caused by deliberate social make-believe.

On top of this, the path that he chooses to find the ultimate reality will have equally confusing cobwebs, although of a different type. These latter cobwebs will be the result of a relative mind-system's attempts to work with word-symbols in the abstract fields leading up to an awareness of the Absolute, and in describing to others his findings, once he has reached it.

If we take time out to change society, so that it will make a place for the mystic, we will never accomplish anything—unless we have hundreds of years to spend. However, unless we point out the illusions of mass-thinking, and identify them as herd-rationalizations, we may be changed by society into funcitonal parts of it, rather than be allowed to straddle the two paths at once.

Somebody said that it is better to light a candle than to curse the darkness. A candle will not do the job, nor would a battery of klieg lights, if by candles we mean social work, social reform, and a passive samaritan attitude. We may as well curse the darkness if the only medium in which we can work is one of social pretence.

We make much of our "rights" in society. And yet we know, that each individual man finds himself to be increasingly restricted, and compressed into a limited circle of activity. Yet his rights do not guarantee against the invasion of other people into his orbit. The process by which a right is usurped, is often classified as a duty.

We are addicted with the "freedom syndrome". We have freedom to worship. . . only in a church chartered by the state. We have freedom of speech, on certain occasions. But not through the mail, nor in court, nor in the army. We have the freedom to beget children, but once begotten, they are the property of the state. We are free to pursue pleasure, but it must be along herd-lines. We have the right to build a house, but we may quickly discover that it does not belong to us. That which we really possess, is a list of obligations to that property. And when the state, or a clever group of politicians wants it, they will take it—not by legal suit, but by the stroke of a judge's pen.

We are also addicted to the "equality mania". Man cannot be legislated equal, he must be found to be equal. And he will be found to be highly diversified and unequal. Herd-language, instead of becoming more meaningful with advancing technology, has become merely more confusing double-talk. So much so, that nearly all of his so-called liberties and rights have been reinterpreted, his children have been abused or slaughtered, and yet he has come up dazed and convinced that it all came about as a result of the perfect balance and justice that emanates from the very soul of the herd. Human error is still greater than human understanding, and we must always be aware of the sinister illusion that the masses can vote on wisdom, and of the illusion that an elected officer or piece of legislation is infallible simply because it resulted from voting.

Throughout history, gregariousness has produced group-confrontations, and when there no longer remained another herd to confront, it produced repression within the herd. And this led to a lessening of quality of the members of the herd. On the other hand, history shows that the few people whose thinking actually produced some meaning or definition for mankind, were men of solitary habits. . . men who spent years away from the herd, often in the desert, in an attic, or in prison.

In this group of contributing individuals, we find Buddha, who sat alone for years. Christ meditated in the wilderness. Gandhi meditated in jail. Not only the saints and yogis found the need for isolation, but the life-stories of many scientists, geniuses and artists show them to have been recluses at least during the incubation of their brain-children.

I am not so sure that man really wishes to be liberated from the frustrations of trying to guess the will of the zeitgeist in each of his daily actions. Herd-living has become so complicated that each man despairs of ever finding relative sanity, let alone, the ultimate reality. And he also knows that he may lose his life and all that he loves, in the social crosscurrents.

He is able to continue living or to tolerate life, by putting the serious thoughts as far back in the mind as is possible. He consciously encourages himself and his children to be sleepwalkers of sorts, sleepwalkers who will act out meaningless lives, just to be allowed to be mobile vegetables. In other words, if you act like the rest of the herd, you will be allowed your bread, your roof, and the "right" to procreate.

Man compensates for his frustration by posing. In this he does not revert to the womb, but only to childhood, and to childish mechanisms for pretending. By pretending a bit, or a lot, he is able to make his robot-existence more bearable. But, by this make-believe, he thrusts himself so far from the urgency of figuring out the labyrinth, that he simultaneously closes every avenue of spiritual awakening.

We are unaware of this life of make-believe, simply because we live it as reality. Yet hardly any labor or habit is without affectation. We feel exalted by soap and water. We don a clean or new outfit and find ourselves walking a bit straighter, using more careful grammar, possessing more elan, more courage, and more dignity. We view ourselves in the mirror and are utterly amazed at any previous conviction of our own insufficiency. A pair of spectacles may induce a contemplative, scholarly attitude, even though the wearer be illiterate. Mascara may paint tiger-stripes on a kitten. A head, filled with hideous thoughts, and distorted in shape, may appear angelic if properly coiffured.

Perfume and suggestive clothing contribute to cranial confusion, both in the wearer and in the observer. The one who plays the act, and poses, is intoxicated by flattery, and he or she who receives the flattery interprets the flattery as a fiat of validity for the act of pretence. Sometimes the observer is likewise intoxicated, so intoxicated in fact that he has been known to change religion, philosophy, or his way of life, in the twinkling of an eye, and even risk his life in the process of encouraging the make-believe and in enforcing it upon his fellows.

The nudists have a point. There are enough mysteries to be solved without the creation of more by men. A white tunic does not make a doctor, nor a uniform, a general. Strip the populace naked and you will have trouble determining the professionals or the fools. Drunkards would be mistaken for priests, and truck drivers would look like business executives. When stripped, the proud would become humble. The judges would appear as furtive as perverts and thieves. The exhibitionistic sex-offenders would probably be the most at ease. The clergy would lose their mask of austerity, and the pedant would begin to stutter. Only the man who has a deep inner conviction, and a true set of values, would remain the same.

Vanity, and the desire to force respect, determine the type of vehicle that we drive, and the type of house we own. And these possessions should remind us that vanity is compatible with obsolescence. . . for which we pay an endless price. The world will not change its vanity, even though a hundred books are written about it. It may evolve toward a more stable self-appraisal, but not swiftly. Since it takes poverty to realize the importance of wealth, it is equally possible that the pinnacle of wisdom extends from a pyramid of ignorance and despair. Our bicameral brain, and its sensory duality, may also be symbolic of the polarity of all comprehension. So that no thing is fully understood, until all things relative to it are understood, including its opposite. So that in a way, all things have their place and purpose, but it is not prohibited for a mind to understand this polarity, and to rise above it automatically.

The social illusions are by no means the only illusions. The worst illusions (those most difficult to overcome) are the religious, philosophic and scientific illusions. More astute and complex minds draw the blueprints for religious and scientific illusions, and consequently they create more complicated labyrinths. And as we penetrate these, we find that the different sets or kinds of illusions interpenetrate one another, and thus increase complexity and frustration.

There comes a time within the lifetime of nearly every man, when he is aware of the nonsense of life, but unfortunately, this time comes at about the time of death. The knowledge only comes with a degree of relinquishment. The whole cobweb of illusion finds roots in the impressionable mind of man, and is bound to his being by strong motivating forces, sometimes called instincts or emotional drives, which I would prefer to label as *implants*.

Love is one of these, and it probably holds man in slavery more surely than any of the other bonds. We begin by thinking that love is something which we possess, and soon find that it possesses us. Next we recognize it as a sort of capacity for identification with our fellows. We identify in this manner with our mates, our parents, children and friends. And we think it quite an exalted quality or ability. That which we find out later, is that we seek out these relationships, and create them where there is no reciprocity in kind. We can assume that man wishes to be loved, and that most of his protests of love toward other beings, if analyzed, would prove to be frantic pleas for attention. This hunger for attention provokes all sorts of concessions and promises from the protestor of love. And of course, the most absurd protestation, emanates from the mouths of egotistical pretenders who announce their love for God, and His love for them.

Such a pronouncement has double jeopardy, in that it uses the two most misused words in the human language—love and God. Both have too many interpretations. Love can be taken to mean, gentle hypnosis, sex, lust, the habit of reciprocal sex, or self-indulgence which uses another person as a mirror.

It is difficult for a person to free himself from the seeming need for love. Man does not enjoy love more than he suffers from it, and is used by it, or by the forces that implanted love within him. And as he becomes aware of his love-slavery, he merely transfers the love-hunger to another object. He is very slow to give it up entirely.

When sex-love is dissipated, the attachment will turn to children or grandchildren. Sex-pleasure is often replaced by the enjoyment of a feeling of nobility in being both more feeble and more extroverted. Sometimes an old person refuses to let go of his or her ideas of loveableness, even with the aid of senility.

INHUMAN LEGALITY

It has been said that Karl Marx and Cotton Mather both agreed on one thing, namely, that the common man (the masses) is incapable of governing himself. The common man, whether he drinks from the paps of parental monarchy, stern communism, or undisciplined democracy—is still like a puppy in an unweaned state. He has implicit faith in the breasts of that parent. He can be abused and beaten, but he will protect that parent with his life. And it is doubtful if his masochism can ever be erased.

Individual parents prepare their children for the future role of masochist, because state-entities are inclined toward the purging of individualists who might attempt to reform the brutality of the state. It is easier to make masochists out of our children than to see them electrocuted or hung. So we begin by paddling, and with a sort of clandestine and sinister gradualism, finally work up to whipping and beating. I have repeatedly heard local school teachers describe the procedure used to induce a child to take his "cracks" without panic or rebellion. They hit him with less severity at first, so that the surprise is gradual. Conditioning of the body to assault. The pupil may even give his consent to being cracked, presuming that there will not be any increase in the severity of the blows.

By the time the pupil is a man, he is no longer a man. He has conditioned himself to being on the receiving end of blows. Now he is no longer spanked, but is now kicked, clubbed by rifle-butts (in service training) and clubbed by the local police. For failing to act in a cringing manner before some uniformed sadist, he can be clubbed into insensibility or suffer excruciating penalties. I know of two cases where men, who had been clubbed by city police—never regained their sanity, and they spent the rest of their lives in the asylum.

But these are only the evident cases of brutality. And some sensitive souls bemoan this disease of civilization which divides all men into two classes—sadists and masochistic sadists. So that manhood is suppressed and suspended with always the hope that somewhere in the future, the little masochistic boy will grow up to be a sadist. The fraternity or sorority pledge pays with pain now, for the purpose and license of causing pain, later. Sensible parents know that there is no top sadist— there is only an endless circle of people beating one another. Here and there an egotistical sadist overplays his part, thinking he is above the club. But the circle goes on. The man who invented the guillotine, died on it. The general is spanked by the Secretary of the Army, and the Secretary is spanked by Congress. And members of Congress take turns spanking one another. . . consigning an occasional member to jail, banishment or ruin for hiding unregistered graft.

And a few parents, seeing all of this, have decided to bring their children up without beating them, hoping that perhaps their example will inspire others until masochism will be absent from the motivational needs of mankind. They may produce unusual children, but not enough to put the rest of mankind to shame . . . which would be necessary to stop the brutality. And so the madness goes on, and subconsciously all of humanity is so ashamed of brutality that no one will even admit that it goes on.

And the result is, that even as a nation, we react as a masochist. We beat our own soldiers, and shoot them for killing the enemy. We run about all over the world, apologizing for engaging in competitive business, or for offending some petulant group.

Religion helps us with any difficulties which we might have in being good masochists. We are reminded of the glories of being struck on both cheeks. I cannot see too much difference between the school teacher who terrifies with the board or rattan, and the judge who threatens with the gavel.

Perhaps you think that we do not live under abuse. If you have this attitude, it may mean that your turn has not yet come. You have not yet been sentenced by a jury of peers. And of course no one is sentenced by peers. . . peers do not condemn, they commiserate.

While the actor, who plays the part of beater, beats us, he consoles us by telling us that we have rights. This makes us feel that the beating has some meaning. Haphazard jurisprudence now has a meaning. But any of us can, within a half-hour after leaving our homes, find that our vast catalogue of rights has dwindled down to one last rite . . . and it is handed to us as a beneficence. It is the right to make a phone call after being arrested.

We have the right to go to bed, but not to sleep in peace, nor to defend our families. If a fire-bomb comes through your window, you must while putting out the fire, overcome and identify the arsonist without hurting him, and then procede via legal channels. And when you discover the efficacy of these legal channels, you will laugh all the way to the courthouse and back.

You have the right to "legal counsel" if you are willing to put all of your worldly possessions in his hands. Even our children know of the farce that is imposed under the subterfuge of justice. They do not know the details, but they know that the deck is stacked. They look into the faces of judges and see senility, and often insanity, depravity, or an incurable vascular condition caused by alcohol.

Alcohol has been discovered to be a whipping-palliative. It makes the whip more bearable. And of course the judge (and many aspiring barristers) cannot forget the slogans issued to them in their masochistic youth, because at one time they were under the whip, and had to be convinced of its right.

The result is that the judge has a strong subconscious conviction that he should be whipped. By all the rules. . . he has sinned. He has taken graft, or at least, let his friends off easier than the friendless victims who stood before him. Perhaps he has broken traffic laws, and the troopers recognized him and turned their heads. This robot expects a whipping, but no one comes forth to whip him. And the fact that he has wielded the whip leaves him with the apprehension that his turn may come at any time. He waits and it does not come. And so unconsciously he punishes himself. He drinks, and then punishes himself for drinking—by drinking more, and more.

Is the great Programmer, up there in the sky, a subtle sadist? Does He feel that this endless punishment of flesh and mind is necessary to prevent the flesh from precipitating into apathy and inertia? Momentarily, we are aware of our superior status to the animal. . . the animal is beaten by stronger specie, while man is programmed to beat himself. And so the ritual of flagellation is not confined to the flagellantes, or cloistered monks, who in dreary circles, tramp, pray, and whip the monk ahead. All humanity walks a similar treadmill, in confusingly interlocking circles, all fustigating, all in turn fustigated.

And therein lies our only equality, perhaps. Our common denominator is found in mutual misery and helplessness. Each of us is but the space in the circle between two whips. And perhaps this sick orbiting will not be stopped until all of society grows tired of it at about the same time. And when men largely and quietly realize that toadstools have more chance of possessing equality (with other toadstools) than do humans. Simply because the more complex and evolved an organism is—the greater the possibility of variety and consequent inequality.

Of course there is always an escape from whipping. It is suicide. And suicide may be slow. It may be a heart attack, when the body can stand no more. It may be insanity, when the mind simply cannot tolerate any more nonsense, but is not able to plan a suicide. The alternative is mental retreat. The more masochistic humans die quietly. Those who thought that they were the masculine aggressors, are those who are more likely to end it all with an extremely violent form of self-punishment. The general, whose monumental ego had to be matched with monumental power, commits suicide when his whip-arm is paralyzed. The psychiatrist goes crazy, cooked in his own pot. The financier is also inclined to suicide. Suicide is the supreme punishment for superior people. No one is good enough to whip the king, but the king himself. It is possible that the only men who might be considered beyond sadism and masochism, are those who die on the scaffold. This would apply only to those who are convicted for killing the whipper, thus knowingly removing themselves from the circle of sickness.

SEMANTICS

We may smile or tremble at the king of liars who sits on his bench and orders us to tell, not only the truth, but the whole truth—especially when we know the implication of that order. The whole truth would give us all the secrets of the universe!

And regardless of all the misery that is caused to the private citizen by the abuse of words at the hands of his bandit-chiefs—this misery cannot compare to the trouble that we run into in sincere spiritual searching, simply because we have to deal with inadequate language, or the deliberate misuse of terms which otherwise might be adequate.

Many books on transcendentalism leave us confused because of difficulties with their terms. We are aware of the glibness with which some words, such as *God, truth, heaven,* and *love* are used. And we are aware of the bloody battles that have been fought for the difference of definition. Before understanding any treatise of length we must first sense and intuit the author's meanings for his terms. It will do us little good to look in the dictionary. Each book has its own little cosmos, the meaning of which we must sniff out, guess or interpret from the general text, and at the end, we must be satisfied with the author's sincerity, if we can detect it.

Some words have several connotations, all of which are added to meaning-possibilities, arising from inference and interlinear hints. And on the other side of the fence, we have words that seem to have no meaning at all, except to a very limited number of people. For instance, *satori* has no meaning that can be described. It has meaning only for those who have experienced a certain state, and for those who have experienced it, it apparently has different meanings. The curse of Babel is truly upon us, and especially upon those who look to heaven. Let us take the words: *soul, mind, spirit, astral body, super-ego, oversoul, universal mind, Brahman, purusha, chakra,* and *self*. Now if we admit these items to be real characteristics of human beings, we must also admit that man must be a very complicated character, because no two of them are defined as synonymous.

We might take the last word—*self*, to use a word for comparison. Writers use the word profusely, but rarely identify it. The self may mean the body, the personality, the individual soul as distinguished from other souls or soul environments, or it might be synonymous with the word *atman*. It might even be used to explain the super-ego or the mind. The materialist might be describing the body when he uses the word *self*. The modern sociologist defines the self as such visible evidences such as emotions, thoughts and sensations.

No one has bothered to define thinking before making it part of the self. Infallible science when applied to unprovable psychological concepts, simply tightens up the circle. . . thinking is defined as the function of the mind, and the mind is defined as that part which thinks.

We have two more words which are the luxury of idiots and authoritative men. They are *right* and *wrong*. Right is luck, and wrong is unluckiness. Right is today, but wrong is tomorrow. Right is strength, and wrong is weakness. Right is a voted mandate, wrong is wisdom possessed by a few. Or right is the wisdom of the few, and wrong is the weakness and delinquency only of those who know the truth.

There are two other words, *life* and *death*, which have obscure meanings. Life is seeming motion, and death is cessation of action. Life is awareness, and death is oblivion. Yet it can be demonstrated that life may well be semi-awareness, or fractional awareness, and that death may bring us to reality, and real activity.

SECOND PAPER

Psychology and the Truth

The path to truth begins with the self. We cannot properly identify the self, isolate it or analyze it, because it is the subject of which man knows the least. We know that we are talking about "us", but if a convinced monist is talking, to him the self might be entirely different than the self that is contemplated by the dualist. Despite interpretations, we still must try to find out that which we are, and that in turn may involve that which we were, and that which we will be.

Up until now, most of us accepted ourselves without any examination. We did not know who we were, or whence we came, but if anyone dared to challenge the pseudo-reality of our existence, we had recourse to a game of dotting the challenger's eyes with the fists, and followed this by asking the educated recipient for the identity of the person who dotted his eyes. This is a little trick known as parrying a question with a question.

We accept much. We like to call it faith. But faith is a carry-over from the trusting days of childhood when we had no alternative to trust. Maybe there never will be an alternative, but then perhaps maybe we can carry the childish trust too far. We clutch at promises, at words, at euphemisms,—at magic mirrors even!

To wean ourselves we must learn to doubt, to compare, to analyze, and also to synthesize. We must have the courage to question authority. We must have the maturity to wean ourselves from folk-customs, traditions and conventionalism. We need not look too far in our circle of friends and relatives to see the varying degrees of weaning or emancipation that others manifest. How many make conformity a sort of passion? The puppets wish to be dressed just like other puppets.

We think that we think. And then we go a step further and announce that we know. Does a drum think because it reacts noisily when struck? It is possible that all thought is the result of forces or impressions striking our nervous systems, and if there is an essence more subtle than the nervous system, they may be impacting upon that also. We have little to say about the quality of this impaction upon the senses, and hence we have a lot to learn about thoughts. Like a baby hanging by its heels, we do not think too actively until the doctor instills a sensation by slapping the posterior.

A prominent mental concept, possibly an aberration, is that we think with our heads, or in our heads. There is no real foundation for this concept, any more than there is a foundation of any worth for the parallel or resulting concept that when the head decays, our thoughts decay and cease forever.

If telepathy is possible, then it is possible that our thoughts may be sent out as a sort of electronic stream from a cranial broadcasting tower. But telepathy may also function in another manner—as a sort of mental tenuosity. However, with either explanation, we can see that the mind is not contained in or restricted to the head.

Paul Brunton demonstrates several of these points in his books on Yoga and the Overself. Likewise, other phenomena tend to determine that the mind is independent of the body. Dreams that are later verified as being actual (mental) visualizations of something happening some distance away at the same time as the dreaming, are a good example. The phenomenal visions of seers, especially when accurate and the ability of clairvoyants—all give us reasons for accepting the theory of mental tenuosity, or Universal Mind tapping, as opposed to taking the long odds that successful clairvoyance results from guessing.

It is possible that the idea of thinking inside our heads comes from reasoning by elimination, and the isolation of nerve-responses. We can cut away most of the body and still think, or so we are led to believe. But much has been cut away from the brain, by accident and surgery, and this varied elimination of brain tissue has failed to localize a thinking center. A severing of a particular portion of the brain may cause unconsciousness, which would mean that the head contains a switch-box or relay for all body-functioning. Unconsciousness is only a qualification of the thinking process, being a screen that interferes with the observation of the process. That which would appear to an observer to be unconsciousness in another may well be the detachment of the senses from their usual manner of functioning.

We have the anaesthetized body on the operating table chattering distinctly about its dream. The patient is evidently unconscious. Yet when the patient awakes, and remembers that of which he dreamed and chattered, it signifies that unconsciousness as observed by the doctor is not the same as was experienced by the patient. At least not always.

Here we see the difference between consciousness and responsive thinking, and this makes the thought itself very elusive. Of course we can argue about definitions, in the event that someone might define dreams as other than thoughts.

One of the greatest contributors to illusion and confusion is the coiner of scientific words and terms. It is the delight of men with paper laurels in sight to coin a strange word or two in writing a thesis. And it is an ensuing error for students to accept such words without proper judgment, or to parlay them into another vain concept-structure.

Of course, at this point we might indicate that exact definition is impossible. But we can ask for consistency and for the so-called authorities to do all possible to avoid building a fabric of thought and expounding it merely because no one is clever enough or desirous enough to immediately attack it. It is no great wonder that many psychiatrists find themselves upon another psychiatrist's couch—especially if they read one another's writings. We can take the various opinions on the attributes of the mind, and note the divergence of number and types of attributes pinned on by different authors.

One of these attributes is will. There are two schools of thought on the matter—the determinists who claim that things are predestined, which means also that we only have the choice to choose things already fated or chosen—and the libertarians who see for man various degrees of freedom in forming his environment and future.

We should not jump to conclusions in a negative manner. It is possible that there is such a thing as a will. And we have no choice but to act as though we have one. However we can look upon it in the light as to what it most likely might not be. It seems highly foolish for this milling mass called humanity to pretend to have a *free will* of unlimited range. Can we choose the thought that inspires us to think that we are choosing? Does the hog choose the butcher? Those who stand by fatalism are no more idiots than those who claim to be libertarians. There are philosophers on both sides. There are major religions in both camps. And as long as there is a doubt, the least we can do is to refrain from actions that might result in remorse as a result of fanatical convictions in the matter.

The paradox remains. It might seem egotistical to presume ourselves to be free agents, but it also seems foolish to be constrained to eternal shackles, and at the same time to feel separate from our environment. And the fact that man is programmed to yearn for separateness, brings hope that man, by some manipulation, may increase his separateness and individuality. We are almost willing to hold ourselves responsible for knowing exactly that which a Creator created us for, if He will just cut the puppet-strings. He can throw us in the fire if we guess wrongly. The robot bids for life. If the master puts the right amount of electronic tubes in, maybe we will be self-aware.

We can expand the possibility for freedom, even more. It is possible (to borrow words from the Bible) that the truth will make us free. The masses vegetate in slavery, but a percentage, measured in very small fractions, studies freedom. They create, even as they were created. They generate a will, knowing that it is not totally free. Their freedom consists in having "yard privileges" while the other convicts are restrained in the cells. Those kept in the cells may not have to crack rocks, and may consider the yard-convicts to be less free than themselves. There is much labor in working for freedom, and often considerable scorn from the mob that languishes in its destined groove.

It all comes back to this . . . do we really wish to find the Truth? And how desperately? If knowing the Truth means upsetting almost all that we have believed or have been unconsciously addicted to in the past, should we desert the path? Do we seek for euphemistic truth, or for the Truth regardless of how it looks? The desire that energized the beginning of the search for Truth, may be dissipated or deflated by our findings along the trail. Yet these same new findings will create new perspectives and a new, but different, desire.

Does this mean that we should rebel against convention? It would be better to advise detachment from conventionality. We cannot rush out and shoot all the lawyers, judges and theologians merely because their inconsistencies are noticeable. Such public demonstrations might edify the masses, but the masses are not interested in pursuing the Truth, and the masses value rather highly many of the weavers who are able to twist an intangible bit of fuzziness into a great yarn.

A word need not have final binding meaning. But neither is it expressive of a great psychological discovery just because of its prolonged public usage. Thought is a word that is more accepted than defined. Everyone proudly lays claim to the ability to think . . . a process is thereby preempted without the least cerebral stuggle, since man is neither able to begin thinking nor to stop it. His thinking processes originate in environmental suggestion, or from previous thoughts. They end with exhaustion, or by mechanical methods of stopping consciousness.

Sleep is not considered a conscious state, but even in the state of sleep there is evidence that some mental activity continues. Men have been known to work problems in their sleep. Both the psychologist and the mystic consider the observation of the dream-process and different levels of sleep as being very valuable in the study of ourselves.

Scientific men are no closer than laymen to knowing the essence of thought. Most of the technical data gathered by scientists or psychologists are observations of somatic references to the thinking processes. Many of these observations furnish data on reaction to suggestion or stimulus, but these data concern our sensory apparatus, and a field or reaction connected with automatic reflexes more than thinking processes. We have not been able to disprove that our mind may be part of a universal mind, or that our equally elusive soul may be only an extension of a soul-matrix or Brahman.

We hear the words of illumined men but fail to evaluate them. "I have no life, but that God lives within me." "I and the Father are one." "You cannot find yourself unless you lose yourself in me." Great men openly indicate a knowledge of their own insignificance. The authoritative technician struts across the stage of life and bravely postulates himself. Of course the illuminated men have been unable to prove their claim (of union with the God-head) by using the implements which we might demand that they use to arrive at proof, because the intuition does not prove, but aims at direct knowledge. A person may try to translate the convictions of the intuition into a logical presentation, but this is generally for the benefit of another person not yet illuminated. A person of a keen intuitive nature generally grasps the idea with a minimum amount of explanation.

At this point, I would like to reiterate that no particular interpretation is being endorsed. Yet, as long as the theories about a universal mind or Brahman are not disproven, they must remain a part of the answer for the unexplained phenomena of the mind, and one answer is as good as the next one if it answers with common sense, and if neither is proven.

In a way these concepts do not rob us of our individuality. Even as the cells of our bodies relate to us, we may be both a separate entity, and at the same time we may be eternally tied up with all other entities who manifest mental capacity. We must admit and appreciate the paradox. It is possible to think within our heads, yet know that thinking need not be limited to the head. It is possible that we think, but that we are also a thought, a projection, or an extension.

There was once a theory that thought was synaptic. The nerve ends or synapses act like a set of ignition points, and nerve-impulses are forced to jump across the intervening space between the synapses. This type of theory exists only because it is more difficult to disprove it than to accept it, especially when the disproving is attempted with the same coined words of the tradesman who concocted the theory.

Saying that thought is synaptic is giving us a mechanistic explanation of thought. It is an effort to present a tangible concept. We like to be able to get our hands into abstract matters, and we feel safer if our grand theory sounds practical.

However, the same technician or psychologist who pretends to build a tangible concept and who seeks justification in science and common sense, is not daunted by his presumptions. And he will be the first to attack another concept-builder by using not only his entire stock in trade implements, but every pretence of common sense as well.

A learned philosopher, or dedicated transcendentalist, may devote his life to the development of a grand theory. A psychologist may cast a cursory glance at this grand theory, and decide, while using the particular terminology of his trade, that the entire grand theory in question was simply a reflection of some psychotic condition of the writer.

The psychologist pretends to examine the philosopher clinically, and decides that the writer was merely enjoying a mental catharsis. He notes, in additon, that the results of the catharsis, the grand theory, or stool, upon inspection, show such ailments as the God-complex, the narcissus complex, the inferiority, sadistic, masochistic, oedipus, Eros and Thanatos complexes. And he is also guilty of the survival mania.

And, of course, while the psychological high-priest is making his damning interdiction, he manages to miss the point or message, if the philosopher has a worthy point. The chicken may have a mental aberration, yet may produce a healthy egg.

The complexes mentioned exist in all of us but an individual may for a period of time favor a particular complex with more energy than his neighbor. If these complexes and drives are motivating factors peculiar to all of us, they are not abnormalities and are not individual improprieties, but are, rather, functional parts. If such motivating factors were removed from the constitution of man, he would probably die.

I do not wish to justify all of the conduct that results from the various complexes and would follow this by adding that, if a man is really pursuing the truth, his first line of endeavor would be the inspection of any possible complexes or drives, with the idea of not allowing any complex or energy-dissipation to take precedence over the pursuit of Truth. The supposition that he still struggles with complexes should not infer that he is a liar, nor prove that his motives should be regarded with suspicion simply because he displays urges or emotions.

Those which are referred to as the narcissus-complex, the superiority-complex, and the god-complex, may be the necessary pride or self-esteem that is both a motivating factor for an otherwise poorly functioning organism and a purposeful personality-glue, without which the various personality components or drives would become more erratic. When a better balance comes about through experience and maturity, those complexes become less significant and the person is more deeply motivated or dedicated.

Sadism and masochism are carry-overs from our primitive, carnivorous ancestry. The beast of prey is motivated or helped by sadism to survive, and the necessary victim is helped by masochism to become the contributor. True to the patterns of nature, the bird flutters before the snake, and the martyr finds (and describes) the bliss of his immolation.

The Oedipus and Electra complexes, through the conduct so motivated, receive much attention from not only our psychologists, but from the legal department of social discrimination, and from the religious segment of society as well. On the other hand, homosexuality is looked upon by some psychologists as being merely a stage of development. The psychologist, who wishes to serve as the high priest of nature, should realize the degree of usefulness of the homosexual. And the religionist, should take into account that the survival of Lot's tribe depended upon that man's relations with his daughters, while the angry God saw fit to destroy an entire city because of homosexual advances, (which were not even successful, and hence were not homosexual acts).

Various sexual complexes are simply variations of the survival-drive. And if the survival-drive were removed, most of the people on this planet would be removed. The survival-urge is responsible for this writing, and for all scientific and transcendental quests. This does not mean that those who are inclined to search along transcendental lines will still possess the survival-urge with the same urgency which they possessed when they first began the search. The Truth may develop in us a reversal of hope, and our urge may then be one of non-survival, or it may, if nothing else, change our definition of the survival as desired earlier.

A very important point should not be forgotten, in regard to complexes. They are sources of energy, and once they are recognized and their energy is diverted into work-channels, they can aid our upward climb. To denounce them is to negate them, and to negate them is to pull up our roots.

Let us move on to psychological terms that relate to mind-definition. Both religion and psychology owe their origins to concepts of the psyche, anima, soul, Atman, purusha, spirit, microcosm, self, "I Am", or whatever you wish to name the unproven essence of man. Immediately most authors agree on one thing. Consciousness is evidence of the-one-who-is-feeling. Aquinas and Decartes both agree.

But from there on, we have immediate dissembling. It is with great difficulty that we are able to know that which any psychologist-author means by any of the above terms, other than to know that he is conscious of consciousness. And the confusion will become more multiplied when we approach the terms of esoteric religion.

The so-called science of psychology is based upon the study of the behavior of the individual, and is so defined by authors of psychological texts or by the masses. It has little to do with exact knowledge about the essence of the psyche, the essence of man, the limits of the self, or the true origins of the behavior of the individual.

Psychology uses a yardstick which it calls normality. And from that is, in turn, spawned a definition for sanity. Without knowing the true essence of thought or the mechanisms of thought, the psychologist shall presume to know which thoughts are healthy ones. And when the opus-writer runs short of material, he resorts to telling the public that which it wants to hear.

I do not wish to discourage the study of psychological works. I would rather like to be able to create some sort of sieve to separate the gold from the dross, and thus save the youthful seeker a few months or years of labor under the impression that just any book is an authority.

One good test for any work, is the application of the work to actual experience. If there exist cases which are not included in an author's theory, then the theory is lacking. If there are cases which throw the book in doubt, and there is another book with a better explanation, we must, of course, pause and reflect.

So timid and cocksure have the pseudo-psychologists become that they have decided to measure intelligence without first defining it. So what do we have? We have a meaningless charade with which school teachers or personnel-interviewers fritter away their time. It becomes a dignified sort of eeny-meeny-miney-mo. As yet, there is no valid calibration of the mental qualities of men in relation to one another. An I.Q. test determines only that the group being tested reacted as they did, individually, and with varied responses to varied symbols. If the tests have to do with numbers or mathematics, then a person who can count on the fingers may look like a genius alongside of a person who coordinates in generalities, or who reaches conclusions intuitively.

It has not been too many years since psychology lay in the womb of theology. This parent had a peculiar authority in the Middle Ages, and the foetus has inherited some of its parent's facetiousness. At an auto-da-fe, it was left up to the theologian to decide if the victim were to have the devil burned out of him, or be locked up in a dungeon with his presumed insanity. They had various ways of determining his sanity, such as the ordeal of fire, and the augury of screams.

We have the same thing today. Pompous alienists today, who have not the candor or honesty to stand upon a witness stand and simply tell the court that they know nothing about sanity or insanity, will utter jargon in a convincing tone which neither they, the court, nor the victim, can understand or debate. They are driven by a trade-survival urge. If the court recognizes them, they must in turn, not let the court down—when the court needs some help with the hatchet.

I must admit that all legal procedure is designed with good intent, and it must continue until the human family evolves something fairer. However, we can avoid sitting in judgement or posing as alienists. Because the masses have a certain fever, there is no excuse for us to jump up and pretend to be the zeitgeist.

The office of judge is a result of the masses' illusion that they can institute a system that will protect them but never take away their just rights. All this is born of fear. The next illusion is that the judge (and this term applies to a jury as well as to an individual) is able to determine guilt. Not even a guilty plea is proof of guilt. Masochists have been known to plead guilty to the crimes of others. Thus we can see that much suffering results from unclear thinking, and that the tolerance of one illusion creates more illusions. So that the pattern of wrong thinking becomes so interlaced and interdependent that many people imagine the human menagerie to be an articulate and perfect entity just because it is complex. Weakness employs bombastic oratory.

I would like to make a final observation in regard to psychological research, such as is carried on currently. The psychologist would like to copy other material-scientists, so much attention is paid to graphs, and every little whim is polled and charted. This is like making notes on the results of fertilizers upon the growth of grass, when the real problem is to determine the essence of the core of the earth.

A LOOK AT THE MIND

Psychology is definitely in its infancy and infants do some wildly imaginative things. Modern psychology is mostly behavioristic, which evolved in a mercenary fashion, to tempt teachers and persons in supervisory positions into believing that there exists a system of predicting behavior. Of course, the supervisors hope to control the minds of men by utilizing a knowledge of the system.

Then we have the psychology of salesmanship. This is purported to encourage customers to buy things that are useless and enable the diligent student or salesman to profit astronomically. And we have the psychology of war, of aggression. This is the study of the capacity of man to suffer, to kill now but abstain from killing later, to learn to give chocolates today but rape tomorrow, to learn the profanation of human mind (brainwashing), and to learn to build entire structures of gossamer concepts that pretend consistency (propaganda).

There is also therapeutic psychology, which may be anything from free lance group therapy to professional psychiatry. This category has become a pseudo-science of manipulation, using mechanisms to syphon off our tensions (pills), to neutralize tangential or anti-social manias (trepanning, ice-picking, castration), or to give some poor professional a more magnetic voice (hormone shots).

There is naturally some variance between theoretical psychology, and utilitarian, applied psychology. But there is also conflict between the different fields of applied psychology.

We can take the psychology of salesmanship as it is applied to international diplomacy. The psychology of salesmanship functions basically by developing in oneself a positive attitude of belief in the intelligence and probity of the opponent or customer, to such a degree that the customer is ashamed not to live up to the pretty picture that we often paint of him. The salesman-technique or diplomatic procedure avoids direct criticism or confrontation of any kind and employs, rather, a "kill them with kindness" routine and an exemplary patience in outlasting the customer.

The psychology of war, however, is not quite the same. It is based on confrontation, terror and abrupt actions. With no partisan political motives, I would like to point out the trouble that has occurred by exposing our general public to both the propaganda put out by the diplomatic corps and by the war-hawks, which is available on radio and television.

One segment of our society, consequently, thinks we can "kill them with kindness" and instill in the enemy certain virtues by simply proclaiming the enemy to be virtuous. The state department talks of peace, while the generals are trying to convince the public that killing the enemy is the real international social remedy. Both are trying to use psychology as a tool.

We can go a step further and see how a third utility—therapeutic psychology—becomes involved in the confused mess. The military system of training men will impose upon those men and encourage in them antisocial traits (to say the least) that a therapeutic psychologist would deplore . . . traits which the civilian therapist will later be called upon to dispel.

Modern therapy has made the confessional old-fashioned. The sins now are not forgiven, they are blotted out. If you wish, the ability to sin again can be removed (with the ice-pick) and with the removal you may become a civilized zombie.

We are learning to drive our vehicular body but we still do not know about inner motivations. We get inklings now and then but we are reluctant to settle for less than a very complicated blueprint. Egotism would not permit anything less.

In regard to blueprints, there are certain laws concerning the protoplasm and its relation to the programming of the computer and those laws favor the protoplasm. After all, the brain must take care of its house. Action, or reaction, is based upon the endorsement of pleasure-sense and upon the rejection of pain-sense in the flesh. A stand is taken for every experience—neutrality would mean no reaction.

If the mucous membrane conveys to the record-room a perception of intense agreeableness, then the computer might find a pleasantness in the contemplation of such words as will and immortality . . . for the mucous membrane. And if our interacting Reactions (Reason) tell us that the mucous membrane has to go in death, Reason will also find it pleasant to observe the reaction that the system of Reactions with its Perception and Memory will, or may possibly, live on without the mucous membrane and the grey convolutions. And the dallying with this pleasant thought in turn, may lead us to believe in a personally directed potential for survival.

We must not legislate that it is impossible to have a Will. It is not impossible for a robot to become short-circuited by fatigue and begin operating in a way that would be more conducive to the longevity of the robot, rather than according to the intentions of the inventor of the robot. In fact, the combinations of memories and reactions to them, (Imagination) are infinite. However, the perception of one of those possibilities and the naming of that same possibility as Will does not add another attribute to all minds. It would be added synthetically, not necessarily being common to all men—being something like a heart-pacer installed in a particular entity.

The robot, from the beginning, was programmed with a catalytic reminder to keep it working. I prefer to call this catalyst an *implant*. Desire was one. Desire was not an attribute of the mind. The amoeba moves toward pleasant liquids and hurries away from irritating substances. There is a tendency in all living things to avoid irritation and not to avoid pleasant contacts. So that desire is more of a faculty of the flesh.

Another faculty that seems to be part of the mind is curiosity. The amoeba also demonstrates curiosity. Curiosity is an *implant* possibly built in the flesh and mind to guarantee a certain life-span. It may have been inherited in the genes of the species, yet such an impulse poses as a mystery in that it seems to be a continual irritant and lure, capable of projecting the host into all sorts of instantaneous, dangerous adventure.

If the young calf and kid did not possess this faculty to a high degree, they would perish surely before they were able to reason out the purpose of the mother's udders. And this is not a quality in the mind of calf or kid. This is an urge—a force which drives the host—leaving the host with little evidence of choice in the matter.

Curiosity is a factor that is inversely proportional to advancing age. As it ages, the host is less able to receive stimuli from outside or less compelled to because of fatigue. The death-gene would be another implant and if such existed, it would be likely to trigger a series of body changes long before the day of death. This clash of implants would account for the ability of the older hosts to manifest more indifference to the curiosity implant.

Regardless, that which diminishes with proportion and consistency to the aging process may well be assumed to cease after death. I mention this because I think we should seize and use this implant, curiosity, and bend its energy-vector toward the pursuit of wisdom while living, rather than dissipate that energy in the instinctive search for food and sex—procrastinating the day of spiritual efforts and rationalizing that we will be better able to satisfy our curiosity after death.

Regardless of the validity or invalidity of the after-death concepts it is worthwhile to note that of all the reports of infernal, celestial, astral, or just uncategorized apparitions, there are none reported that give the observer an inkling of curiosity on the part of the apparition. Many phantoms have demonstrated an ability to perceive, to remember and to react. But none have ever asked curious questions nor betrayed adventurousness, being more impassive and quietly aware. We might say that the spirits are not curious because they now know everything, but this is not so. I can recall reading many accounts that corroborate the several experiences I had at genuine materializations, where the apparitions were asked if they had ever seen Christ. Invaribly they gave vague answers, such as "We have heard that He is here," or "We have seen His Light," "This is about the same as where you are." But none manifested any curiosity to go look up Christ if He were available in that state. In fact, their attitude toward the question was one of apathy, not excitement or reverence.

These things, though not sensational proofs of any sort, bring us back to the definition of *mind*. Immortality, without including something of the mind, has no meaning. And to just presume that the mind as we are aware of it will remain the same after death is not to face a considerable amount of evidence with honesty. The determination of this book is to locate that permanent state of mind. This is, likewise, the objective of the Zen movement which strives to bring our present mind to its real or unchanging state while we are still living.

In later chapters we will hear much of a technique called *reversing the vector,* or *the law of the vector.* We can see that if our present essence is motivated by almost irresistible burrs or spurs in order to promote a biological destiny—then those implants, or burrs, are not part of our essence nor will they be after death. So that by removing them now, (and replacing them with intentional self-discipline to keep the biological pattern going) we may approach a type of mind that would survive death. It is for this reason that certain schools of yoga advise hatha-exercises (to keep the body going) while contemplating the raja yoga philosophy.

Patterns of Instinct and Curiosity are seen in plants. The growing sprout or delicate tendril of a plant looking for something upon which it might climb reaches and probes. Its roots will search and find cracks in the rocks, and adventure in diverse directions looking for moisture. All of this is built in, as well as a crude form of memory which is manifested when the plant is injured. The resourceful method of plant-repair requires this cell-memory.

If the memory of man has access to knowledge of prenatal incidents and is supposedly carried over in some depths of lower conscious levels, or in gene-chemicals, then we might say that Instinct and Curiosity are merely reactions to a former familiar pattern. Regardless of the origin of implants, any acts which are the result of Instinct, Curiosity or Desire should not cause us to be held accountable simply because they are causes imposed upon us and rarely controlled by man.

We can see that that which religion calls temptation comes from the outside. Yet, the master word-builders and creators of the guilt-complex would notify those being swept down the stream of libido that he, the helpless man, was the creator of libido and that furthermore, libido was evil. Man is expected to feel guilty and he is flattered by the fact that he is able to do such "guilty" feats.

Of course, man reaches the peak of confusion when another authority (behavioristic psychology) courageously decrees that mass-man is always right and that anything done by the masses is acceptable or normal. This does not rescue the man from the idea of guilt because libido is still considered to be a private possession, a quality, and not a prenatal brand upon the genes.

The religionist, sensing somewhere that the computer works better when free of libido-stimuli, decided that the libido should be controlled in the layman and avoided entirely by the priests. They may have had a good idea but they made a mistake in denouncing functions of the body which require glands, since we need glands to continue here. The Church protests that God made us but that the glands are of the devil.

And, yet, there is a hint of wisdom in that protestation if by "us" the Church means our primary essence and if by "devil" it means Nature.

That man may become a true observer is his aim. He may generate a qualified will. In cybernetics we hear that machines have been known to adjust themselves. However, the only machine that is able to adjust the universe to suit itself is the universe. The human will, or the human body, may exert itself upon the environment to a degree, but in the long run finds restrictive limits. And when the power-source is pulled out, we simply have a dead machine, unless by some Herculean feat of magic we are able to create another vehicle for the indefinite extension of mind and observer.

When man talks about having a will, he infers that there might be a sly chance of taking over the computer and being more of a doer than an observer. It would seem appropriate then, to understand ourselves rather than to confuse ourselves in our early role of creator by creating a picture of ourselves which might later prove to be unreal. If we can will ourselves to live, and then follow up by conjuring up immortality would it not be a sad spectacle if we conjured up a stranger to ourselves? Meaning that we would, thus, have immortalized a false personality.

We get on now to the attempt to split the mind. Science must be analytical . . . the mind must be broken up into parts. And many different scientists, or Quixotes, charged the phantom windmill of the mind with their axes, and came away with equally imaginary component parts. Those pieces were called by various names. Subconscious mind, and conscious mind, Id, Ego, Libido and Superego.

And, of course, we must not neglect the modern psychologists and their partners in crime—the sociologists. They came back from the windmill of the mind with the spectacular announcement that the mind was physical—we only have a body.

We cannot avoid any theory that might well be true. And so we find ourselves riding the horns of the paradox all the way. An admitted ghost writes about reality. Yet the system or outline which is stressed throughout this book is no less true if it is found on the ceiling of the Platonic cave of illusion and on some strange world of the universal mind at the same time. We who sit in the cave of illusion will be a part of illusion until we manage to separate ourselves and reality from illusion. Are we the chaos from which shall emerge creation?

Psychology decrees that phenomena that are not explainable by materialistic standards are non-existent. Likewise, all phenomena must be recognized by the senses—the five senses—or an instrument that is able to bring the phenomena within reach of the senses, such as a microscope.

The five senses which we hear so much about are gross and imperfect. Knowledge of this led several authors, such as Brunton and Van der Leeuw, to imply that there might well be an illusory world of experience, and another dimension or state not yet comprehended, or at least not yet describable.

When one man sees a mirage, we do not have much evidence. But when ten men see the same mirage, we have something that might give a hint of the possibility of illusion. All ten men will agree that actually it did not exist. But it did exist, in that it was a Perception.

The phantoms witnessed in genuine materializations by us, or the ghosts encountered by us are not denied existence (although their true identity may be variously defined). And we have many instances where, out of a group of observers, only a few witnessed the phantoms or spirits. This was the case with Joan of Arc and with the little Spanish girls who claimed to have seen and talked with the Lady of Fatima.

In such instances we can conclude that there are phenomena not visible to all eyeballs. Joan of Arc and other mystics must have had another sense. They do not have another attribute of the mind. They have, accidentally, or by chance specialization of being, another channel of Perception. There are, likewise, phenomena which involve the hearing of sounds inaudible to others and smelling things not smelled by all.

The refusal of modern psychology to understand that the mind is not limited to the convolutions results in the failure to explain phenomena of the mind. J.B. Rhine had to laboriously translate this mental ability to his fellow psychologists, although the ability had been in use for many centuries by such primitive peoples as the Australian aborigines.

Many rigid ideas have changed in the last few decades. Memory has been released from its cranial, synaptic prison and is now found to be in every cell. It has been found to be transferable through the digestive system to the animal eating another, as in the case of Planarians recently investigated. There are cases on record of people who have developed a sensitivity of skin that enabled them to identify light and degrees of visualization. These things indicate that if memories are found in the nuclei of cells and in bits of chopped worms, then the mind is not within the brain alone. And if Perception can come through the skin, which is usually the domain of touch-feeling, then visual perception is not limited to the eye.

Complexity may be an inseparable factor of life, but there is no advantage to adding complexity to the study of life by generating complexities when simplification aids understanding. Too many terms have come into existence for their euphemism or palatability.

It is foolish to pretend that psychology will ever be drawn up on paper with mathematical formulations that will enable the layman to understand himself or to plot with graphs and slide rule the distance between thoughts or the fractional spaces occupied by memories. And, therefore, this concept is not designed to answer all or to bring a student to the truth by way of a symbolical comparison of the mind to a camera. Symbolism is used to show things more clearly and to indicate that things are not as muddled as our experts would have us believe.

Psychology, as well as economics, operates according to Burke's law. Complexity in any system breeds experts in complexity, and the sincere ones are hard to distinguish from the selfish ones.

There is only one true psychologist and that is he who is able to enter the mind. Starting first with his own. There is questionable value to debates on proper thinking—the point is to begin to think.

The subconscious mind in the camera analogy is merely the roll of film. The data room in the computer. It is unrecalled memories in totality. It is not half of a bicameral mind-system. To say that there is a segment of the mind separate from the continuous consciousness of daylight experiences is like saying that the big roll of film in the movie projector is not the same film as that which is spinning past the projecting lens.

That there is a relation among memories is not denied. That memories may be cross-checking with other memories while the attention is focused upon something entirely different is not denied, and may be explained. The synaptic theory is denied. These things are denied, not as being totally false, but as being incomplete ideas. We still do not know, and may never know, exactly where memories are stored. The important thing is not to isolate memory, but to prolong that faculty and improve it.

Lastly, we come to Intuition. Reason is a pattern of reaction of reactions among themselves. Many such patterns may form a reasoning. It differs from intuition in that it is a process that is projected through the window of consciousness step-by-step. Intuition is that same reaction, or gestalt interchange, or cross-checking of reaction patterns, without any projection through the window of consciousness of each step of the process. Only the answer is projected.

THE MIND: SOME OBSERVATIONS

My quibble with modern psychology is that it not only poses with inquisitional authority, but also reneges on the basic job of at least approaching the mind. It tries to make of Psychology a materialistic and mechanistic science and in the ensuing efforts, aborts the very meaning of Psychology. It now investigates only protoplasmic and sensory reactions. The physical senses are part of the body which is visible while the mind and its projections are not. Of course, the modern psychologist gets around this by issuing an encyclical . . . "Either the mind is physical or it does not exist."

Either the body is part of our environment and is independent of the mind, or else this observer is merely a chance evolution of flab with some really fanciful concepts about himself. If memory is synaptic, we must reexamine our hopes for immortality or be prepared to settle for immortality that carries with it no memory of living. Likewise, if memory is something chemical in the chromosomes, or cell-nuclei, we are in a bad way at the termination of those cells. I should say—if memory is contained only in the cells we are in a bad way. The mechanics of cell-memory have not been determined with precision. We have known for a long time that the genes were memory-pads but they were thought to be only genetic memory-records and had nothing to do with memories of current happenings. This evidence (cell-memory) helps us to understand that thinking is not limited to the head. And the possibility remains that the mind, rather than being completely somatic, or confined to the head, is an essence with contact-points in various points of the body, but without limits to that body in consideration of form, mass or tenuosity.

The science of Psychology in an attempt to pay its way leaned lately to the therapeutic or exigent approach. It concentrated upon a utilitarian enterprise that experimented with physical media and which brought forth answers, chiefly behavioristic. These findings were limited in that they related only, or mostly, to those media.

The investigations of such media are worthwhile in that some search is better than no search, but they should be classified according to their limitations. They are the study of the actions and reactions of physical bodies, chiefly. It is doubtful if Psychology as a science will ever become a study of the "psyche". You cannot "isolate" the spirit and subject it to tests and measurements.

The student who is trained from childhood to lean upon authority pays a dear price for the false pose of psychologists. Only recently have the colleges decided, in a half-hearted way, to enter the field of ESP. In the fall of 1958 I paid a visit to the University of Pittsburgh and talked with a professor of Psychology. He viewed the field of ESP with some temerity and at the time was playing with ESP cards in one of his classes in a sort of non-committal manner. In other words, the students would have to take full blame or credit for any discoveries. There was an outspoken fear on his part of "authorities."

A friend of mine had been delegated to contact this man in order to persuade him to head a parapsychological research group which had been recently endowed in San Antonio by Tom Slick. My friend's blank check and portfolio of credentials may just as well have been a cobra—to judge by the man's reaction. He had a strange solicitude for his job. Who are these mysterious "authorities?" Why must dedicated research be first cleared by politicians and religionists? Are we to presume that Truth may not be divulged or approached except in a prescribed and arduous manner?

Occultists have known for centuries that telepathy existed and that that faculty was perhaps more important than the more evident five senses. Yet mankind had to wait for the scientific world to partially free itself from the controls of the witch-doctor and prelate. And here as late as 1958 we find science still trembling like a child at the woodshed door. This trembling child . . . that may be allowed to send you to the electric chair with his definition of your sanity.

It is demonstrable to a degree that there is another sense which has more direct access to the mind than through the computer, which is largely a physical apparatus. It has been found that while the function of the five senses depends upon a well-functioning physical body (eyes without cataracts, etc.), the functioning of this outer or other sense seems to be independent of the body's health or well-being. In fact, in some cases, the new sense functions better when the body is ill, almost to the point of death, under extreme alkaline or acid shock, wasted from fasting or disease, or largely inhibited by prolonged meditation.

We should not confuse the phenomena of such a sense with the mind itself. And this sixth sense, while being tactically superior to physical senses, still has its limitations. However, there is evidence to demonstrate that some of the limitations of the sixth sense are removed by practice as experiments have shown with the use of ESP cards and dice. Accuracy increases with practice. With clairvoyance, however, there are discrepancies which no amount of practice seems to remove. This does not imply that the mind (the clairvoyant's) involved was in error but that either its faculty of ESP had some difference or limitation—or that the source of clairvoyant information (spirits, entities) contained factors not yet fully explored by us.

Modern psychologists label most of clairvoyant observations products of mental aberrations. Like the priestcraft of old, what they did not think of first must come from the devil.

We have many accounts of people who claimed to have visited heaven or to have seen God. Examples are found in the testimony of world-prophets, life-stories of Catholic saints, medical records of cases of persons revived from near death, testimony of spiritualistic materializations, (these latter give testimony only about their heaven) and, of course, tales of certain mystics. In some respects, the medical cases are more evidential in that the records are of people who did not approach death with the idea of returning to testify, while the evidence brought to us by mystics is of a deliberate nature. The mystic in so seeking, qualified the results of his findings since minds have been known to create desired results.

I hope that it has been demonstrated that there are illusions in the physical world. The statement that illusions exist implies that there is a true state of affairs which, when correctly seen by all, will have but one appearance. The mistake that the observer (who, incidentally, may well be an "authority" or scientist) makes is in announcing himself to be above illusion after the first trip to the optometrist. He is no longer deceived by mirages or magicians. He may even pride himself with his new perspectives including space-time concepts and the force-field concepts of matter.

Our space-time concepts imply that things may not really be as they appear to be when observed with the telescope. And force-field concepts imply that a situation may exist that cannot be observed with the eye, even with the aid of a super-microscope. The senses are, consequently, inadequate in these cases because they are not able to perceive the ultimate nature of objects under scrutiny. And being inadequate in these cases, are no more commendable as senses than the sense that lays claim to witnessing heaven or God. The varied testimony of enraptured mystics does not imply mental aberration. The stuff was seen through a glass darkly. It is true that some of the testimony of visionaries was caused by a predisposition toward imagination, and some accounts may be deliberate lies. Some may have unconsciously copied from earlier authors. We can, however, accept that those that we feel are sincere did actually witness a state of being if they attested that they did.

The fact of their difference in testimony lies in the difference of the vehicles or persons observing and in their individual difference of faculty that facilitated the observation. When the observer relays that information to us we have still another refraction, depending upon the limitations of language.

I would say that the mind itself is not finite. I would also conclude that the perception faculties and the translation faculties are considerably finite.

And there is some explanation for all of the strange and diversified evidence found in this business of heaven-seeking. Some of the phenomena may well be conjurations or creations triggered by mental tricks. Some materializations actually seen by human eye are, in some ways, less evidential than other concepts because they have been conjured up—ordered, so to speak—as you would order bacon and eggs in a restaurant. Eliphas Levi gives us a hint of this mechanism when he describes the materialization of Apollonius of Tyana. Deeper investigations of Spiritualism infer (with a degree of justice) that the phenomena of ectoplasmic figures are of human creation, being an emanation from the body of the medium, and being subject to certain intellectual limitations relative to the limitations of the mind of the medium and his circle.

It is also believed that the mechanics of the seance are engineered by entities. William Crookes was supposed to have had a Titania for a pet. It has been my privilege to meet one of these entities and it was quite the opposite of a Titania. So there must be other types as well. We come now to the business of entities, demons or angels. They may or may not have substance. It depends upon the amount of substance we claim for ourselves. When we begin to concede that we , as far as our physical aspects are concerned, are to a degree illusory, then we may assume that these other entities may be to a degree illusory. But we should not assume them to be illusory just because it is not convenient to try to identify them. We can take accounts from the *Tibetan Book of the Dead* and find that the book warns of impressive encounters after death with alarming, if not terrifying entities. The book wishes us to note that when these things are encountered they signify that we are still in transition and not yet fully liberated from illusion.

From what we read of Aleister Crowley, he was really not too happy with his discoveries up until the time of his death. Yet his metaphysical career started off with the conjuration of a swarm of demons in a drug-drenched experiment. With easy access to definitely supernatural acquaintances, the prospect of tapping those acquaintances for supernatural information immediately suggests itself. However, the last moments of Crowley signify that his demon friends were lacking as informants. Eliphas Levi, after spending many years in the art of conjuration, is supposed to have had disillusionment that resulted in his return to the religion of his youth.

It may well be that travel to another planet and the consequent study of its people or beings may be similar in value to the study of demons. It is strictly a matter of objective. We may discover that those beings are of another dimension or rate, but not necessarily of a dimension more real than our own here in the human bodies. The worth of contact with demons is questionable in the light of all the information gathered from them.

We come to another type of visitation—the projection. This is a form or phantom projected by another intelligence—perhaps human or perhaps supernatural. Under this heading come the visitations of witchcraft and some magical rites. The inference here is that this type of being has no existence other than mental. They are created by one mind to influence another. Recently an article appeared in a magazine titled "Does Telepathy Cause Insanity?" The psychologist who took note of this particular phenomenon was gingerly introducing the idea in the form of a question.

I went to school with a man who was convinced that he was God (Jesus Christ to be exact). He became convinced of this, he told me with candor, because of voices from beings that spoke to him and addressed him as Jesus. The man was, to all appearances, a sane man. He was homosexual and he tried to copy that which he thought to be the physical appearance of Jesus. He was no apparent lunatic. In college he was an astute mathematician and by avocation he was a skilled fundamentalist. He was very practical except on the subject of his own divinity and on the insistence that he had a vast telepathic following. He had that which the minister in graveside-eulogy referred to as a subtle sense of humor. Incidentally, he believed that he would never die because he believed in himself.

The mental institutions are filled with people who hear voices and see people and animals quite invisible to the attendants. Yet these same insane people occasionally come up with startling announcements. At one time in Russia about the same time that starets-Rasputin came into prominence, there was widespread reverence for idiots that bordered on worship. It was supposed that the miserable condition of the idiots was the price paid for their unusual contact with higher dimensions.

I was startled a few years back by a young neighbor who had been released from a mental institution only a few days prior to the following incident. He sat beside me in my kitchen. Our wives were, for the moment, monopolizing the conversation. Without facing me or even looking at me he read my mind aloud. I thought to myself, "He is reading my mind." He half turned and commented, "I have been able to do that ever since I have been a child."

These were not his only words. He replied for several minutes to my thoughts, and replied in depth, being fully aware of things I knew but did not speak. Nor did I even answer him at the end. I was too surprised. This particular man claimed to have seen God. But God appeared to him in human form. He once mistook the family physician for God and knelt prayerfully before him. The physician, who had recently recovered himself from a nervous breakdown, became alarmed and ushered the patient out of his office. The result was an institution for the patient.

The man who thought he was Jesus had been committed once to an institution. He was picked up for walking the streets of a small town, dressed in burlap, while preaching the gospel. He could laugh while describing the experience. I asked him about his release from the asylum.

"Heaven knows it was a task," he smiled as he replied. "I never knew before that I was an actor until that time, nor did I know the full insidiousness of society and of those in charge of saying what insanity is. Heavens, yes, it was the best acting I had ever done in my life. I had to act sane and if you have never tried acting sane, you must try it sometime, especially when you have to guess what they mean by saneness—what will pass the board. You learn after a while that sanity is basically harmlessness, industriousness and gregariousness. You have to put out the idea that you are just a plain, hard-working chap without a brain in your head and they will let you go. It is easy to frighten them and you must not do that. Questions frighten them as do metaphors and harmless equations. They pretend to be thoroughly logical in their interrogation, but it is strictly instinctive. If you manifest logic yourself, they will manifest fear immediately. I rather think that they are afraid of a reversal of positions if the logical communication is encouraged."

Swedenborg was considered insane by his contempories. He knew St. Paul and most of the apostles rather intimately according to his writings. He had not only visited heaven, but hell as well. His description of these two regions was predominately one of an objective experience as distinguishable from the more subjective experiences of other mystics whose experiences or ecstasies led them to proclaim heaven to be a state of being for the mind or a state of rapport of the mind with a more extensive Being or mindstuff. Swedenborg described not a state of being, but a place visited by beings.

Swedenborg was not too reliable as a witness about other matters on which he spoke with authority. He had written scientific treatises years before becoming a mystic and in one of his scientific books he proclaimed that the moon was a mirror. He also claimed to have intimate knowledge of beings on other planets. We can note without prejudice that his faculty of perception—which he extols as being extrasensory— was not infallible. And was, in fact, laden with error.

Swedenborg is no reason for a wholesale rejection of all accounts of experiences of mystics. And records by celebrated prophets and religionists are not more valid than the information gathered from individuals who have had unusual experiences and who make no great fuss about them. The words of a drunk, a dope addict, or a social derelict are as valid as any other if we are gathering material for the study of the human mind. The prophet, in fact, may have weighed his words while the unimportant habitue of the public square may have nothing to gain and less to hide than the most of us.

I have recently read a book, *Modern Clinical Psychiatry* by A.P. Noyes. He tells us much about mental diseases, but does not give us a definition of the mind. In this book (of mine) it would be impossible to bring to account every other book on the matter of psychology. It suffices to say that I have never found one that properly defines the mind. Noyes avoids that definition until he can smother us with a hanging garden of Babel.

He then decides, "It will be noted that in the definition of psychiatry and its discussion as a branch of biology, there was no mention of the word 'mind'. There need not, however, be any objection to the use of the word provided it is employed as a *collected designation for all those activities and phenomena that occur when the organism functions as a whole and that represent the product of interactions between it and the environment.*"

If you think that that was confusing, he elucidates in the same paragraph and utters an awesome decree like the witch-doctor of old. That which the witch-doctor does not know does not exist. The decree is, in essence, a mandate for religion. Man is monistic. Man has no indwelling soul. Man has to be the soul or nothing. He also abandons the whole field of mind-study for the safer ground of what might be called, "mechanistic observations."

I quote him: "As a corollary to this definition of mind the reactions of parts of the organism would be designated as physiological. Mind is, therefore, the biological expression of the organism responding to its own needs and to the stresses of the environment. Man is a unitary organism or being whose physical, mental, emotional and social reactions constitute but different aspects of one individual whole which functions as a unit. The mind, therefore, is but one of the biological characteristics or functions of the organism and not an entity having an existence parallel with the body."

If you read this the same as I do, this fellow does not believe that the mind is anything but the factory control-room. You will see a parallel to a degree in the concept which I offer that draws a picture of illusioned man possessing capacity for reaction more than for will. Man does react and "modern" psychiatry is biological in its scope. But psychiatry is not then a science of the psyche. This man Noyes is more of a biological mechanic . . . an electrician skilled in knowing brain areas that are likely to be undercharged or overcharged in the cases of varying symptoms and irregularities of behavior.

He tells us that "exaltation" (his word for "ecstasy") is a proper diagnosis for the state of mind (body mind) evinced by Buddha, St. Theresa, John of the Cross and any enraptured mystics. The millions of followers of these mystics must then be psychotic. Yet he defines abnormality or "undesirable functioning" as that which disturbs the subjective state of the individual or his relations with other persons. The serenity of the mystic is surely not a disturbance to his subjective state. And the history of mystics shows that after they reached the "exaltation" they were more acceptable than before. The most harmless being on earth is a mystic. We can note the acceptance of Jesus and Buddha.

We may note here that Noyes relates that which is psychotic to that which is not desired by other people. Sanity is once more a matter of public mandate, not scientific proof. The psychiatrist, having no intuition, has no qualification for piddling with the minds of other men. Unfortunately, it is important only that he helps to build a new infallible priestcraft for courtroom intercourse with the legal profession. And it seems not important that he is not able to help a person who comes to him with a sickness that is intangible as far as a biological examination might show. How would he treat a case of possession? With shock treatments or exorcism? Never exorcism. How would he treat a case of mediumship? To him, of course, the medium is schizophrenic. And to some psychiatrists telepathy itself is only an hallucination. It does not matter to them that the medium or recipient of telepathic messages may have data produced that bear no relation to any prior knowledge or experiences of their lives, nor to knowledge of things happening even as the medium is speaking. This is in reference to astral projection or its equivalent.

We must keep our eye on the over-simplifying methods of modern psychologists. Psychiatrists are simply mechanics. Somatic electricians. It is true that they observe behavior, and have experimented with methods and gadgets to alter that behavior to please society, or its herd-bosses. But watch these gadgets. They include trepanning and ice-picking, pills of questionable after-effects, and mild electrocution for mild resistance and permanent electrocution for stubborn resistance. There are some cases where such a mechanic is useful; but we must always keep in mind that this mechanic who treats our body-voltage still knows nothing about the essence of the electricity of that body.

No man can lay claim to being a psychiatrist until he has learned the trick of stepping into the mind of the other, to think for a while with his thoughts. And any other pretensive approach is peripheral.

We should, therefore, not hurry to define the mind, but honestly try to enter it. To be an authority on life on the moon is expedited best by going there, not by resorting to scientific daydreams.

If the body is the totality of man, it certainly has subtler extensions not visible to the eye.

I believe that the computer is perishable. I believe that most insanity, or that which is diagnosed as insanity, is physical derangement or an incompatibility or impairment of parts by disease, aging or accident. The case histories of many people who have been cured or have recovered from that which the medical profession labeled as insanity show that they were aware of their affliction at the time of their insanity even though they were unable to communicate to others.

I believe that this detached witness to this suffering is the mind. It is the final individual observer. It is not the final Mind however. The individual mind may yet have contact or union with other Mind-substance. The body is the observer, but it is not the final observer. We could accept that memory is chemical, synaptic or genetic (chromosomic) and we still would not account for the memories transmitted by telepathy. We may refer to them as mind-pictures but they are still memories once pictured. We can readily admit that the five senses will decay some day but we do not know if that other sense—the telepathic sense—or sixth sense—will decay. The body, which is like an electrical generator, some day will lose its voltage. That is true. But the relation of that voltage in any instance to the final observer is not established. As we have seen, many of the desired phenomena, such as satori, occur when the voltage is very low or when the wires are badly crossed or shorted out.

From my own personal experience, I have that which may be to the reader a strange conviction. I cannot offer it with any pose of proof. It must be taken as just a case history for what it is worth.

My comprehension of the mind of the final observer is such that it presumes the observer to have neither need of mundane perception or memory to BE. It has a different perspective when the body is negated or removed, in that it no longer particularizes, for one thing. The memories and personality that we identified as being us in the body-coat have ultimately about the same dearness and wistfulness as the characters from a story projected upon a screen for our edification. It might be like coming out of such a dark theater—out of comfort and illusion—this business of finding our real selves. For a short while, the chilly shock of the out-of-doors reality is there.

ROMANCE AND TERMINAL CASES

The different sciences of man are interdependent even as the definition of a word relates it to almost every other word. And in examining the structure of any science or department of human behavior, we find the fallacy of one science rooted in mistakes of another. So that it is now a question whether the symbol of the serpent with its tail in its mouth is the symbol of wisdom or is actually a hint that all pursuit of wisdom will bring us to that embarassing circular position.

Let us look at the looker. Let us examine the postulate that man observes. All of the sciences postulate that man is not only the observer but the doer, and what is more, the doer of mighty things, the possessor of a will, the manipulator of magic, and the artist of logic. He gives himself the accolade of responsibility and a sinister godliness when he slyly acknowledges the power to commit sins. He reminds himself eternally of this prowess by romantic drama, both as an individual and as a nation or race. In the romantic drama he is only seen strutting in the uniform of conquest, in the perfumed haze of a Romeo making boudoir history, or he is seen posing as a saint with eyes averted. The fragile minds of youth observe these romances and are moved to action equally fictitious and to write scenes for coming generations. But death is hidden from the stage. Actually. In some places strong pressure is brought upon movie producers to inhibit them from depicting a man in uniform in a horizontal position unless he is a man playing the part of the enemy.

What does a dying man think of all this romance? In fact, what does an older man think of the ambitious play and toil of his thirty year old son? The freshman is looked upon as being "green" by upper classmen who view the lower classmen as unwise and unaware of the true state of things. And the whole lot of them are tolerated for unwiseness by the bewildered professors. And if the professor is more mature, let us assume that there is a knight or two still more mature. And ask ourselves about his reaction to the big question . . . What happens to the Galahad of a thousand jousts with the windmills when the bell tolls?

Why do they cover a dead man's face? Or pull the curtains around the hospital bed? Why do thy wax and paint the face of a corpse, and murmur in guilty undertones, that the face of the corpse flatters sleep? Why do we pay a man to salve our ignorance with a pointless tirade over the casket? When all romances and pseudo-sciences have failed, there is one last attempt at histrionics. And refusal to part with make-believe.

If we are to look upon man as a computer we must admit that he is beset with many problems at once and at all times in his life. The computer must feed, repair itself and amuse itself, and create other computers, and feed, repair and amuse them. But there comes a time when the computer feels itself coming apart. The lights are going out not only in the viewing screen, but in the whole rotting tangle. Here is a chance for the computer to forget all functions but one—self-definition. If the last burst of energy is not wasted on thoughts of escape, the mechanism might, by shutting off the disturbing environment, and with the automatic decrease of sensory impulses, bring about at least one chance in its lifetime to coordinate all circuits in the memory-bank and come up with a startling discovery.

Let us go down to the hopital and see what happens to the computer when it breaks down. Our evidence must be second-handed because the dying computer loses its communicating power and we can only attempt to estimate its final deduction by the death-bed behavior. And what happens? Some are startled, some seem bored, and some smile— but that smile cannot be always judged as seraphic . . . it may will be risus sardonicus. We do know, however, that long before the communication-mechanism is disabled that the aging computer has a dim view of the romances of the younger computers. Dying is not always a sudden process and some people take many years in the preparation for death. Some repent and are quiescent in their later years, but many a young man and middle-aged man swears off his vices and follows an abruptly different life.

It cannot be denied that the dying man does come up with a momentous realization that he may not be able to communicate to us or that which is not verbalizable even if he were given the mechanism for communication.

Later on, also, we can deal with the possibility of there being no separate observers. But to make a beginning we must first examine the field of psychology with the assumption that it is possible for us to talk about it, therefore assuming that we are individuals or observers.

THIRD PAPER

The Veil of Maya

There is some question raised by various philosophers as to the extent to which we can claim to live or assert consciousness. There is much more evidence to substantiate death. From our present population of two billion and more, we can estimate that close to two trillion corpses are now enriching our soil. And we need only to go back four or five thousand years to accumulate this total.

The statistics for death are monumental. The statistical percentage of those who have died and found a life after death might well be said to be nonexistent in view of evidence available. These odds are very discouraging—so much so that the average person, seeing them or sensing them, throws up his hands and refuses to become concerned about the problem.

There are other statistics, however. These billions of people have built thousands of civilizations, hundreds of thousands of cities and tribes. They have produced scientific marvels that have later been lost and they have written books that have turned to dust. Yet the earliest history shows one great movement which has continued until the present time—the most primitive peoples theorized about a Primal Cause or God and formed some sort of theology to satisfy their questions. And their temples and their theologies all have, in due time, proven insufficient and most of them have vanished from the earth.

We have no more reason to discount theological enquiry on the grounds that historic theology was found inadequate any more than we should discontinue scientific research because of the inadequacy of the phlogiston theory. The living or current efforts to determine about life after death offer some very interesting statistics. There are hundreds of movements, religions, cults, societies for psychical research, brotherhoods, philosophic clubs and ale-house fraternities that claim authority on the knowledge of life after death. If we examine them all—presuming that we possessed the needed life span—we might perhaps find that none of them knew about the ultimate state of things, or we might find that each of them contained a grain of fact, surrounded, pearl-like by a blob of flesh and then a layer of slime. Or we might conclude that the majority of their concepts are valid in a relative sense. Still, these deductions leave us only with theories and ensuing confusion and frustration.

Man will spend hundreds of man-hours paying for pills and he often spends his life savings to treat a terminal disease in the frantic hope of adding a few years to his life. Yet, despite modern medicine and medical research, man continues to die. He invents new cures only to find new diseases or old viruses that have developed greater resistance by surviving man's antibiotics. We live in a Christian nation and era that affirms that man's body is only a coat for a more subtle fabric, yet it never occurs to anyone to study the subtler fabric or essence that is left when the coat wears out. In fact, the Westerner (Christian) is likely to ridicule those who dedicate themselves to esoteric diggings.

It is possible that life after death is more important (so hinted by theologians) than this grubby life. However, in many religions we find those same theologians advocating the grubby life, except for a few, chosen for their hierarchy. If the death-plane is more important and this life is only a preparation for it as most theologians claim, then something sensible should be done about it. We should all do the great work—not just a fractional hierarchy.

Humanity throughout the Middle and Dark Ages remained in serfdom to pontifical dogma. Lately, the peasant is somewhat better educated and the matrix of ignorance that begets faith is demanding more sensible dogmas and a more scientific or logical approach to theism. The worship of fear and the masochistic attempt to create godhead from the mingling of fear and love is melting under the light shed by common sense.

The history of religions, their rise and fall, will afford us a disturbing suspicion. Many great religious movements have eroded away, leaving nothing for our scrutiny but external piles such as the pyramids, Ankor Wat, the temple at Karnak and the Potala. Which brings us to wonder why many great religious dynasties have possessed and lost the drive. It may bring us to wonder if there is not a great natural scheme to prevent man from expanding his knowledge. We have the "Tower of Babel" story and the belief that gods do not wish for men to become too clever.

Man, as an individual and as a race, is unable to continue to fruition—the search for Truth. Man as a race develops great religions but they reach peaks in growth and then begin to wither almost like a living entity. Man, the individual, possesses certain years of his life in which he may dynamically pursue wisdom or religion but then he is overcome by lethargy, circumstances or despair long before his natural death.

If we examine the problem we may surmise that not all of man's inability to pierce the veil is because of the jealous nature of the "gods" who might not wish for man to aspire beyond the pawn stage. We will find that man is, unfortunately, a race of liars, whose status complicates his illusion-status bestowed upon him by nature. The man chained in the Platonic cave, instead of breaking his chains, worships them with rationalization.

That man lies to himself and that these lies are in greater proportion than his efforts toward Truth can be demonstrated if it is not already self-evident. And it is part of the purpose of this paper to indicate many of the major lies that pose as vehicles for Truth and demonstrate how they are manufactured out of smaller dishonesties. The Grand Creed degenerates into a social institution because members of its hierarchy use escapes and rationalizations to cover their lack of knowledge and when we realize the tricks that they employ, we find them of so petty a nature that we no longer feel obliged to punish our children for being truant from Sunday school.

It is doubtful if anyone will disagree with the postulate that the most important thing in man's experience is survival. Survival may be concerned with the race, the family unit, the body, or the nameless essence that might survive corporeal death. Another item of experiential importance, equal to or greater than survival, is self-definition. In the quest for soul-survival we come to the business of defining that which we are and hope to be.

As a result of self-definitive study, there are several camps of opinion . . . we have the monists, dualists and the pluralists. (Ouspensky indicates that we are multiple.) We know that it is important for that which is surviving to know the nature of its survival. Or we might ask—is it really surviving if it does not have the proper self-awareness? And is it not necessary to understand perfectly the essence or soul-matter before we embark upon any formulation for continuance? The old sage who indicated, "First know thyself," may have been far ahead of today's theologians who are the product of a supposed spiritual evolution of hundreds of years. Here and there a solitary sage points out a formula but the masses laugh merrily at him as they crowd into chaos. He does not of a necessity give a useless utterance. Someone heard and remembered him and disciples and biographers recorded a word or two for him. For us.

We might say that the sincere religionist places essence-survival as being of tantamount importance and self-definition for him is less in importance. As a result, he becomes bogged down in artificial or imaginary rubrics, faith-implementations, and priest-formulas. Or in false translations, or questionable interpretations of the sacred writings.

It is nothing short of amazing to note the brashness with which various theologians skip across many passages in the Bible (although they profess to be fundamentalists), especially if those passages appear to challenge the structure of their own house of cards. How many are able to explain the lines in the beginning of the Bible? There was a tree in the garden called the tree of the knowledge of good and evil. And man was not allowed to eat of it under pain of death. Now in our botanical catalogues we find no classification that might indicate a plant possessing wisdom, so we must deduce that the tree was symbolical. If the edict meant that man was forbidden under pain of death to seek for wisdom, then the Master Jesus was giving out some bad advice when he said, "Seek and ye shall find."

There is too large a gap between Old Testament and Talmudic laws of conduct—and Christ's attitude. The former commanded conduct by instilling a fear of a wrathful God. The latter proposed a way of living based on love to raise the level of being. The latter declared for a God of love, not one of anger and jealousy.

There are many puzzling things in the Bible. Careful translation and comparison should be undertaken by sincere Bible students. We wonder about frequent references to an angry God. We hear of a God that is partisan, who helps one little tribe on this little earth to kill off their adversaries. We are enjoined to love and fear this God, although we may well be the descendents of survivors of one of the expendable tribes who found themselves in the path of the Jews. We, who have never had the rare privilege of seeing the hand of God in a pillar of fire, nor heard His voice booming from the vault, nor witnessed a sea opening up to let the chosen ones through, nor witnessed a burning bush—wonder how in the name of a name those living witnesses to all these marvels could ever doubt that God enough to worship a golden calf. It would seem that the narrator of that exodus either waxed hot with imagination or else God made a mistake and allowed the sea to swallow the better people. And in the New Testament (at Golgotha) we could really have used a pillar of fire but did not have one. And the voice no longer roars out of the heavens, but is plaintive and mild. Saul is not incinerated but implored. Sodom and Gomorrah, on the other hand, were incinerated because two messengers were merely insulted, not killed. At the crucifixion Jerusalem was given very little indication that it had incurred divine displeasure despite the fact that the Son of God was the victim.

The human mind is finite indeed. As a few mystics have been honest enough to admit, the human mind is unable to focus itself upon a problem for a very long period. It wearies. It loses its chain of thought and it loses in memory the sequence of important things it wished to remember and compare with continued exploration. It loses track of the definitions it applied to basic word-implements. The brain sleeps at night and wakens oblivious of all the noble intentions of the previous night. The eye of the ascetic blinks when a symmetrical harlot walks by . . . and a year's meditation is dissembled. The philosopher gets hungry and the exigencies of the other survival drive take him away from the attic and into the hotmill.

The question arises as to that which can be done amidst all this failure, uncertainty, and man-made confusion. In a way, it is no more difficult a project to begin than any other. But to maintain continuity and purity of purpose is another thing. If man were to bend a percentage of his energy toward the solution of death's mystery, under conditions that would exclude from the beginning the possibility of digression, commercialization, degeneration into cultism, and have built into the blueprint from the beginning an arrangement for periodical shocks or hypodermics to revitalize or remind the organism of its objective, then a greater degree of success might be attained.

We can always find negative statistics to feed our despair. It is a fact though that prior to Columbus, no one in history wished to venture too close to the edge of the earth. Had Columbus been daunted by the estimates of "bona fide" authorities, he would have made no discovery. And if we wish to discover that which is not already under the noses of the masses, we must expect to extend our necks.

Here are what might be considered some pertinent statistics or facts: Man still dies and is still afraid of death, despite any contrary pretence; yet man will bend large percentages of his energy, salary or time to the taxes that go for making machines to bring death about. Of course, he will argue that this is race-survival. Life is too short to go about trying to convince nations that war is useless and distracting to the nobler work of man, so it becomes a peculiarity to spiritual seeking that only a small minority will, in this era, take the time and energy to divorce themselves from the world's travail in order to do something more important.

The individual man is apt to place too much importance on his gregarious instincts. He is afraid of being unconventional and has fear of criticism from people. He shrinks from prospects of being called a crackpot or fanatic by society. And if he shrinks enough, he will never be able to change or help that society as did men who were monumental crackpots two thousand years ago. Men generally gravitate to a job, trade or profession and content themselves with fighting for more money. With that money they smugly buy insurance. They pay the preacher once a week to soothe or shrive them and when the monotony of their lives sends a ray of truth screaming through their flabby brains, they take their wallet to the psychiatrist in the hope that he will purge them of despair with the proper sophistry. Their only real claim to immortality is their undying faith that no matter what dissipations they suffer, the family physician will come up with a pill to rebuild the fun-machine.

Let us take a poll of that which the man in the street believes should be done about securing immortality. Most of them are depending on their minister to take them to heaven. After all, that is his department. Some will casually note that millions have died before them, and they expect to go to the same place to which those went. Another will smile condescendingly and point you to faith, indicating the magic of simple belief. Another will want to douse you with baptismal water. And still another might press you to your knees and have you screaming sins you never dreamed you had.

Man just refuses to take death seriously. We who are sending rockets into the outer spaces are not yet out of the jungle spiritually. We are still consulting witch-doctors, engaging in frenzied religious revivals, and probing the pages of superstition for our auguries.

We do have need of science if we are to understand the physical aspects of man and if we are to monitor them—for this monitoring may well be necessary before we can do too much on the mental levels. Transcendentalism has need of a system of checks and balances. The intuition must be tempered with logic. And the paradox is eternal.

Both religion and science have their proverbial heads in the sand. Most of the errors in the area of religion result from a refusal to look at any research with other than an inspirational attitude. On the other hand, science would profit by taking on more of an inspirational attitude and realize discoveries with the employment of variables.

In examining the achievements of religion, we can encounter many interesting bits of information not necessarily adducive to truth. We have monasteries famous for inventing alcoholic beverages, but rarely, if ever, has a monk emerged from a monastery with spiritual enlightenment for the world beyond the balderdash that has been warmed over and served for centuries.

We find that the many newer religions born by fission or schism are the result of politics rather than a change of attitude toward Truth. If there is but one God, of whom can that God be jealous? And if there is but one Truth, how can jealousy or any misunderstanding separate men dedicated to the path of Truth?

We find that mankind periodically takes up the sword and hacks the monk or witch-doctor to pieces and replaces whole religions. The mass of mankind, usually stupefied by nature and its exigencies, at times is roused from its inertia by a prolonged abuse of elementary reason. The public appears stupid because it is lethargic. Many prelates interpret this lethargy as ignorance and overplay their mental despotism, never expecting to be challenged. But man does not revolt by premeditated plan always . . . the reaction is generally one of nature, identified often as Karma, or it is the automatic purging by an organism of material that can no longer be assimilated. Automatically, unadaptable formulas will be vomited up from the stomach of mankind.

History is witness to centuries of fat clergy who boldly preached holiness and asceticism. History is full of Friar Tucks and obese brew-masters in hooded habits—and modern rectories are no exception. The layman laughs to find more devils in Loudun than in his favorite bordello and scratches his ear when he reads Benvenuto Cellini's account of the priest who sought gold with the help of black magic. And it is no wonder—when Communism points out the religious affront to common sense—that the peasant indicates that he would rather accept stark materialism to be free of the merchants of stardust.

The theological shell-game is about to be challenged on a larger scale than ever before. Seeds of dissatisfaction are popping through the stiff crust of the brain of the masses. As many are drifting away from church because of the secularization of religion, as are drifting away because of aspects of impossible traditionalism. Some leave on witnessing bad conduct of their pastors while others leave with rational reservations.

Many are opposed to the excessive institutionalism of churches and point out that organized religion no longer looks for God or the Truth. Many such dissidents form the membership of new isms or cults. And these dissidents find everything in the cult, usually, that they opposed in the religion.

Like a physician treating chancres, we are restrained from asking, "Why?" upon witnessing the distress of honest seekers. We can only ask, "How can the distress be avoided?" while we continue to treat symptoms instead of eliminating causes. We can point out the symptoms and hope that future colleagues will find increasingly better ways to search.

Public sensitivity is one of the great stumbling blocks before the Truth. The Truth must be administered subtly. And if we try to offend no one, nothing will be said. Too many writers, motivated by the purchasing power of the public, attempt to inject their philosophy indirectly into the reader's mind by the use of wit, laborious logic, or by emotion-stirring fiction. This type of writing tends to carry both writer and reader away from the importance of Truth, since it appears only in the form of a hint. It also possesses a vagueness that protects the writer from any need to defend himself. If the medium is wit, he can pass his controversial motive off as humor. If the medium used is metaphor, symbolism or parable, he can attest that the reader took the wrong meaning. And if the reader becomes quarrelsome about his interpretation of the moral behind a fictional piece, the writer can deride him for allowing himself to become agitated over a mere story.

If I can create a hypodermic, it has not been intended for any sensitive posterior, but is rather aimed at the heart and head. I feel that time is short and that honest men will appreciate honesty in the long run. I am not so foolhardy as to undertake to awaken people who are using faith as a narcotic, nor to disturb the weavers who are using faith as a matrix from which to weave a better world. I wish to reach those who prefer to encourage wakefulness and who would first define themselves and perhaps even the world before trying to make anything better.

Wakefulness involves keeping an open mind and avoiding prejudgment. If we encounter books that profess to illuminate us, we should not judge them because someone else has attacked them. Nor should we be so blind as to avoid testing the creed upon which we presently rest—we should examine it with the same critical attitude which might be applied to any other creed.

Whatever slippages or erosions Christianity manifests, there is no justification in belittling the image of Christ. The same attitude should apply to any of the great spiritual leaders, such as Buddha and Mohammed, who reached a stature of eminence in their lifetime. Christ's teachings can in no way be held responsible for the diverse organizations that resulted from various interpretations of

His words. Nor can He be held responsible for all of the rogues that operate under His banner.

The progress of a transcendentalist is slow in a world inimical to free thinking. Books are scarce and over-zealous librarians think that they are frustrating the devil when they surreptitiously take certain books off the catalogue lists. Personal contacts are even more difficult to come about because each man must protect his family, even if that protection is only from public scorn or business losses. I hope to see better contacts among honest diggers and hope that some readers will bend an effort to help bring about better referential association among seekers. There must be paths in the jungle. There must be places where men of any faith or fancy can go to meditate or to compare notes with a fellow-seeker.

To live with ourselves we must take some stand, some line of action. Nature and society prohibit the complete vacuum. We have the choice of driving dynamically or being driven relentlessly. We may cease to be a cork and become a ship.

ON THEOLOGY

Let us survey this massive subject that has furnished mankind with perennial hope and eternal strife, mentally and physically, individually and nationally. It would be of scientific value to chart the early origins of religion and the evolution of those origins in order to observe the sequence of changes, as well as the religiously revolutionary figures who expedited those changes.

There are works that deal with the evolution of religion that can be studied by the reader. They include the heavy works of Blavatsky and Max Mueller and *The Golden Bough* by Frazer. Frazer has done quite a bit of research on the growth of a complex God from primitive gods of the fields, of the hunt, or of war.

Thus, we have the possibility that the early corn-god may be the father of current religious thinking, or the possibility that there was a divine emanation waiting for primitive man to divest himself of the corn-god, which emanation appeared on earth in widely separated places at about the same time. The time embraced the period from 563 B.C. to 570 A.D. Zoroaster was born in the sixth century B.C. Buddha lived from 563 to 483 B.C. Then Christ came in the year 1. And we have Mohammed in the year 570 A.D.

And so, bypassing historical research, I would like to go directly to the major categories of religion in order to make a comparative study of different definitions and concepts. We have the Monistic viewpoint, which means that God permeates everything, including the human soul and body.

Next, the dualistic God, or God as a separate being.

The regional God, such as Jehovah, who was considered to be only the God of the Jews, and by some to be a planetary spirit.

Phallic God, a sort of humanized masculine evolution, symbolized from the Hebraic letter *jod*.

God, the undefinable, represented by the letters JHVH.

The God within. The inner self.

God as being the automatic law of the universe, but lacking in personality.

Any of the thousands of gods worshipped by sects or tribes.

Concerning the concepts of multiple Gods, they are difficult to categorize because some of the one-God doctrines confuse the layman with complex sub-theories such as the doctrine of the Trinity. There is an argument also that there is a hierarchy of Gods and some translators of the Bible point out that such is meant by the word *Elohim* which is an intentional plural word. The Buddhists also mention a God-hierarchy which they call the *Dhyan Chohans* or *Bodhisattvas* which are sometimes given an exact number. This brings us to the Asian concept of gods which have evolved from humans, as in the case of Gautama Buddha.

For future reference I wish to list certain concepts on life after death.

1. Reincarnation, either upward toward godhood or toward dissolution.

2. Reoccurrence. A theory more complex but no more provable than the others. This has to do with the reoccurrence of a human being, either by design or accident, identical to a previous human being of another era. The argument is that such beings, if alike in all ways, are the same being. Another version of this theory is that the individual man is actually a life-strand in a timeless continuum, with the only motion being the progression of that man's consciousness along that life-strand. Reoccurrence for him would be a repeat performance of such life-strand travel. In simple words, it means reliving this same life over and over. Some Spiritualists claim that this pastime is available to all after death, but that after a while the game grows boring and is abandoned.

3. Reincarnation. White's concept. This theory supposedly evolved as a result of considerable work in automatic writing

with a spirit-guide doing the dictation. In this theory, the human is born unique, having never lived before as the same being. "That which is born of spirit is spirit; and that which is born of flesh is flesh," is used to identify the concept. One or more spiritual parents manufacture a spirit and then look about for a woman about to become pregnant or about to deliver. The child-spirit thus finds itself a child-body.

4. Spiritualism. Spiritual evolution after death through possibly a half-dozen planes.
5. Christianity's paradise or hell. This belief differs from the foregoing concepts in that it allows neither for another life in this plane nor any further refinement or growth after death. One life, one eternity.
6. Immortality through faith. It is held by some that there is a dimensional matrix that is subject to the faith of men. Levi, in one of his books of magic, gives the formula for creation.
7. Immortality through mechanical means, concentrating upon a chakra, observation of certain sounds, prayers, etc.
8. Translation. This theory claims that some people may develop an immortal body by means of a slow change.
9. Union with the Absolute. Satori.
10. Oblivion.

Can we pick up where Max Mueller leaves off and discuss the ineffable? Still, the hunger in man demands an answer and man is annoyed by the inconsistencies of the mighty. It is possibly true that all is rationalization—even this—but if we are to blush at hope then we must pursue some sort of mathematics and even risk the answer of zero. All of this, in respect for the straw, or any other tiny foothold of a word or sentence that might be an anchor. If all else fails, it shall be effort. And effort shall beget effort. On the other side, silence and inactivity will only beget silence and stagnation.

Let us look for the reasoning in some of the age-old beliefs and begin with Monism. If God is everywhere, then He is in complete charge and the quest for Truth is foolish, as well as the pursuit of any action. We would be only an infinitesimal expression of this Being. Add omnipotence to omnipresence and every aspiration becomes vanity for what seem to be separate mortals. Yet, the religions that preach such Monism still preach free-will also, in order to hold their flocks accountable. Then we hear the old expression that God is powerful enough to stop us, but that He allows us to do evil. This can only read that He allows Himself to do evil. And what could a singular God-entity do that would be qualified as being less than deific conduct when by His absoluteness (by definition) He cannot be adjudged one way or the other.

It is hard to determine if our Christian God is one of Monism or Dualism. The Catholic dogmas and catechisms express beyond a doubt that He is everything. Yet those same catechisms make much of human guilt. Would they blame man for the creation of the human being? Predestination would indicate a monistic concept and an all-powerful God, but the advocates of predestination also preach morality.

It has been said that man makes God in his own image and likeness. Could it be that man, being a bifocal, bicameral, polarized creature feels it necessary to see everthing in a relative manner? Regardless, if everything is God, this writing would appear to be as foolish as any other action, but the efforts to know such Truth (if it be the Truth) or to find our true state of Being should not be arrested. We should not qualify the results of an adventure until the project is completed.

The Summa Theologica pretends to prove the existence of a monistic God by using a dualistic mechanism. It observes that the universe is in motion and ergo must have a mover. The mover must be God. This separates God from the universe and makes Him a sort of chief engineer over the visible, dimensional universe. Being a mover of physical objects removes from God the need to participate in functions of non-visible planes or dimensions, so that such theology is more of a cosmology. Thomas Aquinas lived before Einstein and Ouspensky and, consequently, did not have to argue with them about the nature of motion, which must, of necessity, be relative to time in a timeless continuum.

The greatest bit of frustration in Catholic teaching is to be told on one hand that the Summa Theologica is the "highest theology" and be told by the same theologian that the finite mind cannot ever perceive the infinite.

In regard to Dualism, we find that Dualism at least gives us the privilege of being a searcher with an objective. We must all go along on this tack, at least until we find out that we do not exist as an individual. Yet, as we go, and create concepts, counter-concepts are automatically born and for every virtue that we find, counter-virtue is created. And, thus, is born the devil.

Sometimes the devil is not the only competitor of God. There is a belief involving celestial politics, in which sundry Gods hide behind the curtain of dimesion and try to entice the souls of men away from other Gods. An erudite Theosophist recently stated that he held this to be the esoteric truth behind all religions. In works of magic we find invocations to some of these ancient Gods, and practitioners as recent as Eliphas Levi believed that those Gods are still real and still retain the life which centuries of faith bestowed upon them. It is interesting to note here, also, the efforts of churches in modern times to promote a drive for souls and the exhortations of churches to parishioners to increase and multiply. Why do the Gods need men? Unless this is Dualism, strained to the utmost, why should these celestial beings have terrestial roots dependent somehow upon nourishment from fleshlings?

There is still another disturbing note that is echoed by scholar and clod alike . . . Why do the Gods remain hidden? If there is a personal God, more powerful than man, why does He seemingly impose a set of rules or conditions upon man and Himself? This rule holds that the fleshling must guess the correct name, which he must cry out at night, protesting his desire to be food for celestial roots, or to be a constituent.

The use of logic implies a mechanistic attack upon a problem that has its answer in the abstract magnitude. Knowing this difficulty, many seekers use the methods of the mystics which involve intuitional meditation or some form of concentration.

It would be impossible for a man to choose a path from logic alone. Reason will sway the mind toward a movement but intuition plays the larger role in the choosing of spiritual paths. The theory of reincarnation is an example in that it seems to be more reasonable than the one-life, one-death theory. But reincarnation has not been proven either, even though there are many testimonials of the remembering of previous lives. So that if reincarnation is accepted, the acceptance comes largely from intuition. It is argued that it is a more just system than the concept of eternal punishment or reward for helpless reactions to the circumstances of life. It has an understandable, structural conception of the relation of action to consequences when it associates the theory of reincarnation with the idea of automatic Karma. However, we cannot accept a theory only because it has a conceptual structure that is pretty or that appeals to human standards of justice.

On the testimonial side, there have been people who have demonstrated, honestly or otherwise, that they could recall previous incarnations. Some cases have been carefully witnessed, especially cases where a young person described the place of his previous life or people now living who lived contemporarily with his previous life. There are rituals in Tibet by which the monks determine the identity of a child in a previous life. The Tibetans choose their Dalai Lama by this process.

Hypnosis cannot be considered as a valid means for determining previous incarnations, although it has been used here in the West to attempt that task. Hypnotic subjects have been found to be able to assume many characteristics upon command by the operator and have given evidence about any personality named at random as being their previous incarnation. I have verified this through hypnotic experimentation and several other hypnotists whom I know have witnessed the same results. The subject simply adopts the personality suggested and, at times, amazingly enough, will come up with facts about that personality that neither the subject nor operator knew.

The Rosicrucians have a method for seeing your past incarnations, but gazing for long periods of time into mirrors is not very evidential in method and the results must be qualified by the knowledge that the human eye under prolonged strain is not very reliable.

We come now to mechanical means for reaching salvation or for attaining wisdom. One such is baptism—a sacrament which involves water—and a degree of surrender to divine will. Some who believe baptism to be necessary also believe that without it the soul goes to hell or to a lake of fire. The Catholic church teaches that the unbaptized go to Limbo. Baptism, of course, has fundamentalistic origins but there has not been a valid explanation for the use of earthly water to change a supposed spiritual conditon. I can understand the change of being that may be brought about by the surrender of egotistical aspects of the personality but I cannot rationalize the use of water as a celestial catalyst.

Not only is the Christian religion beset with fundamentalism, but every religion that has inspired writings has the same trouble. And it is not enough that we suffer our abstractions to be handed to us in the form of parable and translated histories, but we are subjected to further confusion by still more tangential philosophies which claim for Truth by the application of symbolism to the Bible, or the application of numerology to the original alphabet of the Bible. And this with the knowledge that the original documents are unobtainable.

Can the Truth actually be this complicated? Can wisdom be rattled loose from the convolutions by the bombardment of the mind with myriad symbols? Yet this is a school of thought. It has been said that all wisdom that is verbalizable is but the result of the juggling of symbols.

With the beginning of symbolism-studies, the intuition recedes from fundamentalism. Emotional games are not enough to keep the people in the churches even though the churches have become social centers, utilitarian crime-preventers, or conduct-inhibitors of questionable value. The mass-mind of man as a computer manifests its decisions more by its apathy than by its interest. Worship consists of a smooth confluence of egos.

That man can be inspired by reading the Bible cannot be denied nor could it be denied that he might be inspired by studying Raphael's Ephemeris. If juggling will do the trick, then why not the Tarot or the I Ching? I wish to avoid any great amount of criticism of the fundamentalistic approach. Fundamentalistic interpretations bog down in the ambiguity and obscurity of both literal and interlinear import, and we could spend endless hours arguing about intended meanings. And it is not valid to take the Bible to be of divine voice merely because the book says so any more than we should fall down and worship a totem-pole because the inscription on the pole reads, "I am God, worship me." There must be valid indications or substantiations indicative of the Bible's authority such as witnesses from outside the Bible,—preferably from an all-able God.

There is an argument that uncertain, ritualistic steps are necessary for beings of lesser development whose nature and karma will not allow them to accept the philosophic side or essence of religion. So that such people are doomed to spend this life by frittering away their time, by singing chorals, or quoting the scriptures. And this is both truth and cleverness. There are people who are unable to seek for truth with dynamic energy and average faculties, but I have reservations about using religion as an anodyne, or,— exchanging lies for tithes.

The time has come when another layer of superstition and fearful umbrage should be lifted. Believe what you will, but do not legislate. Belief is no proof for belief. Belief may even create, but then different beliefs will still produce monstrosities and confusion. God remains forever hidden from mankind, and to believe our elders, He is only able to communicate through material objects or through some high-priest who thinks no more of his altar than to take his meals from it and glorify his animal exigencies with it. Drinking of alcohol has been justified by using the Biblical references of Christ's drinking of wine. Quotations can be found to justify various carnal expressions. You can split yourself like a schizophrenic and let the breast boast that it is no part of that which supports it, placing virtue in the heart and head and giving the devil the hindmost.

It is not possible to understand or follow a system of thinking that begets sub-sciences and rubrics ad infinitum. This paper is directed to lives of less than a hundred years—that hope for light within that span of time. Nor can we study every religion. Such a search would be the equivalent of the task of the demons at a Chinese funeral who must pick up every piece of showered confetti in order to find the soul of the deceased.

We are looking for the most consistent. And we must be justified in abandoning too much inconsistency. For instance in the *Summa Theologica* we find that evil is supposed to emanate from good. Yet the wee, bipolar, bicameral bipeds are supposed to be headed for purgatory, limbo or hell for not avoiding evil. This reasoning is the result of a split purpose by the author who would appear erudite while trying to inspire fear. We are led to believe, by seeing repeated, conflicting sub-theories in great religious writings, that some of the authors were interested in constructing speculative philosophies for the edification of their egos. Cosmologies abound. Some harmonize a little better than others on a point or two, or they combine a complex, exotic idea with that which we wish to believe. And the more complicated the diagrammed treatise, the more it flatters such minds whose pride would not let them settle for a simple theory.

Nearly two thousand years of Christianity have not given us one two-edged sword alone—the blades are like the leaves of grass. Each man's religion is a stranger to his neighbor's. We cannot expect that it will be any different in the next five hundred years, but each who sees this chaos or Babel should want to simplify things a bit. Man should, likewise, have reverence for honest effort, whether it be in the field of fundamentalism, astrology, magic or any other. While threading our way among the many paths, let us do so with respect and yet have the courage to criticize. And let the criticism be as honest and as sacred to us, as that which we criticize is sacred to those who hold the different point of view.

And if there is a feeling of resentment it can only be for those who treat truth lightly or who laugh at the hungry while feeding from their sweat.

Let us have a brief look at hell. Celestial schizophrenia and spiritual masochism. Hell must be the womb of the Almighty from which came evil or the devil. Evil must have a headquarters. If we go back to the ancients, we find that those pagans were more civilized. Except for the Tibetans, they did not believe that the soul was tortured after death. The pagan feared the shaman's magic, not his cosmology. We do not hear of an unhappy hunting ground in Indian lore. Valhalla was not a dreaded place. Hades had no terrifying negative qualities. Gehenna was the city dump. Sheol was the grave, not a fiery pit.

The early Christian church must have borrowed from Tibetan "paganism." Dante's sadomasochistic writings may well have been an attempt at legal pornography in his time. Milton could not admit a Paradise without admitting its opposite. In the book, *Lives of the Saints,* I have read of saints who languished in the contemplation of various body-tortures for the sake of their sins or for the "love of their Lord." Reward and punishment get all mixed up so that the zealot who professes to be a faithful servant of God still expects to be punished, to die on the rack. And God benevolently smiles in approval or chooses to silently ignore this passing of his pawn. The God of the Jews would at least have manifested anger at losing a pawn. In those days, one man holding up his arms could turn the tide of battle, but later a thousand Christians dying in the arena while chanting the allegiance of God, had no power over a handful of lions.

It is no wonder that a sobering period was to ensue. And a trend toward materialism or, as it was called at the time, an Age of Reason. The inquisition was the final monstrous act of masochism that sent Europe and Christendom reeling into the age of reason.

Doctrine was replaced by experimentation. Science looked into everything from magic to alchemy. It was called metaphysics, but it was actually a sincere attempt to find a tangible religion. Witches, astral influences, fairies, magi, werewolves, elementals, incubi, succubi, homunculi, reincarnation and translation were all mixed up together. This was a commendable investigation, being an objective analysis of phenomena with an aim at finding the proper relation between these phenomena and man.

THE SEARCH FOR GOD

We approach this subject with the heavy awareness of our limitations, whether our approach to God be direct as a moth flying into the sun, or indirect and cautious as a tiny bookworm trying to digest every book in every library. And the task is burdensome enough without harnessing ourselves with the load of guilt or responsibility every step of the way and with every mistake in every step.

The old concepts of sin must go. They represented acts which were responses to compulsions whose origins are primeval. We are, for the most part, mobile robots with built-in reflexes. As the *Bhagavad Gita* explains. But we are robots that hope to take over our own computers. And somewhere along the line, someone legislated that if we are to take over the computers, we must first admit personal liability for any decisions of the computer. This would be assumed to be a sensible idea only if we could completely control that computer. And completely controlling the individual involves controlling his destiny which would mean controlling the environment with all of its known and unknown laws of operation.

We arrive now at the conjecture that we are not supposed to presume to know that which is planned by God for us. This may be true and it is just as possible that it is not true. There is always the possibility that all knowledge is available and proportional to our ability to remove limitations. If we are not supposed to know that which God is doing with us, then we are placed in a position of insignificance in which any attitude of ours toward God would not flatter that God one iota. And our existence would be as meaningless and mortal as an expendable, erodable cog in a machine of two billion cogs.

There is also the possibility that there is truly a personable God who is the creator and master of all, but who pays little or no attention to us because He has more important creatures with which to amuse Himself. We like to think that God created us as perfect creatures for reasons of perfect joy. We appraise Him with human standards of pleasure and flatter ourselves into the picture by claiming that we are giving a command-performance for His pleasure. We take too big a step when we conjure up a God that surmounts all time and space and then pretend to know Him on a first name basis. The one-God theory, as meaning something synonymous with a First Cause, can be understood as a concept. But there is evidence that the one-God theory is not the result of personal knowledge or research, but rather a result of clever theology or theological diplomacy whereby all the conflicting religions were ingested and included rather than opposed as adversaries. Even the ancients realized that the system of thinking which explained the most would last the longest. The laymen of ancient times, while not as educated as today's layman, still saw all kinds of advantages from incorporating the tax-hungry priest-craft all under one roof.

Theosophy has many good points. It neglects to define God as a personal being both inaccessible to and yet threatening to man. It emphasizes, rather, the Pyramid of spiritual endeavor and the need to contact spiritual teachers on higher strata of the Pyramid. The word Pyramid is intentionally capitalized here because it represents one of the major concepts of this book. The only hope of man lies in the existence of a source of knowledge or direction that is human. And while some may say that all lies within ourselves, we find that even the cloistered monks find a need for cooperation with other humans to secure their meditation. There are, besides teachers of relative wisdom, teachers of direction which are most rare.

Some mystics depend upon spirits, or angels, presuming that such spirits are closer to God, or in possession of knowledge of other dimensions. We have the case of Joan of Arc. If we are to look at the history of her life we must admit that she was in contact, from childhood, with elves or fairies and later in life with an angel whom she identified as St. Michael. Now St. Michael was not a canonized saint and, in fact, was older than both Catholicism and Christianity. He is supposed to be the spirit that spoke to Moses in the burning bush.

The voices that instructed Joan were knowledgeable. They correctly informed her to identify the dauphin, Charles, and betrayed to her a prayer that Charles admitted was known only to God and himself. With these angels' help she was able to locate the lost sword of Charles Martel, which she used to lead the French. The victories which she predicted came to pass.

Yet, the story has puzzling facets. St. Michael, the archangel, was not her only prompter. St. Catherine and St. Margaret, two ex-humans, also prodded her to take over military leadership. The English were Christian as well as the French. What was going on in heaven? What interest could angels and saints have in the politics of France, especially when the mills of God take care of the destinies of men? We are led to believe that God was in need of Joan of Arc. Yet, if this is true, why did God abandon Joan to defeat, to a trial conducted by men, and finally to a fiery death? Like the daemon of Socrates, when the crisis of death drew near, St. Michael did not lift a spear.

We may say that Joan knew that all of this would happen. Yet the whole affair does nothing to promote faith in God among men. And more so, it is likely to make us think twice before listening to discarnate beings, regardless of their ultra-mundane abilities. If the philosophers and saints were left holding an empty sack, what do we have to hope for? As has often been noted, Christ apparently was abandoned in his final hours. All of which brings us back to the problem of understanding all the sources of revelation, whether they be voices, invisible entities who make themselves known by indirect means, or entities which are visible. The Bible itself warns of familiar spirits, but nowhere do we find a formula for distinguishing between beneficial, honest entities and those which make use of us and then drop us.

In regard to Joan of Arc, I have come to the conclusion that her fate was somehow related to her virginity. It is said that she was rearrested for putting on a pair of pants. Previously, she had been arrested and had admitted certain charges brought against her by the ecclesiastical inquisition. The male attire was taken as proof of her relapse. In looking for common denominators, there is evidence that innocence plays a part in the commerce between humans and entities. The demons invoked by Cellini and the priest demanded that a virgin boy be brought to the next invocation. We find poltergeist visitations to be more phenomenal when there are children of adolescent or pre-adolescent years involved. All of which would mean that virginity was the power that Joan possessed and for reasons unknown to us, it attracted either spirits of stature or spirits that were able to impersonate biblical characters and saints. And possibly, as long as Joan was a virgin, (Prince Charles is supposed to have had her examined) she had the service of those spirits.

We come to one of the great secrets of occult work. As Eliphas Levi advises, the thaumaturgist observes celibacy . . . at least for certain periods of time prior to most rituals or invocations.

The dangers of listening to voices are evident in many publicized cases wherein people have even murdered their children at the command of invisible entities which identified themselves as God. Such was the case of Abraham and Isaac, but an angel or voice arrived in time to prevent Abraham from killing Isaac. I can see the probability of such a sacrifice enacted in modern times by another Abraham, a trusting, fanatical fundamentalist, if the latter believed that God actually commanded Abraham (since the Bible is accepted as the true message of God). It follows that if Abraham did not dare to disobey, then neither should anyone else similarly inspired.

Man has been able to discern that he is not yet fully able to discern. Whereas in previous times, the populace was quick to accept any phenomenon on quaking knees—we now take a calmer approach and look for a more natural explanation. While not being able to categorize and explain all phenomena, we have become alert to the ability of the mind to impose a fraud upon itself—by virtue of its finite nature—and we realize that the mind responds to severe problems with unconscious rationalization and weary surrender to the nearest explanation.

We have approached the problem of knowing God objectively and for many reasons it is impossible. In the first place, we cannot define God until we create a definition (a definitive philosophy) for God. As a result of the many God-definitions, it is evident that the word God is a very uncertain term. Equally portentious is the word gizmogle. A scientist might spend decades sifting the sands of the sea with a microscope with the pretence that he was looking for a gizmogle. And in this charade he might actually find a keytone enzyme containing the secrets of life. This is a fairy tale just concocted, but we should not be surprised, if such a case actually occurred, to find that the scientist was quickly ordained as a prophet by virtue of his new power, and find that gizmogle, which previously meant nothing, would now be capitalized.

It is better to avoid the use of the word God, (or definitions of that not yet ascertained), except in the magical processes of prayer. In our objective or relative search we can only retreat from ignorance and error. We may build imposing conceptual structures whose foundations are hypotheses, but we should never make the mistake for a moment of forgetting that the original hypotheses are still there, still qualifying the whole structure.

So that for any research value we find that *the voices of unseen entities and the directives of apparitions are unreliable* and are no final authority for the seeker. Nor are they of use in the search for God. It stands to reason that if God or any other being of bi-dimensional power desired to communicate with us through an angel, then that God would use its ultimate power to clarify that medium of communication by denying any spirit the means to communicate with man in a fraudulent manner. If we are to presume the existence of an omnipotent God, we must assume that He is not concerned with our confusion.

LIFE AFTER DEATH

Man is more concerned with the problem or possibility of life after death than he is with arguments about God. Yet man, being inclined to believe that which he wishes to believe and to understand problems in proportion to his understanding, is liable to settle for a wide range of solutions to the eternal enigma.

If Christian theologians recognized the need to be more than human in their guesses about divine purposes, they settled for much less and made God to appear as a sub-human ogre in their conceptualization of a helpless life followed by a relentless hell.

And while reincarnation may be more digestible than Christian finality, it still fails to answer all questions and it also bears symptoms of rationalization. For the poor and oppressed there is a hope of a better day for themselves and indirect revenge upon the oppressors. For the superior, or dominant class of people, there is hope for still better and greater experiences, and there is more security for them if the less fortunate majority is placated by a promising philosophy.

Another strange belief is that of assumption. The outstanding cases are the stories of Elijah and Mary. Some refer to the raising to heaven of Elijah as being a translation, but today the word *translation* is used to designate a slower metamorphosis of body material. Elijah and Mary were supposedly lifted up suddenly. The Catholic Church in a recent gesture of sensationalism and dogmatic derring-do decided that the Mother of Christ was assumed physically into heaven and decided that all Catholics were required to believe it. This command came at a time when the Church and all Christendom were struggling with the trend of humanity toward materialism, pragmatism and utilitarianism. It was a very bad time to pull a rabbit from the tiara. If Mary was assumed bodily into heaven then the substance of heaven should be analyzed again.

Is heaven a dimension or a place? Would not Mary's body be a bit of an impediment in a place where all other creatures arrived bodiless and possibly subject to laws of another dimension? Evidently Jesus was able to come back and get his body, since the body disappeared from the grave, and later reappeared on the road to Emmaus. This does not prove that Jesus escaped physically from the grave, but could imply that the spirit of Jesus was able to simulate a body and to discard the mask at will.

To say that a personality has found a means to travel from one dimension to another and to be seen in both is not unreasonable, although it implies a special talent. The SRF movement claims that some of its masters were avatars who had the ability to come and go between the spiritual planes and they were also reputed to have extensive creative ability. This brings us to the word *illusion*, for many believe this world to be one of illusion and that some liberated spirits are able to evoke the illusion at will.

If a person entered another dimension with his body he would either experience body-changes that would replace the present body-exigencies—and hence he would immediately become a different being than us—or he would have to take some of this physical dimension with him (food and sanitary facilities) and this might imply the need to take it all with him.

The business of reassuming the body on judgment day cannot be comprehended even by a simple-minded cannibal. Would the man who ate Captain Cook and Mr. Cook travel through eternity together like Siamese twins, or with interlocking molecules?

Another problem arises with the knowledge that some people die with disease-wasted or crippled bodies. The aged and crippled are supposed to find only a healthy, young body on judgment day. If religion can make this concession to those who see the evident unreasonableness or pointless possibility of rising from the grave exactly as they entered it, then it is possible that the whole idea of resurrection has merely been a concession made to the many constituents of the church who could not visualize any other type of survival.

For those who think themselves to be advanced beyond such primitive dogmas of the early church, and who still cannot bear the idea of leaving the body, there is a group who call themselves Translationists. They believe that a very small percentage of humanity survives death by translating. This comes about by a progress in spiritual growth whereby the body, with each year, becomes less and less physical and perishable until it is really a different substance, immune to death as we know it, and unhampered by the functional exigencies that we other clods experience.

Translation theories bring to mind the many spiritual evolution concepts—theories that involve either a change of being or a growth of awareness—the growth of awareness interpreted as a necessity for knowing the future dimension.

There must be some reason for the many divergent beliefs, which is like saying there must be many types of spectacles for the diverse types of vision. And with this observation goes the perennial struggle to try to make everyone accept a uniformly stylized pair of lenses, or to invent a super set of spectacles that would adjust any and all eyes to spiritual reality.

The initial part of any investigative observation must necessarily involve the study of ways and means of observing. Sometimes it is through the critical eyes of others.

Science would demand a personal witness of one who had returned from the grave if science would ever be persuaded to enter the search for a life-after-death. It would, in fact, demand many witnesses. For this reason many intellectuals, or pseudo-intellectuals became involved in Spiritualism. Some courted ridicule in the pursuit of that which might be called "first hand" information. They sought out mediums and organized societies for psychical research. And they were rewarded with adventures in a very dramatic study.

Descriptions of post-mortem adventures in the *Tibetan Book of the Dead* are not too incongruous with Curtiss' concepts regarding spiritual planes. We have learned, however, that we cannot learn from the vapid wraiths that come through the curtains of a medium's cabinet. Their intelligence is as evasive as their tenuous ectoplasm. They utter euphemisms, platitudes and encouragement but any explanation of the nature of their beings and of their surroundings is vague and indefinite. We hoped to find evidence that the form of man would find continuation, even if it were unproven. And to hear the voices of our departed friends tempts us to embrace Spiritualism. However, the fuzziest minds will feel slighted when they talk to relatives who, instead of awakening into greater realms at death, seem to be less intelligent than when they were living and need to be prompted with every answer. An obscure and somewhat secret brotherhood of mystics gives a very interesting explanation for this lack of intelligence among ectoplasmic spirits. This brotherhood advises that there are beings who are able to imitate the forms of the deceased. These beings may not necessarily be human, but are, rather, creatures of a different dimension. Whether or not they don the masks left by the astral body is not important here because it involves more tangential and conceptual thinking not directly relevant.

For those not experienced in Spiritualistic terminology, the planes referred to are generally listed as seven, with the astral plane being the plane immediately above, or next in experience, to this plane. Many students of Spiritualism are likewise acquainted with the concept of the astral body—a shell left behind on the astral plane—when the spirit goes on to higher planes. In some writings, we find the word soul synonymous with the astral body, while the essence that survives the lower planes is known as the spirit. And, of course, other writings refer to the beings (supposedly on the astral plane) who haunt houses as being spirits, and refer to the immortal essence as the soul. Such confusion results in painstaking definition by all parties on all points.

The lay-spiritualist is not aware that cabinet spirits are beings of another dimension. Western scientists did not suspect that such were "beings." They suspected trickery.

Spiritualism does not explain away or disprove the counter concept that other-dimensional entities manipulate the masks of the dead, and until it does, one theory shall be as good as the other and the foundation of Spiritualism shall be in jeopardy.

The unscientific teachers of India and Tibet are responsible for the first explanations of the counterconcept (or the idea) that beings or entities could manipulate the ectoplasm. The always ultra-civilized Western world managed to kill off the witnesses to spirit-phenomena—so much so that some benevolent entities appeared as deceased saints hoping to protect the medium from ecclesiastical fire. William Crookes treated Katie King as a deceased person. Eliphas Levi was of the opinion that most spirits were somehow created out of the subtler essence of the medium's body which the magus manipulated as he would theatrical wax. We cannot say that Levi was entirely wrong, for there is no way to be sure that some mediums do not have unique talents. The Rosicrucians believe that in some cases man is able to create such entities.

If there is any conclusion that can be drawn from these concepts, it is that the medium's cabinet is not an infallible threshold or two-way, glass door between the different dimensions. We can recognize that Spiritualism and thaumaturgy are valuable means of gathering more information about such entities and their environment.

Spiritualism has degrees of depth as does any religion. The lower levels have to do with fraud beneath a pretence of being a comforting utility. And the messages that came from the mouths of genuine materializations are no more sagacious than those that are relayed to us through clair-audient and clairvoyant mediums. When asked to describe heaven, God, Christ, or even the pastime of the deceased, all of the above sources reply in a sweet but inane manner that might be described as spiritual double-talk.

The matter of materialization is worthy of scientific investigation, both in that it is a phenomenon unexplained and in that it presents a situation in which man seems to function as a creator. The pretence about apports is that they are creations. At one seance which I attended the "spirits" wove a scarf and presented it to a grief stricken, but heavy contributor—a mother from Eastern Ohio. There was emphasis here by the elated pseudo-medium that it was created, woven especially for this mother.

Then if such weaving be possible, is it not possible that the phantoms themselves could likewise be manufactured? The more likely truth is that the scarf actually came from beneath a cheese cloth tunic and never had been anything but material cloth. The mention of "phantom weaving" is not mentioned here to expose a case of trickery but to indicate inconsistency in a movement that would fail to see the full possibilities of such weaving.

The significant thing to remember about spirit-materializations is that regardless of their identity they do not seem to have as much personality or intellect as the living person did, all of which would not be encouraging if we were hoping for mental evolution upward after death. Not that we should look for that which flatters our hopes. I have been privileged to witness several materializations that were not cheesecloth. The figures were recognized by relatives but the control-spirit's voice bore a remarkable likeness to the medium's voice, as did the voices of other emerging spirits. Most mediums admit that the spirits use their larynx, but never mention that the ectoplasm itself may well emerge from the medium's body.

W.J. Crawford spent a lifetime studying spiritualism and table tilting, and discovered that the table was moved by ectoplasmic rods or cantilevers that extended from the solar plexus of the medium to the approximate center and underside of the table. He established these conclusions with the use of a soft putty which was placed on the underside of the table. And he isolated the path of the invisible cantilevers by moving a square piece of cardboard beneath the table. When the cardboard interfered with the path of the cantilever, the table would fall. His book, *The Reality of Psychic Phenomena* is valuable to anyone interested in this type of research.

Spiritualism exists all over the world but under different names. The guides or spirits have different names as well, being demons, djinns, pitris and elementals. Eliphas Levi charts celestial domain and categorizes the hosts of angels and demons. It should be remembered that Levi did not deny the existence of entities or demons, but inferred that the wraiths that appeared as souls of the deceased were very probably ectoplasm only. His real name was Alphonse Constant and it is presumed that he adopted the pseudonym to stay alive. He had been a priest but he left the church, married and became quite an authority on magic. After many years of this research, he is supposed to have rejoined the Catholic Church, with the comment that everyone should belong to some church in preparation for the next life. Evidently, if there is anything to gather from the life's work of this man (presuming that it is true that he did rejoin the Church), it is that his research gave him no greater promise than that offered by the Church.

Levi reminds us that his knowledge of entities came from studies by the Church hierarchy. And this indicates that Levi either left the

Church to marry or else he was restricted in his search by being in the Church. And all of this also indicates that at one time the Church was searching for the Truth before it degenerated into secularization and the apathy that comes from being afflicted with overweight.

Levi, who had lost faith in the Church, based his entire structure of magic upon faith. He tells us that the apparition of Apollonius of Tyana may well have been created by his faith and, consequently, was not the soul of Apollonius which his student would have liked to have seen. This is worth remembering when we encounter the analysis of faith in later chapters. And so we ponder the limitations of faith and the coloration that those limitations place upon the results—the creations of faith.

Let us go now to cases which are known as spontaneous reappearances, or resurrections of the dead, for it now seems possible that their testimony would appear more valid than the testimony of conjured spirits. It is impossible to review all of the cases of this type or to examine them for authenticity. If we are to presume that they have any value at all, we must admit that a percentage of them may well be sincere accounts. Occult magazines are well supplied with letters from readers attesting to this type of experience, and occult magazines do not pay for these letters. Articles written by doctors bear witness that some patients, on returning from states of unconsciousness peculiar to terminal patients, relate strange stories and experiences which cannot be blamed on drugs or delirium.

We can study the many different reports and reach some common denominators on the evidence available. One factor noticed is the inconsistency with other accounts of after-death experiences. Another peculiarity that has been noticed in many medical cases reported is that the patient had no horror of death and often lamented at being revived. As regards variance in testimony, we have cases where a dying man saw his departed relatives but seemed unaware of celestial scenery or environment. Some noticed beautiful landscapes but saw no relatives. We have accounts where exotic environment is witnessed, in which appear strange vistas, colonnades, iridescent geometric figures and many other phenomena. A very few have mentioned hearing exquisite music. The nose seems to have no place in heaven,—I do not know of a single report of reported fragrance. Some have reported a dimensional world subject to the wishes of the viewer,—and these are rare.

All of which brings us back to the concept that man may well have, in a limited fashion, the power to project or create. Man may color that which he sees with that which he has already seen, desired or contemplated. Or he may project a picture of his expectancies upon the matrix of mind, or next plane-substance with an intensity similar to projections on a theatre-screen, so that it causes an illusion that there is a living movie-screen life, when actually the only life is behind the audience (us) in the projector (God). This is similarly maintained but rendered in other words in the *Tibetan Book of the Dead.*

Some Spiritualists believe in a Desire World, or plane—a realm wherein the spirit can create any illusion simply by desiring. This could also be hell. And, of course, the whole concept may be the result of the testimony of resuscitated persons who manifestly were rewarded with objects of desire while in the dream or death state.

A significant factor that should not be overlooked is the attitudinal evidence presented by people who are dying. Medical reports show that a majority of people who know that they are dying relax and show no anxiety. This may or may not be evidence that euthanasia is part of the physiological and psychological progression of terminating creatures. It is also possible that the computer found a sudden comprehensive answer thrust upon itself and was delighted in the accident.

We move on to another type of personal witness and that is the unexpected or spontaneous appearance of spirits. This type involves neither invocation nor medium. Typical cases would be the haunts of old houses, roads or scenes of tragedy. Such cases include solitary spirits, armies of soldier-spirits seen by a living army, and convocations of monks. If their substance is ectoplasm and ectoplasm is somehow dependent upon human energy, then the visible shells of this type of spirit must have drawn from the residual energy left behind by people visiting the spot or as in the case of the phantom army, drawn from those present.

There are also accounts of people who have been accosted and warned by spirits that resembled themselves, the observers. We have often heard of people who claimed to have seen their "double." The so-called experts have laid this type of phenomenon at the door of the astral double or astral body.

The significant thing about all of these spirit witnesses is that they show little sympathy for the momentousness of man's ignorance and the momentousness of any information that might be extended by someone we could understand and who would—once having lived in this ignorance—know that the living yearned for this knowledge.

Yet, what do we get? The spontaneous appearance or reappearance while ranking as among the most informative if not authentic, still is, largely, a visitation of warning. This means that the deceased are interested yet in the affairs of this dimension and either cannot or will not place the wisdom of the next dimension above the need to warn us of an accident pending or of approaching death.

Science, of course, would prefer the conjured type of spirit since this would be a controlled experiment; but the conjured type of spirit rarely shows the intelligence or awareness that might be associated with a being that is supposed to be sitting astraddle two dimensions. What conclusion can we draw except that man is frustrated by what appears to be a directed blocking, by supervisory powers . . . or simply by the stupidity of the millions of seekers?

We come now to the group of theorists who accept the destructibility of the body and believe that the soul rises either to eternal paradise or descends to hell. They borrow from one another and while borrowing, protest that the party from whom they borrowed is spurious. So that while we move from one group to another we can observe several things. We find the common denominator of all seekers to be ignorance. And from the overlapping confusion among cults and religions we find that most conventional movements have similarities and we find a common denominator in them in that they are all offered with ingestible syrup. The seeker's problem lies in knowing how and when to step with courage out of the isms which our computer or intuition indicates as being inadequate for other than a social emollient.

In studying and cataloguing isms that cling to the one-life, one-death idea, we find that there is considerable variance among them. Some do not believe in hell and vary in their ideas of heaven. Each heaven is colored with wishful thinking and sometimes we find a spiteful heaven wherein only the adherents of particular exponents are allowed.

The interpenetration of different beliefs has a significance. We may not be as unique as we are led to believe. Christianity has built up an elaborate theology and mythology that can find no origin in the teachings of Christ. Christianity and the religion of ancient Egypt are similar. The Egyptians, several thousand years prior to the time of Christ, believed in a heaven and an underworld. They believed in the human soul and in an ethical or moral code that would facilitate their meeting with God, face to face. Osiris, like Christ, was a man who gave his life to improve the lot of his fellow man and to secure immortality for them. There was a Judas in his camp that betrayed him and there is mention of seventy-two followers. It is suggested that the Copts, or early Egyptian-Christians, played a big part in adding a few trimmings to the teachings of Christ. Some numerologists and occultists believe that the entire story of Christ is a fabrication or translation of Egyptian names into Hebrew names which would be more palatable to the Eastern Mediterraneans. For them (the occultists) the word Mary means Egypt from which emanated Truth.

In Egypt, they believed in a fellow called Aapep, a double for our devil. In the *Book of the Dead* (Egyptian), a common vignette shows the deceased person speaking to the serpent Aapep. The Christians also connect the snake with their devil. The different houses of Osiris remind us of the limbo and purgatory of the Catholic Church. There is considerable similarity between Catholicism and the religion of Osiris and less proportionate borrowings by the Catholic Church from Asian religions. So that it might appear that geography and communication had some effect upon the ramifications of Christian theology.

The mummies of Egypt and the bodies in the catacombs show no alarming deviation from the idea of universal salvation. In Egypt, the poorer people were cremated or buried, but they had a belief in rising again and it is not clear from the translation of the *Book of the Dead* whether they intended to return to the same or another body. Nor is it clear today why the Christians are so abhorent of cremation or why the Catholics go through the exhausting ritual of blessing and anointing corpses, or of blessing graves to insure a celestial expedition. Lamentation goes up for the soul of the deceased who is not buried on sacred ground. And yet the laity meekly accept the explanation that God bends down with special dispensation for the faithful who were incinerated at the stake or digested by the lions in a pagan arena. And are not these martyrs accepted as saints today and are they not saints in heaven? Incidentally, in both Egyptian and Christian religions there is a belief in a final day of judgment. This implies that heaven is somehow subject to time for these theologians. Death is not an eternal Now, nor is heaven an eternal Now, but is measured by the years it will take for souls to live sun-measured lives up to a certain point in that solar system and then to be gathered—the ancients and the modern souls—for a massive trial.

We come now to Reincarnation. It permeates the Asian religions, mostly. It can, however, be found like a whisper or hint in parts of the Bible. Christ's admonition to Nicodemus concerning the origin of flesh and spirit is one example. John the Baptist is claimed by some to be the reincarnation of one of the older Bible personalities. The insistence that Christ will come again in physical form is noted.

We deal with a new type of divine justice and this makes the theory of reincarnation unique. The earthly sojourns replace the purgatories and limbos and man is not damned for his ignorance, but is required to work the lessons over again. Spiritual evolution is tied to the earth and life becomes more of a classroom than a torture chamber. The weakness in the theory of reincarnation lies in the inability of the layman to understand the objective of perhaps millions of years of transmigration. In other words, where are we aimed and what is the reason for the whole system?

The presumption is that if we knew, we might employ some of this so-called free will to accelerate the growth. Another weakness in the theory of reincarnation is the failure of the believer to remember past lives. Of course, the authorities maintain that this ignorance is a prerequisite for our spiritual growth and maintain that if we knew that which was in store for us we might try to throw our machine into reverse.

We come now to a school of thought which has very little connection with the foregoing isms and which has for its objective the *Union With the Absolute*. There are many terms, eternally vague to the layman, such as *Cosmic Consciousness, Nirvana, Samadhi, Satori, Awakening and Enlightenment*. The implications of these strange words, while being vague descriptions of an indescribable state of being, also point to a change of being for the aspirant. Admitting possibly the need of the finite mind to adjust to the infinite before pretending to understand it.

Among the so-called masters who claim to know about these states of mind there is much contradiction. The words "so-called" are not to be interpreted as being derogatory but denote the uncertainty of the title of master. There is no way to distinguish a master from a neophyte and if the reader knew the difference, he would not need to read this. Buddha once was asked by a candidate-neophyte to prove his claim of being a master by proving to the candidate that the latter would actually reach Nirvana by following Buddha's path. Gautama the Buddha replied that the candidate was unreasonable in demanding an answer to an impossible question. It would be like demanding proof from someone describing a long journey or distant scenery. The only proof would be to go and see for one's self.

So the main weakness in this category is the intangibility of the concepts concerned and the impossibility of checking the people who claim to be masters or authorities. In this category we are not dealing so much with religion as we are with direct experience. We are dealing with systems that have no readily accessible temples if temples exist at all. These systems depend very little on written directives and are so diversified in form as to confuse anyone not simply drawn, as by a magnet, to a particular school. And there is much refutation of authority within some systems.

For instance, P. D. Ouspensky devoted much of his adult life to the investigation of methods for the "expansion of consciousness." He was a disciple of Gurdjieff, a very mysterious and autocratic spiritual master. Yet Ouspensky, while never denouncing Gurdjieff, nor attempting to discredit him, nevertheless disassociated with him and founded his own school. And his books lead me to believe that Ouspensky had the better system.

Gautama founded the movement now called Buddhism yet the yogic masters, who admit Buddhistic origins or affiliations, and some Zen masters, claim that what is now apparent on the face of the earth as Buddhism bears less resemblance to the original message of Buddha than Christianity bears to the true message of Christ. According to one Zen master (who from respect must remain anonymous and may, consequently, not be personally attacked as false nor hailed as true), Buddha really started Zen and Buddhism became a personality cult depending for substance on parables and wise sayings. The number of people who were really endowed with the teachings of Gautama (initiated) were few and tremendously out of proportion to the vast number of Zen Buddhist monks who might lay claim to cognizance of the system. This same man claimed that there was a lineage of any true master that could be traced back to Gautama. This tracing is, of course, not possible. If there were no records kept, then we must take people's word for these things. A man may claim that he was initiated by another now dead. But unless the dead man left a bona-fide proof of this for posterity, we are out of luck.

This category (of union with the Absolute) lays claim to a transcendency over the previous religions discussed. This makes it unique. The weaknesses that mark the doctrines of various religions are not to be found in it. The wheel of reincarnation, if aimed at Nirvana, may have more meaning; but an endless wheel of reincarnation could make lemmings out of humans. Cyanide would be better to live with than the knowledge that man can never escape from the misery of eternally being reborn into the pain of adjustment to nature only to be extinguished each time by nature.

But heaven and hell as dreamed and depicted by Dante, Milton and Swedenborg would have to be consigned to the realm of illusion. They would exist in somewhat the same intensity as the light projected upon a theatre screen that seems to be animated by the projector. Thus, we become not the potted but the potter. We become possibly the projector, but the projections (our physical bodies included) may no longer be considered as any more real than projections. So away goes the grave, Sheol, hell and heaven and with them the peddlers of fear-pills.

And what do we have? Still there is confusion. We have, first, no clear knowledge of the state of being implied when any of the words such as Cosmic Consciousness, Nirvana, Samadhi, or Satori is heard. There are different schools and approaches. The direct approach method is called Zen. Nothing about Zen makes sense unless you have become a Zen Adept.

Then there is the evolutionary approach to the "Union" that may take many years or incarnations. This is found in some yogic groups. Here we have an overlapping of dogmatic beliefs with ideas of "change of being." Personal immanence is shadowed by concept-building. Some reincarnationists believe that reincarnation leads to a state of Nirvana after a long period of evolution through incarnations. Some believe also in a longer period of evolution on a spiritual plane, after the body is finally discarded. Thus, the Theosophist Blavatsky speaks of Buddha as being on a level slightly above the level of the masters Koot Hoomi, Morya or Christ. And the implication from this form of yoga is that these levels are somehow related to duration, or time as reckoned in the solar system, because of the periods of service needed to earn the step of a master and the service time needed to earn still later the step of Boddhisattva. This type of Buddhism is a very laborious climb if union with the Absolute is going to be achieved inside of a million years.

There is much confusion, evidently, between the Absolute state and that which might be called the Universal Mind—a plane which still may be a projection. Yogic schools that protest their ability to reach the Absolute still compile volumes about phenomena produced and miraculous ability over the world of matter. Yet, is not he who is able to mold the wax or reform the matrix of matter still only a mechanic—dealing with material by his own admission? And, consequently, dealing with illusion by his own admission?

Blavatsky has two ponderous volumes filled with the wonders of phenomena down through the ages and with miracles ascribed to occult groups—all offered as incentive for the reader to become a theosophist. But from her accounts, heaven is not an absolute state, but an endless ascension of spirits to nobler and nobler heights. We are dazzled with timekeeping in yugas that makes the entire life of mankind on earth a very small point in the overall time during which the great spirits were building the cosmos.

The progress and time that it might take for an amoeba to become a Boddhisattva may be possibly computed. And that is not all. Somewhere are many masters and Buddhas gone before of even greater spiritual heights, but nowhere is there an end in sight. So that we begin to wonder about the purpose of spirituality.

Also in the SRF movement highlighted in America by Yogananda we have an evolution toward becoming a master or avatar. Yet, we must ask about the extent to which this adroitness as a master might contribute to our state of being. Babuji or Babaji (which, incidentally, only means "dear one") was always popping up in crowds in India so that one of the disciples of the movement might tell of the alarming event. Babaji also performed sensational feats but only for the elect. There is a story told about a party of sorts which was given for one of the chief adepts in which an entire palace, villa or village was materialized for the occasion and if memory is correct in this matter, an immense amount of gold was materialized. Would not such a new religion bring the poor peasants of India on the run?

In America, no group has contributed more to the researching mind about the religions of India and Tibet than the Theosophists. Where, in some of the Indian cults that have invaded America there is uncertainty, there is a dynamism and a strong appeal to human reason on the part of the Theosophists. Besides whatever conclusions we may reach about them, they have provided humanity with an invaluable service—they have stimulated curiosity about the origin of things and about the nature of man and they have laboriously compiled information to exercise the scientific mind.

And if there is one who might be considered a voice or authority about Theosophy, it must be Blavatsky. Theosophy would incorporate all religions, echoing Max Mueller with the claim that all spring from the same hunger and all are aimed at Truth, despite the fact that some along the way become either sectarian, venal, or are limited by the understanding of the devotees. Theosophy does not deny Christ, it enlists Him and places Him in a harmonious relation to Theosophy. Theosophy's attempts at a marriage of the utterly profane with the utterly abstract philosophies is interesting to note.

That Blavatsky decrees the understanding of the Absolute to be the basic reality can be found in the proem of the *Secret Doctrine,* on the 15th and 16th pages. She likens it to the Parabrahm of the Vedantists, inferring that they have a similar concept. Displaying an unusual familiarity with the relation of man to the Absolute, she goes on to describe it as the causeless cause from which first emanates the Logos and from the Logos comes the next emanation, Life, and finally, Intelligence.

There is considerable confusion to be found by cross-checking the writings of Blavatsky. Here we are concerned with the confusion that exists in heaven, or at least Blavatsky's heaven. She also speaks of a war in heaven. The first cause, or the Logos, should not have too many meanings. Anything that is first, absolutely, should not have more than one meaning. At different places in the *Secret Doctrine,* Christ is supposed to be the Logos. Jesus (if there is a significant difference) was supposed to manifest the Logos in Himself as being the Son of the Logos. On page 232 of Book 2 of the *Secret Doctrine,* he is described as an Initiate, a Saviour and a parallel of Krishna. In Book 1, page 264, Jesus or Joshua is referred to as representing the fall of spirit into matter so that the war in heaven is only allegorical. In Book 2, page 231, footnote, we find that Jesus and the Father are meant to mean soul and spirit. The Logos is not a spirit, as we noted earlier, but the First Cause, antedating spirit or Purusha.

In works other than the *Secret Docrine,* Jesus is looked upon differently. Blavatsky places Him on the Master level with Koot Hoomi. In *Isis Unveiled,* much space is used to discredit Jesus. In Book 2, page 201 Jesus is described as a wise adept of the Rabbi Elhanan who travelled into Egypt, studied the Kabbala and was later hanged upon the cross. This, according to the Talmud. On page 566, Book 2, of the same *Isis,* Christ is not the Son of God but only a high priest. (Here goes the Logos out the window.) On page 574, of the same book, Professor Mueller is supposed to prove that Paul was the real founder of Christianity and not Jesus. "For Paul, Christ is not a person, but an embodied idea." Page 239 undertakes to find that Jesus, or Christ, was a man and only a man.

So much for the compilation of confusion. If, by running between the raindrops, or by treasure hunting in confetti, we are supposed to find the Truth, then Blavatsky may have some system. The vital issue is time. How much time do we have to fumble with the variegations of symbolism? Is there not a simpler way? If man is to become united with the Absolute in a million years, there is no value in the present contemplation of sacred writings or histories of erroneous and incomplete movements.

In summarizing the various approaches to *"Union with the Absolute,"* we first encounter the slow evolutionary theory. Secondly, we have groups of people, or cults, that endeavor simply to expand consciousness, and whose ultimate aim is Cosmic Consciousness. Gurdjieff and Ouspensky may well come into this category. Thirdly, we have the direct method which is Zen. The Zen method is supposed to be quicker and supposedly brings the individual into maximum enlightenment. We might also mention another group who expect to join the Absolute in a state of unawareness by becoming obliviated and returning to the electrical field of the cosmos.

We cannot discuss any of these groups without participation if we expect to do them justice. And with the teachers who would lead us into expanded being there is no argumentation or reasoning. In Zen, reasoning would only be used by the Master to run your intellect up a rat hole.

We are left, therefore, with either an emotional magnetism toward such teachings or else we are selective by virtue of intuition, if we need to look for a reason for embracing schools of either expanded consciousness or of Zen. And even after the student has embarked upon one of the two paths mentioned, at every stage along the way he still finds himself unable to translate intellectually that which is happening to him.

FOURTH PAPER

On Gurus and Unique Systems

If there were a movement that would lead man or his soul to salvation there would be no need for books or dissertations. I would simply recommend that infallible system, embrace it, and write no more. When I use the word "man" in the above sentence I refer to man collectively, or every man. There may be a system that will lead certain men, but it does little good to write it down for the general public as a universal salvation, since it is evident that only confusion and reaction would result. The same type of reaction would occur if college texts were forced upon children in grade school. Books, religions and systems that pretend to take everyone all the way in one universal class are generally political.

And there is no doubt that politics has entered transcendentalism. There are two types of books to be found in the field of religion and transcendentalism which should bear watching—they are ones which are either critical or political. Those which are critical are worth the study if they are unbiased.

The critical writer is a thinker, at least. And being in the field in which he is, he must be concerned with the Truth. He may be sharp and irritating to us if we are clinging to a vain hope instead of hoping to keep an eye open. He may show anger and justly so . He may go overboard and overemphasize or pick one religion or cult when perhaps the majority are equally to blame. He may be motivated by personal encounters with fraudulent leaders and he may employ a reference to incidents rather than use a strictly logical complaint. But he must not be taken idly. It is more important to read criticisms than it is to wallow in the endless volumes of literature that only encourage belief, that employ color to enhance ritual, and often extol as absolute Truth a devotion or technique that has only the external appearance of being mentally therapeutic . . . to say the most.

A critic would have no cause, except to pick the straw from the grain—unless he is a political critic. That is, unless he is using criticism to campaign for recruits by attacking the forces which have followers. The man who argues atheism is shunned as a leper, but the men who concoct new and more complicated dogmas to confuse and enslave men's minds receive praise in proportion to their success in gathering a following. The fact is that an atheist is actually a man who is protesting his own insignificance, while rejecting the meaningless and the unproven. The atheist alarms people because he shocks them from the smugness of mass self-deception. People pursue their animal existence and pay some sort of tithe to be reassured that they have immortality. Now they are not guaranteed immortality for that tithe because they are usually told that they must, besides paying the preacher, also believe . . . no matter how hard the job of believing gets to be. So there generates in religion and cultism a feeling that is something like "keeping up with the Joneses." Everybody talks it up. Everybody presumes to presume. Going to church is the thing to do. The results are fat preachers.

Perhaps the public has not really decided to believe everything that is preached, but one thing that the public has accepted as a group is that Pollyanna is sacred. People do not wish to be doused with cold water, nor with words which have the same effect. If millions of people could be convinced that they had been effectively baited, their first reaction would be anger. This anger would first be directed at the critic who dared to shake them from their pleasant dream. If the critic is aided by the coincidence of an oppression of his listeners at hierarchical hands, then the anger may be directed at the hierarchy or the authorities of the era. The remarkable thing, however, is that the first and often fatal anger is directed at the light-bearer. Most of us have heard the sly hint about Lucifer, the early light-bearer. He was supposedly exiled for trying to illuminate lesser spirits.

The critic must be read and an attempt must be made to understand the true reasons for his discontent. The politician must be exposed. The politician is a sapper of souls and a spender of time that is sacred because of its paucity. We must be alerted to the tricks of the politician if we are to avoid being swept into servitude.

The politician remakes religion or philosophy to suit the desires of the most people. This is a sort of corrupt democracy which should not be applied to religion—the Truth is not attained by voting. Financial success and the perpetuation of the church may be attained in this manner, however. Thus, the authorities, or augurs, who pretend to be able to read the will of God, if not His mind, have decided that God is fickle and is liable to change His mind.

A sin is no longer a sin. During the crusades, one of the Popes extended a carte blanche to the Templars, enabling them, for political expediency, to fracture any commandment with impunity.

They were given absolution in advance of the offence.

We find God and theology being warped to fit the occasion. We find that purgatory is not a timeless and dimensionless situation. It is subject to the length of a wick of a candle at the altar of purgatorial souls. And the candle itself is subject to cost.

Meat was once forbidden on fast-days. The gods have now been pacified. We can eat meat at any time. On occasion, religious leaders have inconvenienced the people to an amazing extent. We are bearers of canine teeth. Our faces are not designed for cropping grass. Our limbs have lost the skill of climbing trees for fruits and nuts (if they were originally designed for that). Yet, there are some religions that endorse total vegetarianism, while protesting at the same time that we were created by a God (who gave us the canine teeth) who does not wish for us to kill other beings or eat them.

These people become fearful and over-zealous. An egg becomes a living thing. Some deny themselves fish, others rationalize for fish. Soul-degrees are haggled over and conscience-wrestling becomes the excuse for complex, so-called "theological dissertations." And finally, the hierarchical supreme court will decide that fish may not be flesh.

The rubrics of ritual are so numerous as to require volumes. Yet, rubrics are as important to religion today as they were ages ago when the mumbo-jumbo of the shaman was a closely guarded secret.

We get into the business of soul-identification. People would not pay much attention to a creed that allowed all life to be lifted up into heaven. No one would pay ten percent of his wages to expedite a salvation that automatically happens to all animal life. So the authorities decided that a bit of cataloguing was in order. Some could see God, some could not. Those in Limbo. Some could be prayed out of purgatory or burned out with candles.

And the animals just did not have souls. We could not have dogs and monkeys getting the same privileges as the tithe-payers. Yet, even a casual observer may encounter congenital imbeciles who have less sense than Jocko the monkey. Of course, we find ourselves in much of a dither about this thing which we like to call the soul. It is like a car that is the most recent style. Everybody just has to have one. No one dares to be second-best, but we must all seek out some unfortunate being to denounce as being less equipped—like Jocko. Now this will surely make us feel more secure, once we find out that there is someone else that is not so secure. It never dawns on us that Jocko may have it all over on us in that his simple life may bring him closer to Truth, while our highly specialized computers of confusion-data may produce kindred hells and errors that emanate from our fatigue and frustration.

We have observed here just a few indications of the confusion that permeates the major religions which have held sway over mankind for a long time. Wars have been fought over the identity of God's representatives, with the conviction that one was authentic and the rest were spurious. God allowed his signature to be given to the winner, even though it was written with the blood of devout unfortunates. Man was vociferous. The heavens uttered not a word.

People have become less devout—perhaps as a result. Crusades of children are no longer available. Monks and nuns are becoming secularized. Heaven is smitten with liberalism, if we are to believe the mind-readers of God. The minds of men are no longer swayed by threat, nor are the minds of children inflamed with pious terrors. New techniques have been devised. Democracy has become the Way, and man is upon the altar as the deity. The congregation has been invited to partake of the sacred ceremonies. Deep theological arguments are avoided. The individual ego is assuaged by allowing it to get into the act.

We have fewer wars with religious motivation. The religious way at least served as an instrument of regulation which kept the theologian on his toes and served to liquidate movements which had grown too monolithic or cruel. Today, however, we have a growing synthesis of all the grand old failures. They are flocking together and want to be recognized as a way of life. No longer touting their singularity or their solitary efficacy, they now cling to the shred of hope that they might survive in a socialistic world as order-promoting agencies.

New isms and religions, coming up out of the ashes of the old—meaning new concoctions and variations—have taken the cue. They do not criticize. Nobody criticizes. People proudly assert that they are above the odious practice of talking about religion.

Thus, we have reasons for rejecting nearly everything until we can substantiate things for ourselves. It is not enough to have a child's devotion when it comes to religion. Children of all religions are devoted. Only the philosopher who has endured the disillusionment of several isms will fully understand this need for a priori rejection. Each time the philosopher has changed temples he may have done so with a new, refreshing vigor emanating from the conviction that he has found the end of the rainbow. Each time he has lived long enough to be disillusioned.

It is then that we come to realize that we did something too hurriedly. We may have purchased that which looked like a beautiful new coat, when in reality it was just an old coat made over. The fact that it is usually tailored to fit the new wearer does not arouse the buyer's suspicion.

We find Christianity with its Hell and half-hells to be godless or not commensurate with our ideas or propositions concerning God. We find God no longer just by human standards and while admitting that God may have His own standards (perhaps totally incomprehensible), we, nevertheless, also realize that any other than human standards are not comprehendible. We realize that the burden of proof lies in almighty hands, not human hands, so that if there are other standards, man cannot be held to account for not understanding them. For man has learned something about himself. He is finite. He has no hopes for miracles that might enable a finite man to converse with transcendental gods or beings, with the assurance that his senses are not playing tricks on him.

So man looked around. The Christian religion became diversified and various new ideas were added, such as fatalism. Fatalism, or predestination, seemed to answer some of the unanswered questions. But we know that answering questions is not enough. For instance, we might proclaim a kingdom of gnomes or angels and scrupulously answer every question about details adroitly spun from our imagination. Proving the existence of the gnomes and angels would be overlooked in the process of examining a portrait of possibility. And possibility is later confused with probability. And then when certainty replaces probability, we have the necessary fanatics for a new religion.

Man's desire to improve on Divine Justice resulted in the theory of reincarnation. The ancient theory of an angry God disappeared in the Orient long before the scientifically advanced Westerners gave the second appraisal to Christianity. Even now, the theory of reincarnation has gained only a slight foothold in the West.

For the Western man, flaccid tolerance seems to have overshadowed any dynamic curiosity that might exist. This tolerance can only be a sign of weakness, as it is a tolerance of ignorance and deception. The Christian hierarchy in its previous refusal to compromise was at least respected for its vitality, even if that vitality was trapped in dogmatic assumptions. The modern Christian hierarchy has relented because the peasants are no longer ignorant, uneducated, or stirred by colorful stories. The peasants' descendents no longer care if the hierarchy decrees or utters curses ex cathedra. The new breed of peasant reasons that you cannot reason with an unreasonable God. Regardless of the possibly sublime language or motivation of God, the peasant only knows the language of the peasant.

It is likely that the hierarchies of the sundry Christian sects have decided that they have merchandise no longer saleable. The Catholics tried for several hundred years to deny the heliocentric system in order to maintain a particular interpretation of the Bible and to maintain the infallibility of the pope. The telescope—a very simple device—threw the chains of ignorance aside and threw a doubt upon the whole pretensive system of authority.

Since each church has a window and the window is glass, a truce has been called. There is a new approach to the business of religious competition. Each may decorate its window with any variations that might attract the eye of the passerby, but it must not damn the efforts of the others.

The word has gone out to protect all the hucksters. They are doing a good service. They march for noble causes and keep the neighborhood children from growing up to be convicts. They promote obedience and passiveness. But they do not mount any crusades to liberate man from his ignorance. The ignorance of man is their asset and the experience of several hundred years has taught the priests that any whittling away of the ignorance of the peasants may cause reverberations in the membership—if not in the payroll.

We must beware of the movements that proclaim their alliance to the syndicate with such admonitions as "There is truth in all movements," and "Different religions suit the different needs of different peoples."

The brave theologians are all gone. Perhaps Martin Luther was the last brave man and for all we know, his bravery may long since have been forgotten. Brave men are born from the necessity for an answer to tyranny or some similarly impossible situation. In those days the cross was the general and the sword was its lieutenant. Now the cross has no rank at all. The sword has it for a hireling. The church has offered to be a civil servant. The church cannot live as an entity without a state charter and the man who issues state charters is a politician. The state secretary will decide that which is a religion and that which is not. And he usually decides that the accepted, or well rooted religions, shall be the ones that shall have a charter. Let God bow down or lose his share of the tax money.

If we were to believe in a devil, or enemy to the soul of man—we might view the situation with alarm.

An interesting note is the matter of faith as a factor in religion. The exhortation to have faith to many seekers seems like the lament of a hopeless lover about to lose his mate.

It is true that the devotees of almost every religion encounter the word "faith" somewhere in their career. I wonder at the need to exhort men to have faith. Is the religion in question so lacking in appeal, intrinsic value or in evident virtues that one must be exhorted and reminded to believe or that we must constantly remind ourselves that we must be in an accepting frame of mind?

Most Christian schools teach that believing must come before knowing. But if this believing is nothing more than prolonged self-hypnosis—how can we be certain that the knowing is not also a result of auto-suggestion?

Man cannot be damned for doubting, if man lays his existence into the hands of a creator. If man believes that he was created by God, there then must be a good reason for the intellect that hesitates, doubts, dares or chooses to reject.

This is one of the absurd positions of the Christian hierarchy. What sort of theology is it that makes us creatures fashioned by a personal Supreme Being, Who, after fashioning us as He is supposed to have done, with free will and an obligation to choose Him and endorse Him or be forever lost—at the same time denies us the right to doubt and, consequently, choose?

In other words, we have freedom of choice as long as we do not choose anything but Christian recommendations. We have free will, but if we do not heed mysterious and unproven demands, we shall become eternal, cosmic criminals.

The emphasis on believing lies most heavily upon the Christian and Mohammedan religions. Another thing that marks the teaching of both is the exaltation of a man as a Savior or Prophet and the further demand that belief in this man is necessary to spiritual survival.

We know, of course, that both of these religions presume the other to be false. Both used the sword. And strangely enough, both survived the long confrontation with each other. If God is interested in either geography or membership, He did not give the human race much of a clue as to which of the two was His chosen one and which was, consequently, the liar and betrayer of man's trust.

The Eastern religions demonstrate themselves to be generally systems of self-betterment, enlightenment, or liberation. However, many of them, if not the most of them, employ the "Master" idea and the belief in total submission to a human master. This has the same conflict with common sense that the requirements for "belief" in dogma have.

This is no attack upon faith. Many things may well have been created or recreated by faith. And it is possible that most of the dynamic nature of faith has not yet been fathomed. But it must be emphasized that the mechanism of faith is not a guarantee of wisdom and that we must be on the alert for any and all movements that demand it in preference to sincere searching.

Likewise, when we fasten ourselves to a "Master," we presume that all that is to be learned shall emanate from the bounty of this man. This does not mean that there are not or have not been eminent men who have walked upon the earth. It means that when a man demands total servitude and obedience, he may either be something very special or he may simply be a hypnotist.

And we have no evidence that entering the valley of death under a spell of hypnosis is any more efficacious than entering it as just an honest and ignorant being.

CULTS AND OTHER SYSTEMS

All of the movements that concern us in this work were the result of questions about the following items and they should be judged by their answers that ably or poorly enlighten us about the same question-items.

1. The nature of man, especially the inner man.
2. Life before birth.
3. Life after death.
4. Relation of man to nature, the world and the visible cosmos.
5. Relation of man to the Absolute. Most people, and this includes philosophers as well as humble lay-seekers, put the cart before the horse and proceed to try to understand the universe, or life after death, before understanding first their own nature and how they came to be here.

The following are keys in analyzing the isms.

a. Of the many isms that take on the tasks of explaining any of the above five items, we determine to gauge for the least unlikely or those nearer to the truth.
b. We take note of the avatar or other original exponent of the ism, and we look for personal inspiration and perhaps miraculous evidence of his being a superior and, hence, wiser being.

c. We study writings of the isms for contradiction.
d. We look for isms that explain more phenomena than other isms.
e. We pay heed to isms that appeal to our intuition.
f. We watch all isms for most common factors in the business of equating that some truth must accompany concurrence by a number of faiths or movements.

So we look for a workable system or discipline superior to other disciplines. I would like to take some of the movements that are in a sense esoteric and in a sense unconventional or of lesser popularity than the organized religions. In regard to item one, which deals with man's knowledge of himself, we have already heard from Psychology and Psychiatry. Chapter three also dealt with principle religious ideas and I will try to discuss the offerings of movements not discussed in chapter three.

When we approach these more or less esoteric groups, such as Zen, Yoga, Rosicrucianism, Theosophy, Kabbalism, various forms of thaumaturgy and predictive systems, such as astrology and numerology, we find that they fall into categories as far as their primary function is concerned. These are:

The Systems

1. Mechanical means to Spiritual or Truth-bringing end. (Joining the right church, whirling the right prayer wheel, prayers or magic.)
2. Physical means to Spiritual or Truth-bringing end. (Pilgrimages, praying, yoga exercises, fasting, physical mortification or punishment in the hope of spiritual gain.)
3. Mental means to a Spiritual or Truth-bringing end. (Meditational exercises as produced by many cults, raja yoga routines, concentration upon supposed spiritual centers in the body, analytical approach to religion or the analytical conceit that man can by solving the definition of matter automatically find the secret nature of that which caused matter. Or any system that postulates that our finite mind possesses or will possess the breadth of scope to evaluate all problems and the concomitant infallible faculties that would make that mind's conclusions dependable.)
4. Direct union with the Spiritual end or Truth. (Dying-while-living techniques, techniques for Satori or Enlightenment. Or accounts of experiences of those who have died medically and regained consciousness.)

We know that most movements encompass several of these four systems. So it is good to know the degree of thoroughness with which these movements satisfy our enquiry.

Naturally, I am not implying that the purpose of any movement should solely be the satisfaction of our logical enquiry because our enquiry is again being carried out with that same finite mind with its weaknesses, but we still can employ some yardsticks to save us decades of time. Our enquiry must be first tempered with another faculty besides our analytical sense, or else we will be perennially chasing our tail.

Yoga

Yoga is a wide word. Under the various yogic systems we find all four paths or means. It would be good at this point to note that these four systems are all presumptive of a Spiritual nature for man, or presumptive of man's ability to learn or reach the Truth. We might say that all philosophic systems herein discussed imply that there is at least an inadequacy of state of being as far as this present life is concerned or an inadequacy of our ability to properly appreciate the state of being now experienced

This book presumes, in other words, that there is hope for man and that it is possible to better understand both the state we now experience and that it is not unreasonable to contemplate future states. In making this notation, I am sidestepping a lot of materialistic thinking and writings, but as explained previously, if man is limited to a materialistic existence, without any aspirations for immortality tolerated, then writing any manner of books (except possibly hedonistic books) would surely be taking up time when we might be vegetating.

Our chief aim in this chapter is to somehow indicate the diverse paths or metaphysical directions that result from the many unanswered questions. The many questions that possibly result from diverse unexplained phenomena, as well as diverse desires and elaborate hopes, somehow become all tangled up and the different paths or systems somehow become all tangled up by trying, it would seem, to cure all with one system. So that we find a religion or a cult springing up, pronouncing its findings as being all that is necessary to bring man to a condition where he will not need to question any more.

We hear of hatha yoga, which is somehow a yoga of health. The main argument of hatha yoga is not a pretence that by various postures a body can be made immortal, but that if we wish to progress in any higher enterprise, we must first have a healthy body. Some teachers of hatha yoga slyly hint but never prove that some yogis live for several hundred years. This was one of the themes in the book *Lost Horizon*. Various books on yoga have hinted at marvelous phenomena performed by yogis, such as bi-location, astral-projection, dematerialization and rematerialization, projection of the body, and quite a repertoire of magic.

It is worth noting that most of these books came out in the eighteen hundreds or very early in this century. Colonel Olcott and Blavatsky may have stimulated the public's interest in this type of phenomena by their works and caused lesser authors to try their hand at even more sensationalistic fiction and half-fiction.

Blavatsky wrote the *Secret Doctrine* and *Isis Unveiled,* and other books. These two are encyclopedias of occultism. If Blavatsky ever recommended a system, I failed to find it in either book, or in the *Voice of the Silence.* I get the impression that Blavatsky believed that gurus or avatars were the only ladder to wisdom or spiritual ends. And since Madame Blavatsky never gave us the address or phone number of any of these gurus, we are left with her guidance alone and her scriptural interpretation of their words. She was an admitted amanuensis.

The movement that resulted from Blavatsky's efforts is known as Theosophy. Its derivation implies that it is a god-science. Blavatsky's gods are of human origin. She distinguishes them from the Absolute or universal mind. Theosophy maintains that there is a spiritual evolution of men toward godhood, which involves such levels as adept, master and boddhisattva. There is supposedly no limit to the height to which these levels extend.

Theosophy is a very worthy work in that it inspires people to look deeper into the nature of things. Theosophy is commendable in that it attempts to help man to understand himself, before making him submit to wild dogmas. Many of Blavatsky's writings betray an attempt to save the student some time by debunking some of the less meritable systems to which we are exposed. She spends many chapters explaining the origin of matter from non-matter and in explaining the evolution of primordial atoms into humans, and the evolution of the planetary systems.

She does, however, leave little hope for the neophyte-seeker. She gives no system, except to advise the general pursuit of the theosophical wisdom and the search for masters or avatars. Perhaps this omission (of a system) is a passive gesture of honesty, because we receive the hint that man progresses only in the appointed hour, and for man to try to accelerate his development too prematurely would be foolish—according to Blavatsky.

Let us look at the manner in which Theosophy answers the questions listed at the beginning of this chapter.

Item 1. The nature of man. Theosophy explains man as a reincarnating, evolving, immortal being. But it does not explain how we may prove this to ourselves. It, consequently, utters a most detailed concept to answer Items 2, 3, 4—but leaves the gap of mystery about the highest form of god-man and about the Absolute or universal mind (Item 5).

And as I mentioned before, in regard to the systems, it does not really qualify as a system. Theosophy seems to be about the business of synthesizing religions and looking into them for their common factors. It is weak in giving us an invisible avatar, saviour or guru.

Theosophy has received considerable criticism by many pseudological minds who claimed Blavatsky's writings were filled with inconsistencies. I must also confess that I did not check every foreign reference or bibliography and translate it again to double-check her, but I did agree with most of her general criticisms of other movements, even though I felt that she may have allowed her own intense personality to color some of her rhetoric.

Theosophy flourished for a while and I believe now that it is waning, even though there is an increase in interest in occultism. This waning is, I think, attributable to its lack of any system or detailed blueprint for becoming a master or adept, and attributable to its lack of any sensationalistic advertising, such as is employed by other movements. In my estimation, the books of Blavatsky are some of the most valuable handbooks that a student of esotericism might own.

While Blavatsky's mentor or guru appeared to her in his astral form, most schools of yoga recognize only a living guru or master. While hatha yoga promises a healthy body in which to meditate, Krya yoga promises a system of mental means to a spiritual end. Krya yoga is a system of meditation upon nerve-centers or chakras as well as concentration in a prescribed manner to attain physical objectives. Raja yoga and Krya yoga are often confused. Some Indian systems employ Krya and Raja techniques without ever mentioning the word yoga.

It might be better if we referred to both as Mental Yoga or mental disciplines. Steiner's Rosicrucianism is a Christian form of mental yoga. Steiner's system engenders the concentration upon the chakras.

SRF, or Self Realization Fellowship, belongs to the Krya yoga, or Mental yoga class. With the death of Yogananda, it appears to have changed from a guru-enlightened movement to just a plain movement.

The Vedanta movement is a similar movement. In it there are still to be found living gurus who are the spiritual descendents of Ramakrishna.

These last three movements are some of the more "respectable" groups that practice Mental yoga. There are at least a hundred more of the same type, but their origin is recent and the honesty of some is questionable.

The living-guru systems are a nebulous chain. Mental yoga systems do not always promise Satori or Enlightenment, but refer at times to Samadhi and Moksa. As has been pointed out before, exotic words like Satori, Samadhi, and Moksa may have a definite, limited, intended meaning, or they may have all of the unlimited meaning that American and peasant-Hindu minds can conjure up. Satori bears more the connotation of final liberation, while Samadhi is used to determine the point at which the yoga-attention joins the object of his meditation.

The mental yoga systems presuppose that man must first experience a change of being before being able to experience Moksa or deliverance from the wheel of illusion. So, perhaps very shrewdly, most of the systems of mental yoga introduced into the Western world, emphasize yoga as being a discipline of change without ever explaining the end result of the business of being changed.

I am not opposed to the idea of change. I realize that our being must go through much catharsis in order to get rid of erroneous thinking. If nothing else, we are to advance upon a Truth-searching drive.

But many good people, also sensing this need for a change of being, lazily and blindly seize upon any cult or turbanned guru that promises a change of being. Most of these gurus, when questioned about end-results, refer you to their guru or quotations from the predecessor. We obtain a mental cartoon of a staircase with a guru on each step, pointing to the one above him.

I observe sometimes with amazement that that which the enquiring mind finds satisfying is too often a mere seat in the shadow of pretension.

Nearly all of the cults in this country are maintained by a solid upper layer of professional people and a low proportion of working-class people. We find doctors, lawyers and scientists paying humble tribute to an illiterate swami who in turn has very little philosophy outside of a catechism of his own particular sect.

I visited the Vedanta temple in Hollywood and met the Swami in charge. His name, I believe, was Probhavananda. He was a dignified, quiet, priest-like man. He was, however, living in the shadow of his guru and eating from the table prepared by a man, dead quite a few years—one Ramakrishna.

Ramakrishna was not a dignified or priest-like man, judging from his picture. We all know that external appearances are not measurable for picking a man who lays claim to spiritual enlightenment, but on the other hand, spiritual enlightenment leaves its mark upon the recipient and there are, consequently, traits that would cause us to doubt spiritual enlightenment for a particular possessor of such traits.

Ramakrishna looks wild and almost idiotic in the picture of him that is in the Vedanta temple. Probhavananda looks serene. Those in search of advice and paternalism might well be inspired by Probhavananda. But that swami points upward to Ramakrishna and the latter is deified as a sort of avatar. Ramakrishna, as a figure to be deified and meditated upon, had a negative effect upon me. I am sure that he would never have been deified in the United States, nor would he have ever received a fraction of the welcome that Yogananda or Probhavananda have received.

Ramakrishna was chosen in India. And in India, some gurus are chosen out of emotion. It is good to note that at this point, Ouspensky indicates that "man number two," (the second from the bottom) is the emotionally oriented man. If you read the accounts of some of the young yogis in their early encounters with their "Masters," and listen to accounts of Europeans and Americans who have witnessed enough of India's spiritual procedure, we find that the reason a young neophyte in India chooses a particular Master is love. Now we can confuse this love with intuition, which is often the projection which we are supposed to seize upon as the meaning of the word love in these instances. However, we must also bear in mind the mores and general philosophy of India in which, despite emancipating laws, the female is still thought of as an inferior and the male as a superior. A young mind of homosexual inclination in a country that looks kindly upon homosexuality might well also be inclined to worship the male godlike human so deified by his imagination.

This deduction has been proven true in some cases recently investigated by two Americans to whom I talked concerning one of the gurus who now holds a fairly high place in American minds. The guru in question managed to find himself and his movement listed in *Life* magazine as the head of one of the more popular movements. But this guru had about him, in India, disciples that not only worshipped the feet of their guru, but the body-wastes of that guru also. Of course, when this guru comes to the United States, he does not get this sort of attention . . . he is satisfied with our money and the publicity. We fail to go back a step and realize that were it not for this abject attention by native disciples in India, and their blatant, nauseous masochism, or eroticism, his popularity would never have grown beyond the borders of India.

Of course, the perennial optimist (or rationalist for possibly effortless, tantric salvation) will indicate that perhaps underneath all of this "natural man" there is a duality wherein atavism and avatarism live side by side. So I must leave the observation for what it is worth, having in mind only the purpose of looking for reasons for the growth of cults—thus looking for qualifications that might make cults valid or invalid.

To get back to Ramakrishna, he was not in any sense the top guru. The stories about his career tell us that he had gurus of his own. The man who initiated him into mental yoga is rarely mentioned. Ramakrishna had been worshipping another goddess when this man happened to witness Ramakrishna's limitation and introduced him to the higher yoga—Krya yoga or mind-chakra meditation. About this life-story are woven many other stories to give it wonderment and to form the body of the Ramakrishna movement.

The Ramakrishna movement and the SRFmovement are mostly pious systems of hero-worship.

We can take the kernel out, which is chakra-concentration, and forget all about Ramakrishna, Yogananda, Lahiri Mahasaya, and any of the others in the two movements. In SRF, I find the stories that embellished the movement to be too fantastic. In SRF there are hints of ever-living avatars. Yogananda hints of having met Babuji once or twice. There are tales, of golden cities created for the entertainment of adepts, and of the translation of the "Masters." Also stories of levitation and teleportation.

The main criticism of these movements is not their outward structure or possible internal inconsistencies. The main criticism for them is that their yoga-function is like a rope that would hold the ship to the shore, or a rope keeping heaven in contact with earth, but apparently having anchorage at neither end. They seem to be systems unconcerned with a valid foundation and negligent of ultimate aspiration. They are systems that go nowhere. If concentration upon a plexus makes a better artisan, or poet, or mathematician out of you, then your interest is in being such . . . not being a changed being with a spiritually scheduled aim for changing. If any yoga system brings you peace of mind, and peace of mind is what you want, then you are getting what you pay for. And cult lessons may well be cheaper than tranquilizers. However, if your objective is the understanding of the relation of man to the Absolute or even the understanding of post-mortem existence, then we will not wish to linger too long under the influence of tranquilizers.

We now come to Rosicrucianism. There are several schools of Rosicrucians. In the investigation of Rosicrucianism we encounter from the first the obstinate insistence on a mythical heritage.

I use the word "mythical" because most Rosicrucian movements obstinately protest that they have a beginning which they are both unwilling and unable to trace. The heroes in the stories of Rosicrucianism are "Elders" or "Elder Brothers" whose secret hideouts are somewhere in Central Europe. And we cannot help but enquire . . . why Central Europe?

We are reminded of some of the stories about the avatars and adepts mentioned in yoga-literature who supposedly lived to be several hundred years of age. This appeals to people whose instinct for survival leads them to believe that immortality must of a necessity include the body.

Rationalization, like temptation, comes to the human mind in ever changing form.

I expect that this book will largely appeal to people who are dissatisfied with organized religion and the paths thereof. If you ask an occultist or plain cultist for his reasons for abandoning the church of his ancestors, he will give you fairly reasonable answers. He will generally point out what he considers to be the childish or absurd tenets in the faith of his ancestors. But when he joins an esoteric cult, he begins to practice even more absurd rituals and relays to the listener even more childish dogma than that which enthralled his forebearers in the organized "old-fashioned" religion.

I would like to take a moment here to indicate that in many movements we will find absurdities that should be explained by the promoters of the particular cult, or eliminated. The first yardstick that we apply to any movement is simple truth and when our intuition tells us this simple truth may be twisted or prostituted, then there is no further reason for following such a cult.

ON GURUS AND UNIQUE SYSTEMS

I can see no reason for the emphasis on fantastic claims that are always impossible to validate. Many discerning minds have abandoned Christianity because they could not believe that Jesus was divine. They may have come to this conclusion after studying Josephus and personally translating the New Testament. Yet, after doing all that work, they will trot out and join a cult and accept its tenets merely because this new movement promises a form of immortality that appeals to them, or for even lesser reasons.

This may seem inconsequential—this business of lamenting the failure of the seeker in his second try for the Truth. However, the purpose of this writing is to try to help the people on the ladder, whether it be the second or third rung, or attempt. It may well be a wonderful thing to rebel against the almost concrete restrictions of hereditary religious thinking, but it will do us absolutely no good to rebel if we do not have, or determine to have, discernment.

It seems that every movement wants to be rooted in antiquity. This implies that the modern mind is somehow feeble and that men were either very wise or very holy back in antiquity, and in those days were able to meet saviors, avatars and master-gurus face to face. This must be recognized as an evident bit of rationalization. In such rationalization we are clinging to "authority" by virtue of our own mental fatigue.

Capitalizing on our mental fatigue and love of authority, many new cults inculcate bizarre history into their philosophy—almost to a point where the fantastic elements are more emphasized than the factual ones.

We find that different Rosicrucian orders make different claims. One group spends fabulous sums on advertising, leading us to believe that they believe that advertising brings proportional business returns. The claims in some of these ads alone are enough to throw a shadow on their claims to honesty, much less any addiction for Truth. *The Encyclopedia Brittanica* lists some of the claims of the Rosicrucian order. One is that their arcane wisdom is the result of a pilgrimage to the East by one Christian Rosenkreuz in the fifteenth century. The encyclopedia also points out that there is no supporting evidence for this claim.

There is evidence that in the eighteenth century there were many writers who manifested dissatisfaction with the doctrines preached in their time. Luther's intrepidity led other minds to speak out. Because of violent, repressive measures practiced by ecclesiastical powers in those days, secrecy became a requirement for survival, especially if your philosophy ran counter to those authorities.

However, in later years the bloody power of the church was wrested from the church of Rome. And, yet, the secrecy continued.

There is no need to have secret orders now, and secrecy gives us a sort of foetus-complex.

It is possible that many political coteries possessed and needed to possess rules of secrecy. The fact that they were both religious and political complicated the material that was kept secret. We must surmise that this material, passed on to followers in secret, was of a rebellious and theological nature. It is natural that in any rebellion against Rome the promoters of rebellion would use more ancient authority, or more exotic authority, to replace the Roman church in the minds of men.

Once the church of Rome began to crumble from different schisms and was relieved of the scourge and sword, the secret lodges lost some of their reasons for existing. However, no entity gives up its life once it begins to function. I surmise that many of the secret societies discovered that they could maintain their life after the politicians deserted them by encouraging the type of people who love secrecy for the sake of secrecy. How many adults among us are still children! I have been to encampments of cults where the members seemed only to know that they had a secret and were part of a secret organization. The Rosicrucians, in some instances, are so secret that they do not give out names of brother-Rosicrucians even to members.

My reaction to this is that it is a protective device not intended to protect the individual members from pests as much as to protect the mother lodge from the results of intercommunication of members.

Another claim that is occasionally employed by a movement is the hidden manuscript trick.

How often have we heard this. God gave so and so tablets of gold with the law written in His handwriting. Another found a manuscript giving all the secrets of life. However, when we ask to see these heavenly "apports," we are told that something happened to them. The gods were displeased and took them back like petty, resentful playmates. Or the manuscript is kept in the temple and is only available to the higher adepts . . . who have paid in for twenty years.

We proceed now perhaps from the trivial external appearances of Rosicrucianism to the inner core of their teachings. In doing so we abridge a few bales of lessons and mandami.

What do they really have to offer? As far as I can see, one group offers a symbological philosophy and a promise of meeting a Master in his astral form.

As for the symbology, it might be valuable if you need something to occupy your mind. But, again, why do adults need complexity when simplicity is possible in the exposition of ideas? I am reminded of Nostrodamus' prophecies in which we find prophecies that concern an eagle, or a lion, or a symbol such as the crescent. Of course, we immediately conclude that he means Islam when he speaks of the crescent, but in the event that the prediction does not fit Islam, then we can never accuse him of being in error. For all that we know, he may well have been referring to anything or anyone else. The book of Revelations is filled with symbols and I have never heard Revelations explained in such a manner as to give a composite picture wherein all of the symbols have incontroversial interrelation and meaning. Revelations has been used, as a result, in a very uncharitable manner by many zealots who occupy "authoritative" places in theological circles. Revelations has become a cudgel.

Let us now get to the matter of the living master. Or master in astral form. I have over a period of thirty years talked to every Rosicrucian who would talk to me about the matter. And most of them were frank. None but one had witnessed the "Astral Master." The one who had was an old lady who had spent her whole life in the movement.

She said that he allowed her only three questions and she only saw him once. There was no elaboration on the questions. He gave her a simple answer of "No." And that was all she had.

There is at least one Rosicrucian group that protests that it does not charge. I visited the grounds which evidently are the main center for this group in the United States. This is in Oceanside, California. These are followers of Max Heindel. I visited the place more than twenty years ago and it may have been changed since then. In the main reception room stood a table with some books on it. I asked about the price and the lady in charge said they had no charges, but that I could donate something in return for any books I might like to have. I took their *Cosmo-Conception* with me.

I told the lady that I would like to communicate with them since they told me that their instructions were free. When I returned to Ohio, and wrote the letter as directed by the same lady, I never received an answer.

The book, *Cosmo-Conception,* pretty well explains that which they are about. As in some forms of spiritualism, they believe in subtle physical vehicles, such as the astral body, and they believe in reincarnation.

Of all the American forms of Rosicrucianism, this is the only group that I think I would care to look into further. I know very little about them because they did not correspond with me—but I have never seen them advertise, so I feel that they are not spending their supporters' money on pulp-advertising.

There is yet another group which is very select and it is located in Pennsylvania. It seems to be run from behind a cash register. In my communications with them, they had things to sell, but no explanations.

Rudolph Steiner founded a school of Rosicrucianism in Germany and wrote a series of books. Steiner is widely read in this country and I am somewhat surprised that someone has not by now commercialized his name. If a student wished to get a fair idea of Rosicrucianism without spending too much time and money on lessons, he might acquire some of Steiner's books. (I am not endorsing Steiner or Rosicrucianism by that remark, but am merely making an observation for the benefit of any researcher.)

One book in particular brings you to the objectives of Steiner's Rosicrucianism—*Knowledge of the Higher Worlds and its Attainment*. This book was published in 1947 in London. His signature is appended to the preface of 1918. In this preface he refers to "anthroposophical spiritual science" in discussing his own work. This gives us an inkling about the trend in human thinking that draws mankind into the fold of cults that might be of pseudo-scientific origins.

It is evident that mankind, or at least the better educated segment thereof, is somewhat tired of the childish fantasyland of threatening devils and angels with wands all supervised by a very sick (by human standards, I'll agree) God that incinerates any microscopic human that makes the wrong guess.

It is possible that this type of anthroposophy as seen in Rosicrucianism and other yogic cults, is not a long submerged Truth at last revealed, but a creation of new fantasy, palatable to a hungry mouth with a bad taste therein from former digestion.

In the beginning of this chapter I have listed, alphabetically, a series of keys to gauge any ism that we might be investigating. It might be good to list a few of the keys that we should avoid.

A. Does it lessen your fear or raise your hopes by means of concept-building?
B. Does it hint of sensual license?
C. Is it cheaper to subscribe to, or to follow? Is it venal, or

more expensive and are you deluded into thinking that it, being select and, consequently, more expensive, is only for financially successful people (perfected men, meaning the select)?
D. Does it have a power structure that may bring you to power some day?
E. Does it appeal to any other vanity?
F. Did you join it because you were too tired to go on looking?

Philosophic movements have failed to replace Christianity, because for all of our education, we are still like cavemen grovelling in the sand at the sound of thunder. We are still waiting for a sign or a Messiah. We refuse to have the sense to simply start looking and working while applying simple yardsticks to the business of investigating.

Annie Besant and other Theosophists saw that mankind might respond to a new Messiah and were accused of attempting to endow Krishnamurti with divinity. Aleister Crowley and Gurdjieff tried to endow themselves.

Gradualizations of Eastern thought did manage to make a pretty sound and lasting foothold in Western thinking. As a result of these, we have Mary Baker Eddy, who kept Christianity, but inculcated in it the idea of Universal Mind and the potency of man's mind. Universal Mind is similar to that which is understood as Brahman. Steiner also kept Christ, and spent much of his time building an image of Christ. Swedenborg retained Christ while formulating a new Jerusalem along esoteric lines.

The gradualization was not quick enough for the peasants of Europe. Under communism they threw out many nauseous peccadilloes and shook the very dogmas that supported the church.

We are entering into a new era and I am not convinced that it is good. It is the era of the Man-God. From many Gods, to One-God, to Man-God. The Man-God era was not created by communism. However, the followers and promoters of both communism and the Man-God theory have common ground as a foundation for the structure of their thinking. The communist is weary of being exploited by the state powers that are reinforced and justified by a venal church. Mysticism and metaphysics find too many followers weary of the persecution of common-sense postulates by organized religion. Organized Christianity, while professing to believe in One-God, has fractured itself until its polymorphousness is not much different from polytheism. Whenever tithes are the rule of the church, ten men in the congregation will support a minister in a manner even better by one tenth than that of any of the supporters. So every potential minister is inclined to create a schism and look for ten members. Tithing becomes a schismatic factor among the many other factors.

These ministers place themselves above their objective, which is God, and they too hurry along the Man-God trend. Another trend is for the Christian world to produce healers rather than for a preacher to lead a group of men in the studies that might lead to wisdom or to lead a group in meditation that might bring them to a better mental condition, or change of being. In this respect, most healers become expediters of the Man-God concept.

Nearly all of the yogic movements are conducive to Man-God production. The master-chela relationship in some Raja yoga groups plainly states that the only chain the chela has to immortality is the link he has with his Master.

Somehow, I believe that most yogic systems are emanations from the Krishna movement which is older than Christianity and may have suffered or enjoyed a sort of evolution of its own.

The Krishna movement is still alive but it may have changed a bit or evolved into other schisms also, when some observers took the courage to point out the inexorable fate of a bald-headed man, or to note that the hair goes up in smoke with the body on the funeral pyre.

The tuft of hair has since been replaced by things more subtle and more difficult to evaluate, such as the astral cord, the sound current, or the fixing of the master in the pineal chakra, so that we will have his picture with us after death and, thus, be able to recognize him.

Rosicrucianism, while borrowing much from the East, failed to bring the concept of the Master-chain with it. It could only have been out of fear of massive reaction from a Christian-controlled society that claims Christ as its living master. And if this is true, or if it is reasonable to accept the Master-chain concept as being a valid means to immortality, then Rosicrucianism is entering into a compromise rather than bravely bringing out a new system of thinking.

With the advent of the Man-God cults, we fail to observe that they may well appeal to our vanity to the point where our heads are turned. That man is finally becoming more radical and appealing to man is very commendable. However, before we legislate or indulge in too much concept-building, we must be aware of our vanity.

The fact that mankind may well have created most of his gods and other entities does not exclude the existence of real gods or entities, nor does it make him a creator of any merit. When man looks upon himself, witnesses his own unsureness, his finite and relative nature, then it behooves him to double-check anything traceable to human creation. It has been hinted that the materializations that occur in a medium's cabinet are human creations, with or without the help of other entities. If this is possible, then the astral master or the guardian of the threshold might bear a second glance, if for no other reason than to check ourselves for their origin. Eliphas Levi, the expert on magic, tells us that he suspects all of the phantoms that he produced may well have been mental creations!

Let us summarize or evaluate Rosicrucianism according to the five possible functions:

1. About the nature of man, Rosicrucianism offers a concept.
2. About life before death, the theory of Reincarnation.
3. About life after death, the theory of Reincarnation.
4. Relation to nature, vague, nothing definite.
5. Relation of man to the Absolute, no tie.

In response to the tests:

a. Subject to your judgment and lengthy comparisons.
b. No avatar or outstanding original prophet.
c,d. This would be a lengthy undertaking as the writings are not scientific.
e. There are things about it that appeal to our intuition, but some of the very foundations of Rosicrucianism do not.
f. It has common denominators with Eastern religions.
g. It does usually extend a discipline and lays claim to efficacy for the system in relation to spiritual growth.

Let us take each cult and each movement and ask ourselves these same questions about the functioning of the movement, apply the tests and test it with the keys A., B., C., D., E., and F.

I do not wish to imply that this is a complete system of evaluation. You may wish to add a few keys of your own, since the reasons for a person's joining a movement are not six alone. This will give you some idea of the weak spots in any movement and may help you decide the direction in which you wish to apply yourself.

Magic

The world of magic comes under the first of the systems—those which use mechanical means. This is not a field to be ridiculed because it seems to be rooted in things tangible or materialistic. Under the many categories of magic we find scientific results once the unknown processes are understood.

Hypnosis and mesmerism were once in the province of magic. But there is no better lever than hypnosis to understand the human mind. The herb of the medicine man often becomes the life-saving drug for those who ridiculed the medicine man.

Much magic is rooted in intuitional procedures so completely intuitional that there would be no logical way to explain the rituals that are used to bring about predicted results.

We might say that Magic is in many cases the science or ability that goes directly to nature for the understanding of nature, rather than an aloof, perhaps impossible, appraisal with rubber gloves and scalpel.

Magic has one great stumbling block. It can become an endless trip to fantasyland. And many of the so-called discoveries of deeper magic have never been properly explained.

Let us take some of the cases. Benvenuto Cellini relates one in his autobiography. The priest was able to bring up, literally, legions of demons. It is difficult to believe that the priest would be interested in gold alone, and that Cellini would be interested in seduction alone. There seemed to be no great interest into the nature and origin of these demons. All we know about them is that they were very powerful, that they (or at least the speaker among them) liked virgin boys, and that all of them had an aversion for asafoetida.

Eliphas Levi, perhaps the foremost author on Magic, leads us to believe that Magic may well be the utilization of mechanical levers to facilitate mental creativity. It is said that a lifetime of magical studies and exercises did not bring him happiness and he supposedly rejoined the Catholic Church later in life.

The life of Aleister Crowley is another instance of a very unhappy man. A life that began perhaps as an earnest drive into high magic soon became mixed with drugs and sex. His historians indicate that his direction degenerated quickly into a combination of nature-worship and witchcraft. And to all appearances, most of the rituals were sex-sessions, stimulated by drugs.

The magus should never allow himself to be absorbed into the experiment. We find magic to have been perhaps a factor in older religions that spelled for those religions permanence or transience.

We find the Jews gaining power with the rod of Aaron (which ate the snakes from the rods of the Egyptians). We find the magic of the apostle Peter frustrating the levitations of the magician Simon.

Miracles come under the heading of Magic and we find that almost every major religion finds it necessary to list miracles performed by its members at one time or another.

Miracles have been somehow accepted as the external form of divine contact on the part of the practitioner. If we were to remove the changing of the wine at the wedding feast, the raising of Lazarus, the feeding of the multitude on insufficient bread and fish, and the casting out of devils—the message of Love may never have gained the footing that it did, nor would Jesus have gained the stature of Saviour.

There are limitations to Magic, however, and this fact or phase of Magic has not properly been explained to the devout followers who imagine that the powers of the magician are without limits. A hint of the nature of Jesus' works of magic is given in the thirteenth chapter of Matthew, verses 53 to 58. The last verse reads: "And he did not many mighty works there because of their unbelief." Jesus had gone back to his home town to do a little preaching and met some skepticism.

Miracles do not come entirely from a divine source, if at all. Even those miracles brought about with the aid of the faith of the believers or followers are subject to natural laws. The phenomena that are listed as miracles are mechanisms that do not upset any natural laws, but are, rather, natural phenomena just not yet understood or explained by what we understand to be scientific explanations at the time.

The question has often been raised concerning the reluctance or inability of Jesus to embarrass his enemies with magic at the time of the final agonies. It is argued that since he predicted His death, it would have been unwise for Him to have escaped the enemy. But the fact that He predicted it may well mean that He recognized inexorable karma or natural laws that could not be breached. The argument has often been brought forth that His success in centuries to come depended upon the spectacle of an ignominious self-sacrifice being imprinted upon the mind of mankind.

Such a display was not necessary for Gautama the Buddha and, in fact, Gautama advised his followers against using magic. Let us suppose (with justifiable supposition) that the changing of the water into wine was done with hypnosis, that Lazarus was either hastily interred (an epileptic or hypnotized cateleptic), that the feeding of the multitude was either hypnosis or sleight of hand, and that the casting out of devils was simply exorcism. Exorcism has been demonstrated by many primitive shamen since the time of Christ—these shamen being not even Christian converts, let alone priests.

Every magician gathers belief about him like a snowball and as the belief snowballs bigger and bigger, he is able to do more marvellous things. But, as I said before, all the while the magician is dealing with a science of which he knows very little. He plays by ear, as it were, until one day he almost surely tries some trick that does not work. The factors which made his success vanish like a puff of smoke. These factors are his ever-inflating ego and the belief of the audience. The factors which he does not know, and the ignorance of them, brings about his failure.

Some of the magi have come to the conclusion that the visible world is an illusion. This can only be understood properly when viewed from the position or attitude of the Absolute. And this is saying little more to relative man than to assure him of a possible situation that cannot be proven. From the material standpoint, we cannot argue that the material, visible world is illusory. However, the magus presumes that proper knowledge of the nature of this illusion will somehow give him power over it.

Those who have really experienced sentience of the Absolute and have viewed life from the direct appraisal of things—lose all inclination to change any part of the theatrical mental reflections. An adult simply loses interest in the toys of childhood and it matters not who has the marbles now.

The Qabalah

I do not wish to deal extensively with the Qabalah because I have encountered too many diverse authorities or pseudo-authorities on the basic value of the Qabalah. There are evidently two uses of the Qabalah. The lesser of these deals with magic and the higher use is in pursuit of wisdom. MacGregor Mathers lists four forms of the Qabalah: Practical Qabalah, or that which is devoted to talismanic magic; the Literal Qabalah, or that which deals with a numerological analysis of the sacred word; also, the Unwritten Qabalah and the Dogmatic Qabalah.

If you are not interested in talismanic magic, or in playing with word numerology, but in the part that deals with man's relation to God and the universe, you will want to go on to the Unwritten Qabalah. The wisdom of the Unwritten Qabalah, or Dogmatic Qabalah, is practically an endless study, especially if we are to launch into Literal Qabalah as well. If the great secrets are transmitted orally, I conclude that years might well be wasted in study . . . when a few words whispered into the ear will do the trick.

We are here again faced with the negative aspect of a movement—which is secrecy. Discovery of which is always followed by the question, "What are they hiding, an explosive fact or an embarrassing ignorance?"

Additional Yoga Comment

I would like to omit any evaluation of the various types of hatha yoga. And if possible, ignore the hundred or so cults that have sprung up in this country whose only evident aim is to collect money and delude their supporters.

I would like to presume that if the reader has read this far, he will be aware that I have no interest in any movement that does not honestly work toward the Truth. I consider it foolish for those who work for power to subscribe to any "power system" that lacked the functional wisdom for managing the power promised or that failed to forewarn the student of all results of their actions.

I would also like to avoid, as much as possible, the endless and confusing use of Indian terms. It is my belief that wisdom is not the property of one race alone and, hence, it can be expressed in any language. If at all. I borrow some words from the Indian language, such as yoga and karma, because they are almost lay terms.

While we are memorizing new symbols to understand a chapter, we might be reading an entire book. The same thought applies to Qabalistic studies. Many seekers are over-impressed by Hindu terminology and lose their way through the woods by studying the trees. For instance, the word transmigration is easier to understand than the word samsara because, for one thing, the latter word is too often confused with samskara which means karmic memory.

There is much to learn from the various Hindu schools. India is split up into many religious factions which made for competition and stimulation. India is situated close to Tibet and Tibet has long been the living stronghold of occultism and transcendentalism. The prevalence of the God-Man attitude, or theory of the evolution of man's soul toward godhood, encouraged Indians and Tibetans for centuries to continue the exploration of man.

If we are to take the axiom-directive seriously ("First know thyself"), then we must realize that the Orientals are far ahead of us. A theology that expects us to know the nature of God when we do not even know our own nature is manifestly absurd. If, on the other hand, the Orientals—like today's Westerners—have taken the Man-God attitude up because of laziness and moral decay or out of rebellion against a priest-craft and temple-taxes, then they are no further along than us.

The prevalent theme of nearly all yogic systems is the upward evolution of transmigration to a better state. Some go as far as to set their sights upon a particular zenith at which they aim, such as Nirvana. In nearly all yogic systems there is a noticeable absence of the worship of a deity. Graduation from the worship of a non-human deity is looked upon as a favorable step by mystics on the path of yoga. Ramakrishna supposedly worshipped the goddess Kali for some time until a monk came along and taught him to meditate upon his own spiritual centers. Thus, Ramakrishna is supposed to have found all within himself.

In this case, the guru-monk became more important than Kali. I have previously referred to the guru-chain—a very significant mechanism for immortality.

THE CULTS

There are many cults flourishing today. Some promise an advantage for the applicant that is similar to mental yoga. I have a filing cabinet filled with papers from different "brotherhoods," "orders," and simply nameless gurus. I am indeed puzzled to understand or evaluate some of them for motives. Some do not have the circulation necessary to bring in any periodic flow of money. I have to conclude that this type of venture had to depend upon a big financial killing by a complete takeover of the finances of the enquirers.

This practice is not unusual. The Radha Soami group, while not asking for money, instructed their followers to place all of their physical karma in the hands of the master. This placing of the "whole being" in the hands of the master would, naturally, endanger any bank account.

I received certain "documents" through the mail from a man who inferred that he had membership in a brotherhood of universal dimensions and ancient origins. Questions by me about seeming inconsistencies were answered with vague replies or confusing allusions to general ethical postulates. Some of the "documents" had interesting information in them, but nothing was in them that could not be found somewhere else. They were unique in their manner of presentation only. One clever "document" tried to demonstrate that wisdom was somehow dependent upon the proportional ability to purchase it. With that one I called a halt.

Another cult professing to be reliquary of ancient wisdom used the trick of mailing me a letter from Greece. It informed me that I would soon hear from one of their "elders" in California.

Most of these cults protect themselves by initially confiding to the applicant that the rest of mankind is vulgar and unable to contain the powerful medicine which the cult is about to bestow. The next step is the swearing of the applicant to secrecy, under pain of causing kinks in the cosmos or his own convolutions, if there is any divulgence to the profane. This manages to screen the operation.

For this reason, secrecy itself has become something to look for if you are looking for indications of trickery. Secrecy appeals to many business men or prominent professional men because, to begin with, they are a bit ashamed to have their colleagues or drinking companions hear about their joining a cult. A person may also be very hungry for the truth, but still wish to check it out before sacrificing too many of his business contacts or risking social criticism.

We should not be afraid of social criticism if we have the conviction that a search is necessary for finding. And the search is more important than static membership in an organized religion.

When there is a liability of hurting the feelings of our friends, it is advisable not to preach an unsure doctrine or cult, but there is quite a gap between discretion and total secrecy. In the days of the inquisition, or the Salem witch-hunt, secrecy was a necessity, of course . . . for students of witchcraft. But too many cults have sworn their members to secrecy, only to be proven fraudulent themselves.

A man, now deceased, who was known to have spent his entire life looking for the truth, spent many of his valuable younger years in a movement operated by a man and wife. This couple seemed very sincere and had written several books that showed no great inconsistencies. Their works did contain a considerable amount of unprovable concept-building. My friend, who had gathered quite a bit of money as the result of inventions, had evidently contributed to this pair for a period of over fifteen years. The couple was involved in a scandal when some unsatisfied victim exposed them to the world. They were found to be drug-addicts and prone to sexual excesses and abnormalities with quite a circle of co-conspirators. And in the event that these things seem inconsequential, the crime was really inconsistency . . . they had been preaching quite the opposite of that which they were practicing.

Too many of us are led to the acceptance of cults by our eagerness to accept strange terms. Many cults are nothing more than a slightly new twist to older speculative theosophies. We are enchanted, as neophytes, by the use of new exotic terms, such as the word, "chakra."

While one group of philosophers is desperately trying to establish understanding of the body that is visible and the mind that has evident relationship with that body, other people are inventing and designing systems, both intangible and vague, and elaborating on details with imaginative, detailed charts. The latter do not bother to explain either their system or their charts thoroughly so that the viewer may clarify the system with his own personal experience . . . outside of twenty or thirty years servitude to a cult.

And the final frustration is that even those who profess to have seen chakras still have no better knowledge than ourselves about the post-mortem destiny of man—other than a vague belief in reincarnation.

An analogy might be given. It is like giving a condemned man a tedious course in anatomy so that he will know the precise functioning of his nervous system when he experiences the gas chamber. The thing with which that condemned man is concerned is the condition in which he will be after he has breathed the gas and expired. This analogy-reference takes into account the possibility that there might be such a thing as a chakra.

There exists a very valid argument that applies to systems that purport to change our state of being or to sharpen our intuition or understanding. This same argument is used to justify a lesser or venal cult. The argument is, of course, that proof of the claims of a discipline aimed at changing our state of being lies in the end result and cannot be demonstrated beforehand.

I do not flatly accept this argument in either case. We still must make an effort to make prior evaluations. And it would appear that a developed intuition is our only alternative.

GURDJIEFF AND OUSPENSKY

In the Gurdjieff-movement we find a refreshing lack of oriental terminology. On the other hand, Gurdjieff has his own unique brand of confusion. To learn of Gurdjieff, you might read Ouspensky's, *In Search of the Miraculous,* and Rom Landau's, *God Is My Adventure.* Kenneth Walker also wrote a book about Gurdjieff, *Venture With Ideas,* which was reviewed in *Time* magazine.

The review in *Time* has little mention of Walker except to say that the latter believed Gurdjieff to be an outstanding philosopher-psychologist. Gurdjieff died in 1949 at the age of 77. Ouspensky, his chief disciple, died two years before. The article depicts Gurdjieff as a gourmet and a "shearer of sheep," or confidence man. The author does credit him as being the container of a vast amount of knowledge.

From reading, *All and Everything,* and from reading what I could that had been written by those close to Gurdjieff, I have come to believe that he fathered an interesting metaphysics and had an astute insight into psychology. Some of his followers lost faith in him and left his Fontainebleau retreat after Gurdjieff became injured in an automobile accident. He is supposed to have led them to believe that his system gave him control over accidents.

I am much more interested in the way Ouspensky deals with the Gurdjieffian philosophy. Ouspensky presents more of a serious, methodical approach. The Gurdjieffian fanfare is lacking in Ouspensky's explanation of the work. With Ouspensky we recognize that learning to think correctly is more important than concept-building, because the latter may lead to fantasy. Some psychoanalytical systems are good, therefore. The self-observing system gives us something to do with our meditations besides just allowing the thoughts to wander. We must indeed observe ourselves first.

Another very good point about the Ouspensky lectures is his insistence upon the School as a means for growth. The implication—a very valid one, incidentally—is that man must have his fellowman, even in the business of spiritual development.

Gurdjieff has now been dead for twenty years and his movement is still alive, but some of the people who are giving lectures with a pretence of authority as Gurdjieffian heirs are either functioning under conjecture or inaccuracy, because their movements are fanning out in all directions.

I heard that lectures were being given at Virginia Beach a few years back and decided to make the trip. I sought out the lecturer. He was a young man of twenty-five years, if that. Twenty minutes of conversation with him started me in a homeward direction without listening to any of his lectures. In a brash manner he announced that he knew all there was to know about the movement. I protested that he was only in his twenties and could not have known Gurdjieff in his lifetime. The boy had a ready answer. He announced with the same blandness, that he had quite a start on me, since he had known Gurdjieff in his previous lifetime, or incarnation!

There are about a dozen pretenders to Gurdjieff's throne and none of them flatters the memory of Gurdjieff. I had a particular encounter with one such self-appointed guru of the Gurdjieff line. This encounter may serve to demonstrate the extreme caution that a person must exercise in order to choose not only a teacher, but each acquaintance or co-worker. This man came to me practically out of nowhere. He came unrecommended and unsolicited.

This fellow did not write and get acquainted by mail before making his appearance—a custom required for those coming to the Ashram. He made several flamboyant phone calls and had his "disciple" make one. He next sent a very wordy and flattering telegram and followed the telegram in person, accompanied by two men—one crippled and the other hirsute.

I picked them up at the nearest train station and drove them some forty miles. Their smell was an ordeal in itself. Had it not been that part of this smell was an alcoholic one, I might have excused their untidy condition as the result of travelling and poor accommodations.

The leader was an oily, hairy man with a weak but cunning face. I listened to his tales about Gurdjieff for several days before I realized that he really knew no more about Gurdjieff than myself. He was an unctuous name-dropper and at first some of the Ashram-residents were impressed by him. Soon I noticed that the other residents of the Ashram were leaving and new arrivals were dissuaded from staying. I also learned that he was running a confidence racket. When questioned, he did not deny it and claimed that Gurdjieff had certain sincere students whom he did not charge, but that Gurdjieff, like himself, had no qualms about fleecing "the little old ladies." With an affable smile he would spread his hands and remark that Gurdjieff extracted large sums from people because money was the only contribution that some people could make.

This imposter, whom I shall call Mr. A, took a few pages from Gurdjieff's history that were to his liking. He consumed a quart of wine a day—if he could get his hands on it. "For his low blood-sugar." The crippled man was receiving a small pension and I discovered that the other two were using and abusing the crippled man. Finally, the crippled man left.

The younger companion, Mr. J. G., was a very clever disciple. He constantly sang the praises of his leader. He would drop little tidbits regarding the long wait that he had to endure before his teacher answered any of his questions. They spoke nonchalantly about raising the dead, about curing with herbs, and about their common Master who walked through walls.

Then other little stories began to trickle out. They told of having a sort of commune in New York in a condemned building. The police evicted them. Mr. J.G. bragged that he had shot a policeman in San Francisco. In one city on the West Coast, Mr. A. had his followers carry him upon a horizontal cross upon which he stretched, dressed in sundry clerical vestments, and wearing a crown. This travesty he considered to be very comic.

He also told of serving thirty days in jail for contempt of court. I decided that I had two imposters on my hands and possibly two extortionists, judging from the money that came to them through the mail. So I moved them out of the house and told them that they would have to leave the premises. They asked for permission to stay a few days in a house trailer until some important mail came, which they were expecting soon. I agreed, mainly because they did not argue about leaving.

It was very close to Thanksgiving and they asked me to meet the bus in town and pick up a young lady who was coming in from the South to spend the holiday with them. They had no car. I picked this visitor up late in the evening before Thanksgiving. Since neither of these men believed in work, there was no adequate fuel at the Ashram, so I suggested that this girl stay in my house in town for the night. I found that she was sixteen years of age and that she knew many startling things about Mr.'s A. and J.G.

She told me that she did not wish to come and visit them, but that she came out of fear . . . of physical violence and black magical powers. She had met them in Colorado. J.G. had encouraged her and a group of hippies to join with Mr. A. This little colony was evicted from the area and they began to hitchhike toward New York.

When the group arrived in New York it only consisted of the two men and this young girl. They immediately tried to put her to work as a prostitute and when she resisted they beat her and broke her nose. And, yet, this same girl was ready to go back for more punishment. The girl's mother had been sending them large sums of money. When I talked to the mother by phone, she admitted that the money was sent out of fear.

When I ordered the two to leave the trailer they threatened me and burned the trailer completely as they left. This is the price that can be paid for being impractical or being slow in setting oneself up as an arbiter of people coming to stay and work at the noblest of undertakings.

I believe that the only way to get anything from the Gurdjieff system is to study the books by Ouspensky and the other disciples. After having done quite a bit of research, I fail to find anything about Gurdjieff that would give him the position of a spiritual leader. That he had wide experience is true and that he was also gifted with extraordinary common sense is also true.

He comes in with a new approach. We do not have to listen to an interminable symbology of no worthwhile meaning. We do not have to memorize a foreign vocabulary to study Gurdjieff. Yet, he says many of the same things that we could learn if we labored through oriental philosophy and transcendentalism.

Gurdjieff furnishes us with a system by which we can escape mechanicalness and find self-determination. He also proposes the school, or brotherhood. He is one of the few authors that emphasize that man is victimized by nature.

The theory of Kal tells us the same story that Gurdjieff tells but in a different way—about man's hopeless condition as a slave to nature. Gurdjieff also reaffirms the "Many are called but few are chosen" line that relates to the percentages of people who have evolved sufficiently to desire to escape or search for an answer. Gurdjieff categorizes the evolvement of man as having seven steps and claims that most of mankind falls into the first three steps or numbers. Thus, man number four is the one most likely to escape from the net of nature. Gurdjieff also places significance upon that which he calls the "sly man."

This little reference that we find in the Gurdjieff teachings is often overlooked. It has significant meaning. It means that we do not get to heaven by being saintly, because trying to be saintly is a fool's endeavor . . . a fool who pretends to envision the will of some invisible deity and to judge that that deity sees mankind acceptable if sweet and gregarious. Likewise, in ancient times the same class of fools butchered human sacrfices because they thought the act of sacrifice to be pleasing to the gods.

The Gurdjieff-system teaches that a man must first have common sense and must discover the many, many ways in which each human being outwits himself about the most serious of subjects—self-identification and survival. It is worthwhile to note that if a man does not know the looker—there is little use in looking. The evidence which has been brought back by lookers whose cognitive apparatus has not been checked out is not very reliable. In fact, down through the ages the masses have chosen to use their emotions and desires as eyes. The Gurdjieff-system automatically places man as the field of study. This is nothing new either. There is a very ancient adage, "First know thyself."

The Gurdjieff teachings have some inconsistencies. Much of the writings consist of a complex cosmology and this comes as a bit of extra padding—if his system is designed to bring man into the exaltation of being fully "awake." Knowledge of the universal cosmology has no value to us if we cannot utilize that knowledge in the direction of our own immortality. Also we can only conclude that being "awake" in the fullest sense is synonymous with reaching the Truth in the fullest sense. And since Gurdjieff does not describe for us this ultimate goal, but recommends a path similar to the three-fold directive of Buddha, we can only assume that the goal must be the same in any case. And if the goal of the Gurdjieff or Ouspensky system would be (even without their intention) cosmic consciousness—there would not be much use in categorizing, cosmologically, an illusory world.

Unfortunately, neither Gurdjieff nor Ouspensky tries to describe the condition of the man who is fully "awake." We do learn that man number seven is more awake than man number four. But a person almost gets the impression from the writings of both and from the lives of both that they were not sure about the state of being that might be expected from a "man number seven." In other words, the goal is never really named. And for this reason, I have come to the conclusion that the Gurdjieff-system is a good and worthy system for a person starting out on the path of self-liberation. But it is not complete. Perhaps there was a personal teaching that was not recordable because it would naturally differ in each student-case. If this latter supposition is true, then, of course, the Gurdjieff-system would be more complete, but it would still leave us in the dark about the reasons for the complex cosmology which is part of the writings.

I realize that many opinions have been given in this book and only a little information has been given as to the manner of collecting the information that must necessarily have led me to my inflexible conclusions.

When I was about twenty-five years of age, I began to meet other men who were of the same mind as myself about the search for Truth. Since I do not have their permission, I will not identify them. Not that they would object to being known perhaps. But they have grown families and children and grandchildren who may feel that such divulgence would not be compatible with a particular game of life that they may be playing.

We were not many . . . the more faithful ones numbered six or eight. Then there were other contacts who knew of our interests and these friends also supplied us with information and attended our meetings. We decided to prospect in separate environments for systems and for people who might know more than ourselves. In the early days of the search we were afflicted with the "Hunt the Guru Syndrome." We promised one another to learn all that we could, and then compare notes. Each of us joined different sects and became initiates of those sects which held initiation requisite to learning that which the sect claimed to be valuable, esoteric knowledge. Needless to say, on many occasions we were diasppointed with the trivial offerings of most sects.

In this manner we learned, as a group, that which could not have been learned in three lifetimes by any of us alone. We became acquainted with the initiation rites of SRF and Radha Soami. We obtained heaps of Rosicrucian private lessons or mandami. One of our group was "opened" in the Subud movement. Two others attended latihan sessions.

We made lone trips to investigate materializations, spiritualistic phenomena of all sorts, and individuals who had particularly unique talents. We visted witch-doctors, priests, Protestant ministers, and fortune-tellers. One member took time out to help set up a scientific research group—the Mind-Science Foundation of San Antonio (endowed by Tom Slick). We worked with smaller "psychic research" groups whose investigations were along the lines of ESP, table tilting and hypnosis.

We subscribed to magazines that dealt with occult or transcendental matters and occasionally placed ads in them to contact people who might be sincere.

We had several things in common besides ignorance and the admission of it. We agreed that moneyed cults, power and glory cults, and movements with excessive secrecy were not worth the bother. Of course, we argued among ourselves over the relative worth of some movements.

I feel that the history of our search is secondary to our conclusions. The history of our diggings would include many movements and teachers not even discussed in this book. Some are not worth mentioning. Some were found to be created out of whole cloth. And a few of those mentioned in this book are not worth the following of one day, but they are examined here, nevertheless, to demonstrate the negative effect they have upon the minds of too many people.

By the same token, there are individuals who were instrumental in either encouraging me to continue my work or who were directly helpful, and who, beyond a doubt, held the rank of teacher, who will not be described here because their value was recognized only by their conversations and their manner of working. If any sort of bridge has been built by our collective labors, a picture of the bridge is more important than a portrait of ourselves.

And still, in this chapter devoted to observations of teachers and unique systems, I should admit that those who played possibly the most valuable role for the most of us were not the teachers of any cult or well-known system, but were individuals largely unseen by the general public . . . whose real value to us was forever unknown to their next door neighbors, employers and associates.

To give them justice would require a chapter or a book for each of them. And to write less would leave the reader with fragmentary evidence or would give only the human picture of mistakes made, and blind struggling. It might be interesting here to give a sort of summary conclusion of our group as regards the systems encountered.

I am sure that nearly all of us would agree that systems that aid in "becoming" rather than "learning" are endorsed. The real science, we concur, is knowing the self, which we somehow sense is the door to Reality. The observation of magic or the study and classification of phenomena is mostly an interesting divergence for the mind when it is too tired to do anything else. The study of phenomena and phenomenal men does us no good if we cannot relate that study to the better understanding of our self, or at least formulate laws of phenomena by studying them.

An example of one of the phenomenal men is Edgar Cayce. I made a trip to Virginia Beach to see his place and talk to some of the people who came there. I did it only as part of a family vacation. Edgar Cayce was dead and his son Hugh Lynn manifested none of his father's psychic ability. And Edgar Cayce, while living, gave reams of advice and perhaps issued some semblance of a philosophy, but he left behind no system nor explanation of his own peculiar powers answerable to scientific investigation.

Nor did he give a formula for a student who might like to be a psychic doctor or even finder of lost items. Cayce was a phenomenon, not a teacher. And now being gone, he is only a history of a phenomenon. It is good to read of him and to read his writings. It is not wise to make of him a religion or a solitary path to Truth.

Phenomenal men are more valuable contacts than are phenomena. The study of phenomena includes the wide range of flying saucers, Fortean research, spiritualistic phenomena, magical mantras, astrology, numerology and thaumaturgy. None of these deserves an all-out application of our life's energy, but they are more commendable pursuits than remaining inert on the soft bed of organized religion.

FIFTH PAPER

Obstacles to Transcendental Efforts

ARGUMENT FOR TRANSCENDENTAL RESEARCH

Transcendentalism not only provokes more negative argument than positive argument, but it also provokes more ridicule. The ridicule is inspired by the comic or pathetic appearance of some transcendental poseurs, fanatics, and psychic ripple makers who make up some of the motley classes of transcendental effort. We can never be sure, except in certain individual cases, whether occultism and transcendentalism causes or worsens the mental conditions which are likely to be described as "sick" or "crazy". And it may be true that some sincere people may have submitted themselves to deprivation, asceticism, or some painful experimentation which may have left them in worse shape than they were before they became transcendentalists. In any event, we should not criticize this latter group, until we have walked a mile in their moccasins.

As for argument . . . it is not hard to find arguments against spiritual or transcendental prospecting. The arguments come in from all sides, and especially from those well-organized groups whose concepts might be jeopardized. Religion is content to bed down with the politician and sociologist and make any sort of compromise to protect its slumber. Religion evidently wants no amateurs adding to its enlightenment. Psychology is alarmed by various transcendental findings which might upset the entire psychological pretence.

We can dispense with the arguments from religious sources, because we should know by now that transcendentalism is actually religious research, and most of the criticism from religion is recognizable as sectarian or political—meaning that some sects embody in their religious practices things which other sects persecute.

That which diverts more minds from psychic research than anything else is the persistent scientific sophistry of pseudo-scientific writers. It might be said that material scientists and those esoteric groups which specialize in mind-science or systems aimed at states of being, are the most polarized. The material scientist claims that the transcendentalist cannot prove anything, and implies that the latter makes no sense. The transcendentalist, on the other hand, often does not try to make sense, because he feels his development to be superior to logical processes. And he, in turn, also accuses the material scientist of being only a sort of animated slide rule, without the necessary feeling-ability to actually do research work in dimensions other than the apparent one.

However, both work from the same base. Neither denies the existence of man, and their sciences or meta-sciences are the results of and concern for, understanding man's relation to environment, whether that environment be the visible world, the invisible and molecular man, or the still more invisible, and seemingly remote God-spark, of which molecular man may only be a reflection.

We must abridge all such argument and admit that man is a fact, and in being a fact, immediately is assured of the immortality and indestructibility of the fact-state. Whatever his limits are as regards his immortality or mortality, or as regards his degree of consciousness, his fact-status is permanent. Of course, the concept of the nature of, or the exactness of, that fact-state is interpreted differently by the two polarized groups, and therein lies the root of the misunderstanding.

Man is a physical fact in that he, (particularly the material scientist), recognizes as man, only that man-being, or man-object, which is witnessable by the physical senses. And it is true that man is such a fact for such an observer. However, the transcendentalist may go as far as to say that the physical body and the senses themselves are both illusions and the results of illusions. Yet, the transcendentalist (as in the case of a Zen student or aspirant to Satori) still views man as a fact. The amazing thing is that this latter group (of transcendentalists) views their concept of man's fact-status as more concrete and real than any other. Their fact-man is indestructible and complete. The fact-man of the material scientist is a transitory creature and a limited one.

Another argument against transcendental work consists of complaints of supposedly infinite and insurmountable difficulties involved in such research. This argument bears some truth, but it is not valid in the long run. An equivalent argument might have been handed to the cave men to discourage them from embarking upon their primitive and seemingly hopeless research, which must have ultimately led to our present technology. In other words, it is better to look back upon the successes of past programs if we need assurances for future efforts, regardless of the field.

It is true that we are working with abstractions, but it is also true that even in abstractions, patterns have been discovered. These patterns, in turn, lead to either a better understanding of the phenomena involved, or to new angles from which the phenomena can be studied. The sad evidence remains that such patterns have been discovered decades and centuries ago, but the material scientists, ever on the alert for things apparent, failed to see these apparent patterns. Such a pattern is expressed in ancient occult books with the words, "As above, so below." This ancient allusion to the relation of the Microcosm to the Macrocosm is still missed by many physicists who are aware of the orbital systems of both atoms and solar systems.

Hypnosis was practiced by primitive humanity, but it was many centuries later that either the scientist or medical practitioner of our quasi-civilized society admitted the validity of the phenomena of hypnosis. And it was probably a half-century later, after that admission, that it was used as a therapeutic instrument as well as a parlor pastime.

If it was possible for primitive peoples to come up with such an instrument long before Galileo demonstrated his lenses, (he was belabored by the Church of Rome because he was unable to prove, as in a court of law, beyond all cavil and doubt, that the pope was not the center of the universe), then there surely must be hope for the modern researcher. All the latter needs is the courage and basic intelligence of an aboriginal shaman.

We find another argument which claims that all occult phenomena are the result of fraudulent manipulations, and that all transcendental cults result from the hunger of the needy layman and from the greed of the dispensers of nostrums and gimmicks. And I must admit that this argument has a true bearing on ninety percent of the cult movements, for if I did not recognize considerable and manifest fraudulence, I would have omitted much of this work.

Yet, even in some of the movements that have been proven to have fraudulent directors, we find some material borrowed from other sources which, in their own right, were not money-motivated. And often, if we submit to dig through this type of re-digested material, we will eventually come across evidence of historical research and note-taking, so that even the charlatan hacks of such evidence may have some value.

Above all, no man should enter transcendental work with fear-expectations. He should attack it with the same energy that he would apply to mastering calculus, and with the knowledge or conviction that he can study either calculus or esoteric philosophy and still be a man. There is no reason for any man to anticipate any metamorphosis of his physical body or deterioration of his mental processes because of such a search. It is possible that preconceptions of angelic development for men of the cloth and of saffron robes alike have resulted in their acting the part to a point of affectation of strange poses and states of mind.

If we are male, we should advance upon the battlements of ignorance with the tools of the male, with aggressiveness. The female may find the mark better with passiveness. In any event, there is no danger of her becoming less feminine by being passive, and, less danger of losing her femininity. Both parties should never lose sight of human exigencies, right up to the day of final victory or cosmic-consciousness. Until that final day our role can only be that of the fact-man that is knowable.

THE CURSE OF INTELLECTUALISM

We are continually subjected to the fallacy that an intellectual is a wise man. Let us ask ourselves about the nature of our real objectives in pursuing the study that leads to being an intellectual. And then after this self-scrutiny, let us ask our neighbor-intellectuals, our colleagues, about their motives for becoming scholars or experts in an intellectual field.

The human being goes into higher education because of primitive drives. The main factor in a young man's decision to fight his way through college is competition. To strive with greater facility for the material things of life . . . which is the same as saying that he is putting a bit more effort into satisfying his physical senses, his appetites, or his fears.

An engineer will have twice the earning potential of a shoe salesman, and perhaps three times the earning ability of a farmer. With that proportion of earnings he is better able to afford the type of fear or desire that might stimulate him. He does not specifically enter into the study of calculus to find the Truth. And too often, once he has become a "qualified" engineer, he is apt to scorn anyone who overlooks his importance, or who might question the infallibility of science as the engineer sees it.

In days gone by, there was a tremendous reverence for even a school teacher. Anyone who showed a love for learning was automatically presumed to be wise. A school teacher is little more than a memory bank for the community. They are the custodians of information. They memorize, but the nature of their work causes them to fall into the habit of acceptance of authority, which does not make for philosophers or thinkers. They drill themselves as well as their students.

The college student who takes up a more scientific course and avoids the teaching profession may well become an efficient slide rule or computer to enhance the environment, or to aid the interminable scientific pursuits of society. But once the engineer has mastered the slide rule and become an extension of it, he has little time left to look into the nature of life and reality. The difference between the intellectual and the farmer (besides their earnings) is that the farmer sells his physical energy while the engineer sells his mind. And for this simple reason, the mind of the engineer is of less value to his Self, or to that part of him that depends upon the mind to evaluate itself.

Go among your colleagues, if you associate with intellectuals, and ask them for the reasons for their pursuit of education. And ask them for their opinions about the scientific investigations of phenomena as yet unexplained by our sciences . . . such as are approached by transcendentalism. Ask them to define themselves, or to give reasons why they have not bothered to define themselves.

You will find that nearly all intellectuals and scientists see no urgency in defining themselves before they define the material world about them.

The appalling thing in the world of religion, and up or down to the world of psychology, is the manifest confusion. We have a painful weakness in regard to authority. Even the most absurd concepts will, by some twist of statistics or intuition, appear to be valid. And on the other hand, those concepts born out of reason, or legalized by pseudo-authority, will be constantly attacked by unexplained phenomena or contrary evidence. Of course, the main weakness of both categories is that they are both mostly concepts rather than discoveries.

Frustration besets us at every starting point and at every attempt at definition. We start off proclaiming nobly that we are in search of the Truth and are determined to find it. Immediately there are authorities that will rise up and denounce us for fools, saying that the finite mind will never perceive the infinite. Yet, the same theologians who utter this also attest to the teachings of Christ, Who advised us to seek in order to find, and Who also declared that the Truth would make us free. I am not eager at any point to ridicule the honest theologian, nor to belittle any effort toward genuine understanding. We may justly lament the fact that there are people who stand in the pulpit of authority whose only cause is their own, and whose words are geared to manifest their cleverness in argument, and whose arguments are oriented toward profit. These people are not always itinerant, back-woods preachers or curb-stone orators. Some of them have dictated the policy of major religions, and others have dominated entire nations.

Which brings us to another facet of terrestrial thinking. We are inclined to think that that which everyone believes in must be true. We have carried our gregariousness over into a massive respect for mob-opinion. Eminent theologians will proudly cant in tones acceptable that there is immortality because everyone believes it, while the truth that they hide is that everyone desires it. Of course, we are immediately open to confusion, even with that criticism, because it is possible that if everyone really believed in immortality, that belief might create some form of immortality, if it were not otherwise a fact. However, we immediately come back to the factual statistics of the number of people who sincerely and unwaveringly believe that we will survive death. Many honest theologians feel that the only immortality-hope lies in keeping the masses reassured, so that their faith will be mountainous and creative to the point where the post-mortem status of their own particular religious group will be assured.

I am inclined to believe that about ninety percent of the people *desire* immortality. There is a small percentage who do not even think about it, or who desire the eternal rest of oblivion. I doubt that a majority of the human race actually believes in a life after death. I think that even the zealot has a moment of uncertainty or light, whichever it might be, when he senses his own gullibility and gains a bit of insight into the complexities of his own rationalizations.

I ask nearly everyone I meet to give me their beliefs on immortality and their reasons for thinking as they do. I am always looking for an account that will manifest conviction, and I am aware that perhaps I am seeking for some sort of magic that will give me a pattern of the Truth that I had not previously contemplated. Regardless of motives, the answers that people gave me, although possessing little of the magical or the illuminating, betrayed the trend of the thoughts and aspirations of the masses. It can be summed up best by the expression, "Me too." They do not presume to know that which is going to happen to them, and they do not presume to be big enough to find out. The layman points out that billions of people have gone on before him, and he expects to go to the same place with them. He might even remind me that he is paying his minister a salary to insure his celestiality. If we approach the professional man, or those who might be labelled the intelligentsia, we will obtain some really complex rationalizations or indications of very brave futilism. The layman is often more honest than the well-educated man, because he is conscious of his lack of learning. His intuitional doubts are equally as valuable as those of the pedant or philosopher. The layman is lazier because he allows another man to do his theorizing for him, but his laziness may be also intuitively inspired, since for some it is just as well to begin with frustration as to end with it. And it is human to clutch at straws.

We are reminded of the force called Kal, which in Radha Soami literature is mentioned more frequently than the name of God. And I think that the one-sided amount of emphasis is appropriate. Kal is the force that keeps men in darkness, and when we start to recognize him, we see him all about us. God is not so apparent. I have always been conscious of the existence of opposition to spiritual growth, and I prefer to label this negative force as "The Forces of Adversity." I prefer this label over such limited words as Kal or Satan. These items also imply personal opposition or the conspiracy of a particular being against humanity, and when all the evidence is in, we have no foundation for such a belief. In the search for reliable translations of the Bible, we find that Satan should really read as "adversary."

I am opposed to advocates of "positive thinking," and to disciples of the omnipotence of belief. I maintain that we are relative creatures. We have not yet merged with unity and lost our identity. We look at all things with two eyes, a bicameral brain, a mind that appraises with alternate logic and intuition, and we wallow in the misery of the paradox and the confusion of the polarity in our thinking. We attempt to utter our anguished message and we find that we must use a relative language, and we are snowed under by heaps of words that can only express the difficulty of trying to say something accurately before we have lost the thought that fathered the effort.

There are those who deny negative powers. Yet, if man can conceive of positive powers, he must admit the negative. All is not sweetness and light, unless somewhere there is bitterness and darkness. I cannot visualize a time when all will be wise simultaneously, for wisdom depends upon ignorance. Nor can I visualize an era when all men will share alike in a great economic brotherhood, because wealth depends upon poverty.

If positive thinking means negating of negative forces, then I can concur. But I cannot place my head in such optimistic sands that promise for my leaving my unfeathered rear exposed, that no harm will come to me. Nature has a way of gleefully awakening the ostrich-type. Those who have too great a faith seem to encounter disastrous opportunities to test that faith. One great Christian controversy centers around the despairing words of Christ upon the cross, since some feel that even Christ had a loss or weakening of faith. The type of "positive thinking" that has been offered to us as salutary in spiritual endeavors is better adapted to salesmen and persons who wish to free themselves psychologically from some mania or habit with the help of auto-suggestion. "Positive thinking" does not bear the characteristics of a law, but rather identifies a technique or psychological lever.

Kal is supposed to permeate all human thinking. Of course, this may leave us a bit confused. But, when we first begin to read philosophically we get a hint that much of the world in which we live is an illusion. Kal says that religions themselves were invented and diversified to dismay the sincere and persistent seekers. We have the Biblical tower of Babel. There is a story of a sort of Maya that resulted from the eating of the paradisical apple. (The desire to be like God.) These little legends seem to indicate that for a long time man has had a whispering feeling that the game is fixed.

We generally go through several stages of dismay that might be interpreted as education. We align ourselves with a religion or are aligned with one at birth. Then we notice discrepancies of dogma and the hypocrisy of the clergy. We become disgusted with yesterday's beliefs, and we are attracted to another and often opposite system of thinking. Then we find the second system equally as transparent as the first, and we increase our despair. But our attitude is broadened. We start looking for the good points of various movements, and from such an optimistic endeavor, plunge into a way of life that may reward us temporarily with a great feeling—one of bliss or illumination. However, it must be emphasized that such exaltation is temporary. We cannot understand this bliss, and when we try to analyze or prolong it while living the vegetative life, it leaves us. And when it goes, we stand and wonder if we have not been the victim of self-hypnosis or hysteria of a sort caused by the chemical changes in the blood or glands wrought by the spiritual practice engendered. And then, suspiciously once again, we look over our shoulder to see if Kal is standing with his feet in our hip-pockets, laughing.

In the early stages of enlightenment we look with pity on the old lady who takes her pennies to church for the padre to buy beer. We think we are smarter because we can analyze her blindness, or because we have been lucky enough to catch the pastor tippling, or overhear the preacher confessing to be only an oratorical emollient. Yet, while we are convinced that the cult to which we are paying tribute is beyond suspicion, and often think ourselves fortunate to be picked by one that makes masters out of muttonheads . . . it will be good to pause and remember that it may be the same with the semi-exalted as with the lowly lady supplicant. As above, so below.

It is often the case—when a seeker is dismayed at the lack of truth in his native religion—that he is very easily satisfied with a foreign creed that he understands even less. A new hypnosis is established, and the person who smugly thought he was above being hypnotized, again is entranced. The Christian religion generally pictures a benevolent God who has scattered us like seeds, some among the cockles and stones, and some on warm manure where we will prosper. In the Christian religions we do not feel very important, so when we hear of a system of thinking that endows us with a godhood of sorts, we lift our ears readily. It is not the ignorant layman alone who is responsible for oriental leanings. Some of our eminent lodges borrow from Indian literature and pass it on to their applicants as arcane knowledge. Many serious philosophers founded schools based on systems studied in the orient. And sitting in the chair of the Western hierophant, we again see Kal waving his wand and laughing. The lodges employ secrecy, even as the quasi-gurus of India. The secrecy is treasured with the same zeal as the horseplay at the initiations.

Those who decide to join an Indian cult may agree to an even more blind servitude to a teacher who speaks in a jargon more confusing than Latin. And while the candidate may have previously bought beer for one teacher, he will be possibly now buying hashish for another teacher. And after paying years of his life into a cult or lodge that promises everything in the line of secret revelations, he may discover that Freud was a greater revelator than any of the high-priests.

I have labored through some very dense writings in which the wisdom pretended therein was certainly circular, and like the symbolical serpent, managed to continually bite its own tail. And yet, most of them stand abashed in the presence of a simple story like the *Bhagavad Gita* or the *Rubaiyat*. We attempt to analyze the worth of a theory qualitatively and quantitatively, and in the process invent a storm of complex words, each bearing a dozen facets of meaning. Although the writers, too, must become confused—those abstruse, scholarly writers on esoteric matters surely must enjoy the confusion that they know the reader undergoes in attempting to first understand them, and then to seek the loose ravelling that will enable the reader to pull the whole cloth apart. I think Kal invented all the big words . . . and maybe is responsible for inventing all words.

The inquirer goes out to seek understanding of these creeds or movements that promise immortality. He is often awed by the first books that he picks up, or the first "authority" he meets on the subject. I wonder at this point how many people would have pursued the study of yoga and kindred subjects, if certain words of the original Indian language were omitted and instead were replaced by simple synonymous English terms.

For instance, let us take some of their words and place them alongside an English equivalent. We have a juvenile abhorrence of the word "teacher," but we will climb the Himalayas in search of a guru. And by uttering the word "guru," we manage to add another point of argument to our dictionary.

Cultists talk glibly of Nirvana, Devachan, Brahm Lok, and Sat Desh as though the use of the words took them there magically. Heaven has lost its magical sound. Another term used with much abuse is the word "chakra." Cult-students will use the term with a glibness that would hint that they had actually seen one. If the word chakra means a nerve-ganglion or gland, then we might as well call it that. On the other hand, if the word signifies a luminous focal point in the astral body, then, of course, we must presume that the speaker is quite sure of the mechanics of astral bodies, and we must be convinced that there is such a body with such points.

The cultist is hard to retrieve. He embarks upon the path of cultism because of a disappointment with conventional faiths, or because of a particular intuitive appeal from the cult's ism. He is taken in because the cult has a pretty composite blueprint that explains much that his old religion did not explain to him. Let us note here that explanation is not a system of proving. There are many concepts which are structurally symmetrical and congruous, but which bear no more value than a pretty picture.

It is not enough to create a creed that fits together like a jig-saw puzzle. It must also try to prove its point and be beyond being simply desirable. Let us divest ourselves of the deluding dignity we assume at the instance of uttering a string of alien words. It only adds to our confusion and to the increment of the "forces of adversity."

Not only does a concept need to be structurally perfect to be acceptable, but it must be more all-inclusive and explanatory than any other concept.

As long as there can be no philosophies that are proven beyond uncertainty, then we can only keep replacing new ones for old ones, and the new ones being those that by their propositions explain the most unexplained phenomena, and satisfactorily answer the most questions.

It is not enough to explain that the finite mind will never perceive the infinite, we must prove that the finite mind can or cannot ever be less finite. We must keep on looking.

We know not where Truth resides. There can be no paths to Truth, only paths away from untruth. There is nothing proven for us in advance. We must experience for ourselves, and at best can only begin with a "working hypothesis." And we cannot spend too much time developing yardsticks to measure all the hypotheses for workability. We must find a yardstick that can be applied to all situations, and that yardstick must be very reliable.

This book does not profess to solve the riddle, or to be orderly in the presentation of a philosophy. I doubt that you could call it a philosophy, nor would I want it called that, because a philosophy, in attempting to be orderly and systematic, tries to build words upon words and syllogisms upon syllogisms. And I fear that such building involves sophistry. Being clever is commendable perhaps for survival, but being clever for the sake of ego or for the entertainment of others will not help the cause of Truth. And although I may try to get my point across with some skill, or with an accent of humor, rest assured that my main motive is to hold the attention, not to entertain. I hold that these things which I say are those which I have come to believe, and I consider any medium or expression inadequate to the serious compulsion I have to communicate them.

In this careful attempt at honesty, there shall be no attempt to prove absolutely. And truth, (with a small t), if it is to have a definition, would be that which is the most consistent, and that which is the most inclusive of all human findings. For no matter how consistent our thinking may appear to us, as long as there remains a single phenomenon unexplained by it, or there remains another system in which there are no more flaws than our own, but which may have alternate or opposite claims to ours,— we must continue to search.

OUR SELF AS AN OBSTACLE

Most obstacles that inhibit the research or search for Truth find their roots in the discrepancies in our evaluations described in previous writings. The greatest difficulty for man lies in his imperfect vision. We need to see things more clearly. The philosophy of the past has been beset with confusion by taking a positive approach to this business. It is impossible to state our aim beforehand. It is foolish to assess the utility-value of religion or philosophy. We are dealing with the essence of things, not their effects. "By their fruits you shall know them" does not belong here, regardless of its piety as a quotation.

We are not interested in greasing the axle of the wheel of Nature with utilitarian platitudes. We must not tremble that our search and our discoveries cause unhappy ripples in another man's religion, or in the fashionable thinking of any particular era. We are busy with too many obstacles to bargain with anyone, or to gamble away verities or the possibility of arriving at verities, out of tender solicitude for venal and transient religions or mores.

The first obstacle is ourselves. We are limited. Our limitation is demonstrated, not by our cosmic insignificance alone, but by our mental uncertainties, by the extremely qualified aspects of human comprehension, and by the emotional apparatus with its inclination to wear the respectable mask of intuition.

We are inclined to seek out that which makes us happy. And as a result, some of the "happy boys" with scholastic knighthood and title get things mixed up with their own adolescent unhappiness and decide that happiness is the goal, the god, and the way. Momentarily, because they have studied about aberration, they imagine that knowledge of the disease of rationalization makes them immune to rationalization.

We must be aware of the influence our desires have in motivating for us our choice of religion or life's work. We must put some time into observing our limitations and determining, if possible, ways to allow for the percentages of error caused by these limitations. Now this sounds like a bit of formulation, but it is not. The business of such observation is not to be evaluated quantitatively. It means that a man groping in the dark must learn to protect himself, not only from uncertainty, but from his own reactions to the gropings.

Physically, man imagines himself to be the supreme animal, but his sensory efficiency is often inferior to lesser animals. He cannot smell as well as most animals. The dog seems to be able to hear sounds that the human misses. At least the dog reacts to such sounds. Let us take into consideration the powers of lesser animals and contemplate our status if we had them.

In rooms where poltergeist-phenomena or spirit-like manifestations occur, dogs have shown by their attitude and bristling hair that the manifestations to them were real. These dogs, incidentally, had not been previously brainwashed by books or theories. Their reactions were spontaneous. Perhaps if we could see with their eyes, we could evolve better spiritual concepts.

It has been demonstrated that many animals have telepathic ability. Stranger still is the homing instinct of pigeons, and the habits of birds and animals that are generally labelled "instinctive." These abilities are fairly accurate mechanisms similar to radar. Some of these talents are most noticeable in fish. The animal also has a direct and quick understanding with other animals. The herbivorous animal knows the propitious moment for eating and for running at the approach of the predator. Specialization or other skills has lost these abilities for humans.

On the other hand, our senses are often deceiving, besides being weak and inadequate. Vibrations and rays must surely have a wide range of meaning for different animals because of diverse sensory apparatus in different species. Which means that the human appreciation of what he sees and hears is not by any certainty a real understanding of the projection or projector.

We do not know if having animal intuition would help us in any great way. But we can lose a little of our stuffiness if we observe the animal. We may sit in a church or lecture hall for twenty years listening to the same preacher and never know the most elementary thing which we need to know—namely, the veracity of the speaker. Whether or not he is a liar. The twenty years would be spent in evaluating, arguing, and weighing one elusive sermon against another . . . when it may have been possible to have gone directly to the mind of the man. I did not mention that the man may have been misguided. However, if we cannot determine if that man is a liar or not, what other evaluation has any validity?

But let us look at word-evaluation. This is necessary because we might spend our twenty years taking correspondence courses in salvation, or we may be obsessed with fundamentalism or the intrinsic value of some manuscript. Words are like refractions and bear to the perception or perceptee a variation of refraction in proportion to the position and capacity, and to the conductivity of the environment which stands between the meaning to be projected and the perceptee.

When the idea of this language barrier comes into view, I immediately think of the tower of Babel. I find it easier to believe that this story is an allegory of early theological frustrations brought on by language barriers of the era, rather than an account of a petty God dispersing His supplicants. Christ advised us to seek. But the Old Testament execrates the seeker and almost implies that God was alarmed at the height of the tower of Babel. Since there has been no celestial reaction to the sending of rockets to the moon, we must reappraise the significance of God's anger at a pile of rocks.

There is another explanation to the story of the tower of Babel. It may be that the early Hebrews or inhabitants of that region were being directed by an entity that posed as a deity, which or who, being desirous of maintaining its powers over the tribe, resorted to noisy manifestations to keep the people in line. Thus, we have a hint that the "Lord" of the Old Testament was human, which would account for the descriptions of personal appearances, instructions given vocally and heard by the multitudes, besides other phenomena attributed to God.

The physical body also places limitations upon the mind of man. William James makes quite an issue out of this aspect of man. He calls "medical materialism" that school of thought that looks into the human body for disturbances that limit the mind and religion of each man. He infers that it might be possible to diagnose a man's physical diseases by listening to his philosophic or religious protestation. Medical Materialism may well have a point, but we, in turn, may diagnose *it* as emanating from minds diseased by egotism and laziness. While it is true that a person's religious zeal may suddenly increase with old age, it is also true that we can find many religious zealots in healthy individuals under twenty.

We cannot trace the zeal of man to a disease, unless we admit that disease to be common to all protoplasm, if we wish to call it a disease. Such diseases would be curiosity, and anything that might help us to overcome the obstacles listed in this book. The amoeba manifests curiosity. Curiosity is found in all forms of life where any degree of individual consciousness is found.

If we presume ourselves to be of divine origin, then curiosity is a divine mandate. If we are considered to be evolutionary products of lesser beings of accidental origins, then that curiosity is as normal as any animal function, and is of tantamount importance to any animal's survival. And a goat need not have a diseased liver or mind to have the compulsion to climb to the top of a barn roof just for a look around. The medical materialist fails to take into consideration the ramifications of curiosity. And he implies that a man is sick if he is neither eating, working, or being happy according to the restricted pleasure-code of society.

Still, we must not miss a good point. There are people who are quite a bit off base, and some of them gravitate toward transcendentalism. Yet, I still cannot see a clear line drawn that would make all seekers out to be sick, any more than to presume that all sick people are trancendentalists. Not long ago, a seemingly healthy ex-marine shot and killed about a dozen people from a tower of a Texas university. Despite his previously normal behavior, a post-mortem examination showed that he suffered form a brain tumor or lesion. On the other side of the fence, I knew a man who lived outside of San Antonio who was respected as a psychic healer. He was just an ordinary fellow, until a kick by a horse caused a brain tumor. The accident happened when the man was young, but he lived beyond the sixty-year mark before the tumor killed him. He ascribed his healing ability to the kick in the head. If we are to judge him from a functional viewpoint, this second man helped thousands of people and had visions as a result of mind or brain impairment. He was not irrational, unless we wish to define the whole healing system as being irrational. He maintained that diseases were caused by demons or entities, and he had the ability to banish the entities. It was simple, and it evidently worked to the satisfaction of thousands.

We find that some sects candidly admit that a spiritual breakthrough is often coincidental to a mental breakdown, or follows on the heels of somatic suffering or disaster. In the history of the Zen masters, we find that one fellow applied to the monastery and was rejected. He tried to pry his way into the gate. The attendant slammed the gate and cut off his leg. "Whereupon he received enlightenment." Evidently.

Our smile may not be justified. I have been acquainted with quite a number of people who were striving for Satori. Some of them were taken right to the door of death by some cause, and after operations or a damaging siege of illness, they came out with the claim that they had reached the state beyond concern. One man had colitis that nearly killed him, and I presumed at the time that his stay in the hospital was for a colostomy. I think I have mentioned elsewhere in a previous writing, the case of the woman student of Zen who attempted suicide. There may have been such attempts that were successful. However, all movements have their share of suicides. There is no prophetic pattern, and Zen does not require colitis, ulcers, or amputations.

The sedentary life of a clergyman is liable to produce an occupational peculiarity or ailment. A trend toward effeminacy may be a corollary of clerical occupations. Even as a coal-miner may develop silicosis, so a priest, whether he preaches asceticism or Pollyanna, may come up with ulcers, thyroid trouble, or prostatitis. It does not follow that all priests became priests because they had prostatitis.

There are hazards to each profession. The metaphysician has his share. And I do not intend to brush aside either the motives for becoming a seeker, or the illnesses that result from the work as a seeker. We can be too careful of being guilty of some complex or other, and inhibit our drive down to zero. On the other hand, we must be able to recognize the signposts given us by the medical materialists.

We must neither work too hard nor sit too long. With the former comes callouses of the mind and body. With the latter comes sleep and fatalism. With excessive preoccupation with the works of others, or with scholastic successes, comes an intellectual conceit that is a web as effective as a concrete wall. And with such also comes the confusion of words. On the other hand, abstinence from books and teachers results in a lack of source-material, source-material that might save us years and health. We cannot do it all with our intuition alone.

We must know ourselves in order to find the obstacles that find their roots within us. Too often our decisions are influenced by emotions. When this happens we will pick a teacher for his personality and pick a system that harmonizes with our appetites.

Another obstacle within us is fatigue. The mind goes to sleep after so many hours on a subject. The mind retreats from problems that hold no hope of immediate solution. Our attention goes tumbling off, accelerated by desires and rationalization.

Some physical and mental obstacles can be surmounted by observing and correcting chemical conditions and glandular secretions. When we take into account the enormous amount of and weight of factors that influence our thinking, and hence affect any spiritual drive, we are apt to throw our hands up in despair. We might, in fact, decide to throw the entire world's library into the flames, presuming that everything could be discounted by virtue of possible chicanery by the authors, or by virtue of our susceptibility to hypnosis, manias, and body chemistry.

The coffins of Poe, Coleridge, and Oscar Wilde may contain nothing but empty dope capsules and alcohol bottles, but their writings give me the feeling that they experienced something that the ordinary "normal" citizen does not find. Their occupation had its hazards.

Naturally, the experience (of permanent physical disease) is not desirable, in that it is surely not necessary for spiritual enlightenment. We find that alcohol can immediately change the conviction of the user. And the same is true about the user of narcotics. An alcoholic sometimes develops two or more attitudes or personalities. When the great thirst is upon him, he will be vindictive and full of praise for the grape. When the thirst is softened by a few drinks he develops a second personality, which may be the dramatization of a personality that he wishes to possess. The hangover-stage introduces the third personality, in which physical conditions render the alcoholic despondent and remorseful. He now hates the grape and himself for the alliance.

Strangely enough, out of all of this conflict of attitudes have occasionally emerged men of great spiritual stature. I would not advise anyone to take the alcoholic path in order to find spiritual amazement, for the simple reason that the gods seem to desert alcoholics in great numbers. The percentage of alcoholics that free themselves from the depths of addiction is very small in comparison to the number of alcoholics that die in the addiction or commit suicide.

OBLIQUE DOGMATIC SYSTEMS

Various authors and systems, whose works fall short of being valuable in relation to the pursuit of Truth, are generally not aware of their particular tangential direction which removed them from the functional position which they covet. These sources digress along recognizable lines, and can be identified by their chief feature or style.

There are, first of all, the Utilitarians, of which we have heard. To them, religion has a value if it serves as a social lubricant, if it heals, if it aids in business ventures, or if it comforts the troubled.

Healing itself may often be recognized as a vain implement for the healer's glory or monetary gain, in exchange for a health-gift to those who do not even seem to be grateful. If, as some believe, the energy for healing actually comes from the combined energies of the minister and the congregation, then healing may well be a prostitution of valuable energy on a lost cause, or upon a person who will, in turn, only spend it again with poor spiritual thrift.

To this group (Utilitarians), we must consign the pollyanna of Unity which labels its periodical, "Better Business." To it also we must consign almost every organized religion that boasts of its value to society by keeping its members in line, and those which seek survival and acceptance by virtue of their social usefulness.

A second category of thinkers are the Psuedo-Practical Critics. They are the scientists who have momentarily invaded the field of transcendentalism, or are the various tumid reporters who exude the attitude that they are able to look at all things objectively. They tackle every concept with a sort of conservative attitude. They might excuse ESP or other phenomena as not being illogical, but they would be careful not to associate their own beliefs with the issue, and they employ a detached literary style to give the impression that they are a popular and irrefutable medium of common sense.

They who manifest this attitude are the literary barristers who would rather settle out of court than admit a position that would require a vigorous defense. They are not barristers of hope or principle, but men of glory in a show of intellectual cleverness. They go into the court of human reason half-heartedly and are very careful not to establish a position that might indicate that their own thinking is on trial. They are careful not to endorse anything that might at a later date undergo a qualifying change. If they endorse the field of mysticism, they will do so timidly.

A third category of pseudo-authorities are the Piddlers. These treat mysticism as a hobby, or as an excuse for social gatherings. They are often part-time mystics, or are those who indulge in the solemn-faced mummery of lodge-work. A few will be extremely well-read in many different philosophies, but will treat the whole field with little more respect than they would bestow on fiction. They may become engrossed in a cult or ism whose main substance is the endless juggling of symbols with questionable results. They may become so engrossed in the juggling that the pleasure of juggling becomes an intellectual titillation and conceit, rather than a potential means of finding Truth. And yet, the juggling of symbols, under control, may well bring us results in the scientific field, and in the sharpening of the faculties that aid in direct experience.

Thus, we have astrologers who only tell fortunes, and numerologists who would predict our political or amorous compatibilities. These are the augurs who examine the flights of birds and the entrails in the slaughterhouse for a hint of heaven. They are the strangely inspired, who allow superstition to overbalance reason and intuition. They will write books filled with symbols and invocations that do not work. They will compound secret codes that will consume years of the reader's time before their meaninglessness is exposed. To compound the mystery, these authors will assume pseudonyms, or may even remain anonymous.

The Concept Mechanics are piddlers of a more complicated type. They build new concepts by borrowing choice tidbits from the old ones. They observe the dying of current religions, and fancy themselves to be phoenixes that will sprout from the ashes of the dying religions. Their inability to supplant current religions or theories lies in their inability to think with their intuition, or to realize that another, the reader, might penetrate their processes and reject such concept-building. For the Concept Mechanics are fabricators, not believers. They speak with cleverness rather than sincerity, and they are rewarded with our admission of their cleverness and little more. They note the discrepancies of other concepts, and their limitations. Then they go about dreaming up a celestial science that will answer all our hopes and desires and will explain some previously unexplained phenomena.

The writings of Concept Mechanics are generally very complex, but in the last analysis are no more than presumptive formulae and utopian air-castles. Their concepts are built upon accepted axioms which we are more eager to accept than to deny. Yet, the numerous cosmo-conceptions that result from the same set of axioms bring the student to much bewilderment and leave him wishing he had examined the foundations first.

Instances of concept-building may be found in most Rosicrucian literature, in some Theosophical literature, and in most cult-literature that borrows from or pretends to borrow from Hinduism, Eleusenian lore, Essene wisdom, the Qabalah, from any ancient religious writings, or from combinations of any of these sects.

Readers of such concept-structures are often, besides being misled, titillated by suspense . . . and come to expect that the Truth will come on the next page. The actual subscriber will hold his breath waiting for a Master or for Initiation. Steiner writes profusely, describing a way of self-development which he admits is all meanignless, unless we are initiated. Yet, there is a discreet silence about the nature of initiation, so that that which might bring some element of verification to his writings hangs like a golden plum, always beyond our grasp. Tantalization becomes the chief feature of the cult-vendor.

Another category is that of the Quoters. Here are the writers who shrink from standing alone, even as the critics do. In their writings, they seem to be trying to tell their message indirectly. Some will use only occasional referential quotations, but others may compile entire books of copied material. Such is the style of Aldous Huxley's *Doors of Perception*. There is a subtle cleverness in this attempt to inspire conviction by summoning another's ghost, and forcing that ghost to testify for your cause, while inhibiting and limiting the testimony so that only those words are taken out of the text that will flatter the Quoter.

The thundering fundamentalist is an example. Occasionally the sacred books of the East are quoted, and then often in an apologetic manner. The chief feature of the Quoter is his manifest cowardice and inability to outline in his own words, that which he believes. His main tool is the inference that backing by important people makes for the Truth.

The Gimmick-Users are a very subtle group. These have discovered that which a scientist would call a law, and they gain either fame or following by either demonstrating the law, or by extolling it with more significance than it deserves. Thus, some are unselfish and devote the knowledge of the law to the betterment of mankind, but some become so enthralled with their discovery that they do not bother to progress further themselves—to the discovery of more laws or to self-improvement in general.

There has existed in occult writings, for centuries, the explanation of the law that governs healing. It is not the sole property of Christians. The Mohammedans recently challenged Billy Graham to a healing contest, which he politely rejected. This supposedly happened on his tour of Africa. Mr. Graham may not even profess to be a healer, but if he were, he would have difficulty in a Moslem country, or in an area where people strongly disbelieve in Christ.

The amazing thing about some healers is that they do not even understand the law, but use it instinctively.

Another of these gimmicks is the law of love. It has been found that love begets love and hate begets hate, and that hate destroys the hater. Love may also be self-destructive, if we do not know which types of love are to be inhibited. Somerset Maugham hints that Christ may have been destroyed because of his unqualified love (*Razor's Edge*).

As a result of the knowledge of the ultimate value of love, quite a few isms have incorporated themselves around that law, forgetting all other endeavors. Ramakrishna was supposed to have attained a deep spiritual position because of his intense love for Kali. Some Christian mystics have employed the same process to achieve rapture.

Another gimmick is "positive thinking." There can be no denying the power of positive thinking, but we can really run into error if we do not know its limitations. Partisans who try to gauge their lives by N.V. Peale's handbook, find that they still clash with society and other obstacles. "Positive thinking" can mean only "conventional thinking," and is limited as to effectiveness, regardless of the nobility of a purpose, if that purpose is not popular.

Mary Baker Eddy discovered the illusory nature of the material world. However, things get complicated when a person attempts to heal the illusory body of the illusory disease. It would seem that the real project would be to first find reality.

Centuries ago theologians discovered another law, but they continued to misunderstand and misuse it. This is the Law of Proportional Returns, or that which the Indians might call Karma. We borrow from physics and state that any object being struck manages to afflict the striking object with the same force. That which you sow, you will reap. Hate begets hate, and if you hurl negative thoughts you will, in turn, be visited by others with negative attitudes.

All of these things seem possible, but to affix to this law the idea of personal guilt may be the needless weaving of a whip for the already belabored mind of man. There is a considerable amount of friction over the ideas of guilt or degrees of guilt. The fact that there are two schools of thought on Will—Determinism and Libertarianism—means that man cannot quite make up his mind whether he should accept guilt or not. The proponents of guilt claim that guilt is the sense of responsibility that man must accept if he, man, wishes to have any right to function as an individual in charge of his own destiny.

Thus, we have sin catalogued and categorized. We have analysts who have examined sin qualitatively and quantitatively and proceeded from there to prescribe to the gram and grain how much pain or money must be paid to take the vigor out of the inevitable repercussion.

Thus, also in India we have much confusion among believers in Karma. Some Hindus breathe with apprehension, lest a microscopic retaliator gets caught in their intake.

The Oversimplifiers. These are not to be confused with men who honestly try to avoid complexity and verbosity. We get the idea from the Oversimplifiers that the mystic and the transcendentalist take themselves too seriously. The former would have us believe that there is a very simple explanation for all phenomena. They would say that a man did not see an apparition, he merely thought he saw one. And the man who was healed, to judge by them, was not sick in the first place. Precognition to them is coincidence. The man who performed a miracle simply hypnotized his audience. Spirit-manifestations are merely mental extrusions, etc.

Now the Oversimplifiers may be nearly right in some instances, even though they are looking for an easy explanation. They are not idiots, but they are uninspired, even though they sense that others tend to confuse inspiration with superstition. Their chief error comes from being unacquainted with the field which they criticize. To criticize a mystic, one has to be a mystic—one cannot view mysticism objectively and do it justice.

The tired thinker is apt to rationalize with oversimplification. From his inability or fatigue comes a weird sort of bravery. After a prolonged contemplation about life-after-death, he will announce that since there is nothing that can be done about death—it is foolish to give death a second thought. Eat, drink, and be merry.

Let me summarize a bit in the above categories. We cannot speak without quoting to some degree; we cannot simplify without running the risk of oversimplification; we may all be unconscious concept-mechanics, since we may be so impelled by our gestalts; and we are all piddlers when it comes to our attitude toward the Absolute. There is not so much damage in erratic thinking as there is in the conscious employment of erratic thinking and techniques of writing that might promote confusion. And all of this criticism is designed to save time for the seeker.

THE TRAP OF CONDITIONING

There are many obstacles to mental clarity, but the most insidious is mental conditioning. The voice of the appetites is easily recognized, and its form wears little or no mask—but conditioning is subtle. Conditioning probably contributes more to the spiritual inertia of man than any other factor.

Other minds have seen the adverse effects of conditioning. We can read Huxley's *Brave New World* for example. Huxley seemed concerned more with the intellectual enslavement of man and the social results, but he depicts the man of the future as a conditioned zombie.

It is bad enough that we are conditioned by nature to function as well-behaved, potted plants—in this terrestrial greenhouse. It is quite another thing when we start doing it to one another. We begin by conditioning our children to save them a few knocks in life. Teachers use about fifty percent of the classroom time in conditioning children for plasticity. This process is called "citizenship-training." Next, a good percentage of the young men will have to take military training, which process is designed to produce automatons to do any bidding, take any insult or degradation, and be convinced of individual worthlessness and individual inability. They are also trained to be proud of this treatment. Of course, men who are conditioned for the axe should not be burdened with too much thinking, but this is as tyrannical as expecting a rabbit that you are eating for dinner to provide the napkins and gratitude.

Lodge members condition other members with asinine initiations. Mankind is basically afraid of individualistic men. We do not like to face a brave, independent man nearly as well as a harmless, inoffensive one. We elect to office mostly people who avoid positive attitudes and, consequently, we rarely get men of principle. Businesses set up schools to brainwash candidates for sales and executive positions, in order to have a minimum of trouble with the business organization. They are taught to "handle" people. What this actually means is that a sort of professional behavior pattern is adopted, to which they want all people to conform, including both workers and clients.

We are cast into a state of awe by the choice of words used by mere mechanics who are conniving for some justification for public support and for livelihood. One such word was the title "doctor." But let us read the history of the Mayo brothers. A century ago, a doctor was revered almost the same as a priest. But now we find that they knew very little, took only a short course in medical training, and robbed graves by night to get cadavers. Yet, they held their head high by day, and literally commanded respect.

We have conditioned ourselves to accept excesses in government.

We are stunned into silence by "authority" in uniform, in gown and gavel, and by the ruthless glint in the barrister's eye.

And all of this happens for the benefit of Nature, which scarcely needs any help in running this greenhouse. We are not becoming, as human beings, more compassionate and loving, or more filled with understanding for our fellow man. We are only becoming more docile and faceless, out of compulsion.

Everything possible is employed to grease the sloping path to the slaughterhouse, including theology. Such is the calloused efficiency of those who feel themselves called upon to take charge of the propaganda and literature of conditioning. Modern drama now depicts the mother betraying the son, or the daughter betraying the parent for the meaningless codes of the state. At the turn of the century, this betrayal would have been considered an act so base as to invite the hate of all humanity. Now it is noble!

No matter how well it is welded together, the social entity is no better than its individual parts. The expansion of the individual is, in the long run, for the betterment of the state. A shrinking of the individual has already, in our time, begun to show signs that lead to social chaos.

STATES OF PERCEPTION

I have noticed that all (or most) psychologists or claimants to authority on matters psychic, carefully minimize the difference in states of perception, or else write or speak as though every reader should be compelled to interpret their words in one incontrovertible way.

And all the while, most of the difficulties in the social world are the result of differences in mental states and the complete failure to understand the other fellow's state. Marital incompatibilities, both mental and the mentally inspired physical ones, come as a result of different mental states. Factional conflicts likewise have the same roots, whether they be of religious, political, or ethnic nature.

Let us look at the different states of perception. I am sure that when a person understands the wide range of perception-states and mental-states he will begin to wonder if the human mind will ever be able to discern, among these many states, that singular state that might be called sanity.

States of Perception, in turn, affect states of mind. They are not the same. The former involves qualified means of seeing or perceiving. The latter involves periods of conviction marked by related attitudes. States of Perception are those states that may be produced by sensory imperfections, drugs, chemicals, or other conditions.

Anyone who has gone through the alcoholic experience will know that a few ounces of alcohol will change the world's aspect for the user. That which is perceived, is a new state of perceiving. The new aspect may be so different that it shakes the validity of prior states which we identify with convention and sanity. The drinker may find the new, ensuing state of mind, and not be aware that it is caused by an abrupt change in his perceiving apparatus. States of Perception are generally of short duration, and while they may trigger or reawaken states of mind, they are more factors of coloration than lasting states of conviction.

Subliminal states of consciousness are perceptions of longer duration and of greater intensity, and they have the ability to dominate the entire perspective or perception field. More will be said of them later.

To give a further explanation of this mental vacillation (inaccurate states of perception), let us look through the romantic eyes of younger days, when a particular mood descended upon us at sunset or sunrise. Upon entering a cave. Upon watching lightning. Now, these are outstanding incidents which may have changed our mood, if not our mind, momentarily—and which left strong memories behind. Examining the possible causes of these States of Perception may help us to be more aware of their influence.

The sunrise seems to fill us with awe and vigor, even though our training tells us that we are probably only experiencing a combination of the quiet hush, and slow-changing light and color patterns. It may be that that which occurs is the remembering of a primordial urge to go forth in search of food. Also, dawn usually comes when a person is rested, and when there are no pressing worries on the mind. The mind has rubbed out the worries in the forgetfulness of sleep. So, now the mind and the eye have time to dawdle, as the mind of a child, upon such things that are momentarily "new." We now have a combination of "rememberings" that are not conscious memories. We have a combination of vigor, a carefree mind, and an infantile pleasantness, along with the hypnotically changing panorama of dawn. And even after reading and believing this paragraph, if we walked in the meadow at dawn, we would still feel the awe, and the mystery would momentarily put our philosophic attitude to the test.

Our daily life is a concatenation of changing moods, some diametrically opposite to the predecessor of an hour. We are hypnotized by objects and by other people. Some of the spells are short-lived harmless little excursions into a fragrant flower or a poem. But the concatenation literally becomes a chain and our years are bound in chains that resulted from the hypnosis of a few moments that caused us to make decisions that tied up our direction for decades of our short life. Some of the results of such hypnoses, or attitude compulsions, are marriage (or mating), murder, enlistment in organizations, and the development of habits that cannot be abandoned.

You may say, "Oh yes, we know all about the traps" . . . while uttering the words from the midst of several traps that have been nobly rationalized. But, unless we are constantly conscious of ourselves in each reaction to the environment, we will succumb. And I doubt, in all sincerity, that even a select and dedicated group of men could free themselves completely. They could free themselves to the point of knowing their chains, and being able to resist them in incidents really critical to their spiritual growth. The evidence of this inability is observed in religious monasteries and in very active transcendental movements that either pick out one of the traps and rationalize it into deific status—justifying the trap as divinely imposed (such as marriage), or they carefully avoid identifying something as being a trap, if it helps their business. It is hard to find, in non-sectarian groups, any harmony or even desire to work together, because each is laboring under the rationalization of some trap or other. If we were all laboring under the same trap, then cooperation might be somewhat possible . . . as in a factory. But, the different degrees of addiction become at first, an interminable harping point, and finally—a mood of intolerance.

So let us stop occasionally and think of the simple and yet profound effect of color. We find that colors bring certain moods to us, and we find that they do not—always as individual colors bring the same mood to all people. That which elates one may depress another. We are not only the unconscious victims of color, but of many other mood-impellers.

STATES OF MIND

States of mind are like massive gestalts. Psychologically, they have never been given the proper consideration. Most people are not aware of the existence of a state of mind, other than one similar to their own. When they encounter another state of mind, they may reject it as aberrated or abnormal. Normality is always that which we are, not that which the other fellow is. And because of this lack of understanding, friction and even violence result.

Psychologists try to create a sort of universal state of mind, in regard to conduct and behavior. They have recently gone a step further and imposed "sensitivity sessions" upon some of the students of the country to force a precipitation of tensions, and to bring about a homogeneity of reaction-patterns.

The psychologists and psychiatrists will fail because, again, they do not know all the factors, and specifically because they can, at best, be responsible for creating newer states of mind which shall conceal more deadly resentments than the possessor had before.

Some of us are aware that we have different states of mind. However, most of us are unaware of the many states of mind that exist among different people, nor are we aware of the tremendous role that these states of mind play in religion, politics, and war. Some states of mind are easy to see. For instance, similar states of mind are found in close families and among people of restricted social contact, such as the inmates of monasteries and prisons. Inmates of such institutions or families have several other states of mind, besides the one which is common to all of the other members or inmates.

Let us not confuse the term "state of mind" with mood. The mood is transitory and lacking in conviction, and could be better explained as a state of perception, a clouded glass.

We are lucky if we only have two or three states of mind. We are still more lucky if we know that they are there, within us. A state of mind is invariably a fairly composite thinking pattern, which has as its chief characteristic one of the basic desires of the individual in question. A more dominant state of mind may result from the synthesis of two or more desires, and the synthesis of their corresponding philosophic rationalizations.

It is easier to describe states of mind, and the manner in which they are altered, than it is to define them. We may take the case of two men, Mr. A. and Mr. B., meeting at a bar. Mr. A. uses a perfectly harmless word, penguin. Within a few minutes, and with little or no explanation, Mr. B. has knocked him to the floor. Mr. A. leaves, and within the hour is robbed by Mr. C., and finally, in another hour, Mr. A. may encounter Mr. D. and kill the latter when Mr. D. places his hand in his pocket, thus reminding Mr. A. of the robbery of an hour before.

And yet, three hours before, Mr. A. may have been a benevolent extrovert. An analyst might ascribe the violent action of Mr. B. to paranoid foundations, or might say that Mr. C. was a robber because his mother tried to abort him. Paranoia is not a state of mind, but a singular example of a state of perception in which we can see the difference between the two—state of mind and state of perception. With paranoia as a qualification of perception, or as a manner of looking at incoming impressions through bruised sensitivities, there is no doubt that some of our states of mind will be affected, but not necessarily replaced.

Any creature that has been repeatedly injured becomes paranoid. In Hubbard's *Dianetics,* such repeated injury leaves a mental scar which is called an *engram*. This scar or engram must be reckoned with in all future experiences related in any way to the experience that caused the engram or scar.

If the being were not paranoid, it could be more easily killed or crippled as an individual, and eliminated as a species. Paranoia says to the body—people are going to hurt you as they did before. You must adjust and train your personality to either frighten them, or train yourself to be more aggressive.

States of mind are various massive concept-structures which usually come about over a period of years of evaluation and increasing conviction. However, it is important to remember that they can be brought about very quickly as a result of an extreme physical or mental experience. The case of Mr. A. is given to show roughly how this may happen.

We take Mr. A. and suppose that he was a young ministerial student. He has led a rather sheltered life, but there have been times when he was insulted or in some manner afflicted for his gentle ways. His gentle ways were part of a passive state of mind, and his reactions to a life of mysticism helped form his passive attitude. And he may have also developed an additional, tangential philosophy, which saw God's will in his work—and God's protection.

The man who knocked him to the floor was a Catholic. Mr. B. thought that Mr. A. was poking ridicule at the Catholic nuns by his reference to the penguin, and Mr. B. also thought that he was doing God's will.

The violence suffered by Mr. A. caused an abrupt change of mind. And when the threat of continued violence aids the paranoid element in his thinking, he feels quite justified in taking quick and violent action.

The man subject to an abrupt change of mind-state need not be timid. Strong, brave men have suddenly been reduced to tears, and bullies have suddenly become cowards under brutal treatment, or in an incident of terror. Drugs inflict a similar sort of punishment upon the addict, but the metamorphosis is so subtle and gradual that only after the victim is hopelessly addicted will there be any intense suffering.

It might be said that a traumatic experience or incident of intense suffering are about the only things that will actually bring about a change in the state of mind.

The congestion of the population has brought our attention to a sharper awareness of many different states of mind in different people, and the need to understand such states is also felt. Of course, understanding them is better than trying to alter them before understanding them. And understanding them in ourselves is of greater priority—even in the search to understand others.

I think that the study of states of mind is far more important than the focusing of attention on incidental reactions or behavior patterns. Such a study can come about only by direct experience, and the faculty for having direct experience can come about by particular systems of developing sensitivity, or by a change in the being or nature of the observer that will facilitate his rapport with another mind.

States of mind are not easily supplanted, and a person capable of switching quickly to an alternate or opposite state of mind could well be labeled schizophrenic. We are all schizoid to a degree, but not as obsessed as Dr. Jekyll and Mr. Hyde. We do have such obsessions, and they do change us for a period of time. We can examine the act of sexual intercourse, and note that most people (if not all) have states of mind that vary or change with the act. The person who begins is not the same person who finishes. This has baffled people for ages. It can be blamed on abrupt chemical changes brought on by intense physical activity, (endocrine influence) or it may be an automatic governor, which is part of the human structure to alter the pleasure-drive, once nature has attained its goal . . . so that the potential parent will not endanger his or her health in the pursuit of more pleasure, since nature is interested in the children.

It is because the sex act has such a pronounced ability to change the state of mind, that we find so many violent and bizarre murders connected with sex. Sometimes the partner who acts as a devastating catalyst is resented.

Different ethnic groups have different states of mind, and there is no crime in this difference. The crime lies with the psychologist who thinks that he can banish it by denying it. The Negroes are aware of this wall of difference, and protest (this is the admission of the knowledge of difference) that the Whites do not "think black." And, of course, the standard reply is that the Blacks do not "think white."

It would be laborious, if not impossible, to go into all the factors that trigger conflict between states of mind. Some may be genetic, and some may be acquired. For instance, the mouse has a state of mind quite different from that of the cat. And the cat's is different from that of the dog, unless the cat is a lion. The cat has no respect for the mouse. There is no rapport. The mouse is geared for terror. It is numbed or hypnotized by terror and does not utilize any proper degree of resourcefulness when confronted by the cat. Perhaps, like the Christian martyrs, the mouse is also geared to enjoy his own immolation.

The same occurs with people. Those who have been raised for generations to have a contempt for fear will also have a contempt for those whose chief feature is fear. Or an ethnic group that practices sex control may have difficulty in having rapport with another ethnic group that believes in no sexual restraints.

The effect of these states of mind on political levels is not our concern here. We are concerned with those states of mind which stand like towers of Babel between religious, philosophical, and transcendental minds. We only need to pick up some of the books that are being printed today on psychology, sociology, and theology to witness with amazement the many approaches to a common central point. If Aldous Huxley seemed to test our flexibility in reaching out for new understanding, he could not hold a candle to such artists of confusion as Brown and Roszak. And perhaps this writing will come to many as a hodge-podge of emptiness or a surfeiting of deliberate complexity.

Let us examine the drug-state of mind . . . if it is possible to find rapport with addicts without smoking from their pipe or drinking from their needle. Or let us begin to study religion. We may be attracted to a spiritual teacher who is "hooked" on drugs, and despise the teacher who is addicted to alcohol. We may never know that the alcoholic had as much or more to offer. And what's more, we may wind up with an aura of injected needles instead of a halo.

We can take a step further, and presume that men of the four major paths—the fakir, the yogi, the monk and the philosopher—have divested themselves of all obsessions, such as sex, drugs, or alcohol. And we will still be confounded by their distinct states of mind.

The monk, on a lesser level, is a person who thinks he is fully evolved, spiritually. His conviction marks his state of mind. He eats, works, and sleeps the part of the monk. And he finds peace of mind which he identifies as God's hand.

The fakir works on a lower level than the monk. He feels that he will find spirituality by controlling the body and its sensations. He does not understand the monk. The monk may understand him, but will be unable to get through to him long enough to convince the fakir in regards to the efficacy of a milder form of asceticism.

The yogi occupies a rung above the monk, but the monk does not always understand him. The yogi understands the monk. He sees the monk wrapped in the confusion of sublimated sex, and in autohypnotic techniques which seem to be crude. The monk is begging the answer, rather than seeking it. The raj-yogi is looking for the *true* state of consciousness, and is aware that others only think they have it.

Still more free, and advanced, is the Fourth Way Traveller. This is the sly man, or the philosopher. It is apparent to those on the fourth step that they themselves, while they were on the lower rungs, could not comprehend or tolerate those who were later discovered to be on more advanced steps. And now, viewing those, who, in turn, cannot tolerate them, the Fourth Way Travellers are amazed that sincere, dynamic individuals dedicated to finding the Truth can have so much lack of understanding and rapport.

So that the thing to observe, (for each level) is the level upon which you stand. The pursuit of Truth necessarily involves the understanding of present states of mind, first. Then there follows the automatic shedding of nonsense-components of these states of mind, from which comes an evolution of mental purity, approaching, all the while, that state which is called satori or cosmic consciousness. And by whatever name, we can be sure that it is the only true state of mind.

It follows then that this writing is not intended to be an attempt to change human conduct, except in the individual, by the individual. We must first be aware that we are the victims of our states of mind, not proud possessors of them. And we can be aware of them, (to take a page from Ouspensky) by self-observation.

Self-observation, meditation, or self-remembering generally have an automatic self-correcting result. It is almost as though we were operating on a cybernetic law. The circuit is apt to clear itself, once the trouble is located and admitted.

Strangely enough, this automatic clearing of circuits through the application of energy inward, may be the first realization for the individual of free will. This process involves the slave knowing the degree of his enslavement, and utilizing mechanical processes to put an end to his present state of mechanicalness.

When we embark upon a course of self-change in order to purify our consciousness, the first nice thing that happens to us is that we develop a new compassion for our fellowman, and tolerance for his moody moments. We realize that he, too, is laboring beneath circumstances that are not of his making. And his states of mind have been imposed upon him by his environment and by his colored perception apparatus.

But what is more important and more wonderful is that we realize that we are at last on our way to becoming a vector of Truth. We also learn that there are ways to change our dominant state of mind that do not involve the use of drugs. We find, if we look hard enough, that there are helpers, or teachers. even if such are only books.

There is somehow an urge within each man that wishes for him to be whole. The designer of our computers did not program us to be totally responsive to the hypnoses of nature. It is possible that we are, in fact, programmed to periodically resist any dominant state of mind, so that we will be prevented from destroying ourselves in dissipation—thus destroying nature's most valuable herd in the process. This concept finds more meaning if we observe the innocence and conscience of children. And all of this implies that the designer of the computer had no other choice than to let us get a glimpse of those things which obsess us.

To observe these states of mind we need only to sit quietly and observe the present troubles that we have. It is best done when we are troubled, because then we have a high incentive-impetus to use for energy.

We should also do a little remembering and go back to the days when we were able to think more clearly, when our thinking bore convictions by which we risked our lives and our fortunes. Those convictions may have changed, but it is not appropriate that we look back upon those years as being foolish just because we were young. We must remember the factors which made us think clearly then, if we wish to think clearly today. And it is in this fashion that we must become as a little child.

There can be no successful, scientific study of psychology, nor can there be any promising individual search for Truth without a better understanding of these phases called states of mind. Any attempt at analysis by viewing behavioral causes or environmental factors will only bring us to a knowledge of that which causes the state of mind, and then only if we absolutely know all of the factors. These factors include all things in our transcendental environment, as well as the manifest environment.

Most of us have awakened from a convincing nightmare, or have recovered from a very hypnotic love affair. Some of us have been brutalized into accepting a state of mind common to our fellows, such as is found in armies and penitentiaries. And we have shaken our heads in amazement to think that our mind could be changed so easily. Yes, the psychologists and psychiatrists have experienced this confusion of convictions too, or else the high rate of suicide among them would not exist.

Men have had dreams that have shaken their lives. The augury of dreams or the dreams themselves, have caused battles or wars.

It is also true that transcendental phenomena have a great influence on states of mind. Hypnosis is no myth. And witchcraft has been used successfully against people who did not even know that a spell had been cast. We can only surmise that beings of another dimension, being strategically invisible or superior, may have profound effects upon us. If this is true, then the modern psychologists will have trouble finding compatibility with such evidence, because they have agreed to believe that man is only a body, and that transcendental experiences are really somatic maladies.

So that when St. Paul was struck down on the road to Damascus, and endured for the rest of his life a profoundly altered state of mind, we are told by the psychologists through the lips of Huxley, that Paul did, in reality, fall victim to an epileptic attack . . . possibly. We could go a step further into absurdity, and say that Paul had just returned from visiting the local psychiatrist, the witch of Endor, who had just succeeded in purging him of his violent homicidal syndrome. This explanation would prevent any shame for Christianity, by showing that Paul was cured of his epilepsy and violence by the local witch-craft union.

We like to think we are logical people, living in an orderly manner. However, when we experience a change of state of mind, all of our logic and all of our so-called professional and authoritarian attitudes are of no use to us. We find that we have been changed, and it disturbs us.

Jung found it expedient to examine the *Tibetan Book of the Dead*. For therein is a hint that all that exist are states of mind.

And unless the individual finds some stable manner to keep track of the true self, in the many turbulent and often terrifying nightmares of life, what will happen to us hence, when we can no longer flee back into the living body by simply awakening?

I have only found two systems that I would recommend for studying the mind directly. One is the Gurdjieff-Ouspensky system, and the other is Zen.

SUBLIMINAL STATES OF CONSCIOUSNESS AND THEIR EFFECT UPON DISCERNMENT

In matters of religion, a field where the guiding intuition is of subliminal nature (being intangible and inscrutable), we find that many deciding factors for religious judgement are related to subliminal impressions.

There is a large gap between the thinking of the scientist or materialist, and the pursuer of abstract values. There are always doubts in the minds of these two adversaries about their own individual infallibility. The hardheaded materialist may come to doubt himself, if he falls in love or has a precognitive dream. Or if he witnesses a miracle. (Something not explained in his orderly book of rules on the behavior of matter.) On the other hand, the religious zealot who is convinced that the mundane or sensory world is illusory, or illusory to a great degree, will have his faith shaken (if faith happens to be for him an accepted force), when some person closely related to him becomes seriously ill or dies. He rushes out and calls a doctor or lives to curse the beliefs, or to doubt them seriously . . . if he fails to call the doctor.

A subliminal state of consciousness is a state of awareness that is very strong, and yet very elusive as regards scrutiny or analysis. We may be conscious of something, of a force or strange ability within ourselves, and yet not be able to identify it or describe it.

This state manifests itself to people under the influence of certain drugs, under mental shock, under prolonged mental fatigue, and sometimes in the period between wakefulness and sleep. They are not states of mind, if we are to identify states of mind with self-observation and conviction. It is almost impossible, if not impossible, to study subliminal states, except subjectively. They are worthy of mention here, because they invariably have an ability to affect states of mind and affect them in a drastic manner. A person on the brink of a nervous breakdown, or the physical breakdown that is often labelled as insanity, generally is disturbed by many of these subliminal states of consciousness. A dying person, judging from deathbed testimony, has confusion of some magnitude, as a result of strange consciousness-states.

We may correctly decide that subliminal states of consciousness are more dangerous in being blocks to finding our true self, than those experiences which are labelled "states of mind." This would be determined by the recognition that subliminal states are more difficult to apprehend and examine than are states of mind.

I remember the early hours of anguish that preceded the great spiritual revelation, which is described in the *Three Books of the Absolute*. I saw the entire population of humanity, milling upward as a heap of maggot-men . . . . Their pleasures were pathetic. The whole scene, as viewed from my body-consciousness state, was dismal and so filled with despair that I wrestled with my sanity, or that which we call sanity—that which affixes to the body-processes, a pretence of reasonableness and ultimate reality.

Only when my cherished sanity seemed to evaporate did I realize that this vision was only real as regards the perspective of the minds of men. In relation to the Absolute (which is real Reality), the whole thing was a mental tableau. It was a tableau of physical existence as opposed to ultimate Essence. The tableau is very much alive until we realize that it is mental. When we are about to step out of the mental into pure essence, we still have with us the memories of our evanescent intelligence, and the memories of relatives (particularly those of our children) who are but the sad extensions of our game-playing. We are aware that these children still believe that they are real (meaning that their self-estimate is not questioned by them), and this is momentarily torturous, since in our memory they are tied to us with love.

I might liken the situation to one in which a person might fall in love with a mannequin or robot . . . or with a Galatea. In the game of life, such a Galatea has life breathed into it, but of itself, it is nothing, and that which it imagines itself to be is nothing. The being that loves the Galatea is no better than the statue. When the creator of the Galatea comes into the deeper realization, it sees the Galatea as ego-born fiction. This observer still has not crossed over and seen his corporeal self-belief as fiction. The observer is also a statue, except that part of him that is Absolute. For the Absolute is forever impersonal.

A GENERAL SUMMARY OF BLOCKS

Everything cannot be verbalized. And the emphasis upon the "states" above is an attempt to show that things happen to us, and have a great influence on our essence, and cannot always be described with words. Likewise, there is no book of symptoms that covers all of the blocks that may be generated by these "states," nor is there an instruction-book of any sort that will list the manners of surmounting each block. Without perfected intuition, we are lost.

In examining the systems that have endured in whole or in part down through the ages, we find that nearly all religions recognized that a sort of battle had to be fought to achieve anything that might be identified as spiritual accomplishment. Now, we might say that we are not necessarily interested in religion in this writing, as much as we are in thinking and in understanding the essence of man . . . all of which might well come under the heading of psychology or super-psychology. And, of course, when we say that we are interested in psychology here, we are not referring to the pseudo-science that is peddled by the political hucksters of social amenities.

When we find ourselves dealing with mental processes, we find ourselves dealing with the battleground of mystics and theologians. And while we may wish to pretend that we are philosophers, and above all the weaknesses that might be earmarked as having religious origins—we can only so pretend with facetiousness. We are looking for the tool to probe the abstract plane, and we find that the mind is about the only tool we have for the venture. Next, we are looking for yardsticks to gauge and keep a check on the mind, because we have discovered that the mind is unreliable and elusive. We are in extremely bad shape, in fact, unless we can find some way of monitoring this computer which is continually suffering from emotional interference.

Let us look at the advice given us by the earlier prospectors of this field, and consider the things which they considered to be obstacles to progress or success in mental and spiritual achievement.

We have the seven deadly sins. They could also be called the seven obstacles to understanding. Pride, covetousness, lust, hatred, anger, envy, and sloth. These were published by the church long before the science of psychology was invented. Let us look at some of the mental blocks outlined by psychology, and compare them.

What is procrastination, but another form of sloth? Exhibitionism is another term for pride. There are many trade terms for lust, such as satyriasis and nymphomania. Anger is considered an aberration—the result of incomplete knowledge, or frustration with diverse objectives. Paranoia in some diagnoses as such, may be nothing more than envy and fear. It can be seen that the seven deadly sins can be seven obstacles to clear thinking. But there are more.

The first and chief obstacle to the pursuit of Truth is Nature, and nature. Meaning both the nature of man and external Nature—which is capitalized to distinguish the two. The nature of man is such that it hinders his thinking, since he must spend a good bit of his time thinking about survival in its several forms. By that—meaning his personal survival, family survival, and herd-survival. Under the heading of personal survival we may find his motives for seeking immortality, but his immediate daily survival needs do and must have precedence over post-mortem survival.

So, the appetites are a block or impediment. The exigencies of living are obstacles. And bodily or physical limitations are an obstacle to the quest. We will get tired if nothing else. The body may be in pain and while it is in pain, we will not be able to think. And most men wait until they are in pain before they feel compelled to think about life-after-death. Our glands may not be functioning properly, and all sorts of complexes and confusion may result.

We are pretty much at the mercy of our natural limitations, which can be overcome to only a very small degree at a time. Consequently, the major religions hedgehopped the issue of Nature and concentrated on the mental obstacles. Only the priests and nuns undertook to negate the physical, animal nature implanted in us by Nature. They seemed to bargain the spiritual chances of the laity away for a respite for themselves—during which time they practiced celibacy, poverty, and fasting.

As for mental obstacles, the word that expresses the most adverse force is called "Ego." We define Ego here, not only as egotism, but also as being that composite of voices or urges known as personality, which in the final analysis is always false. Because the Ego is such a significant negative force, we will come back to it later to give it wider examination.

Let us examine a few more things which are obstacles. There is the laziness of the mind which somehow must be tied up with physical incapacity or brain-limitations. There is a fugue, or flight from strain of thinking. Our curiosity will take us occasionally to the threshold of study, but something in the mind sees the work coming and takes the thoughts away in flight and escape. There are fears. There is fear of social rebuff—fear that the neighbors might find out that we are standing on our head or chanting mantras, or fear that they might discover that we have joined a group. There is the fear of hobgoblins. Brave men who have survived the battlefield cannot be dragged into a haunted house. There are fears of incubi or succubi. There are fears of spiritual contamination, and even fears of losing the soul (which we cannot intellectually isolate).

Blind faith is an obstacle that comes in the category of rationalization. We should believe only tentatively. When we build on belief, we build cement around our mobile mental faculties. Or in other words, we stagnate.

Robert S. DeRopp recently wrote, *The Master Game,* a very good book for serious researchers, and for psychologists in the true sense of the word. He lists six catches: the think-talk syndrome; the starry-eyed syndrome; the false-Messiah syndrome; the personal salvation syndrome; the Sunday-go-to-meeting syndrome; and the hunt-the-guru syndrome.

Number one and number six speak of procrastination. Number one differs from number six in that the former may never get anything done but talk. Number six wanders from guru to guru, never stopping long enough to work diligently with any. The second syndrome, the starry-eyed, refers to those who, from a combination of emotionalism and weakness, blindly follow a particular teacher or system. This is an example of blind faith and aptly describes some of its motivation.

The false Messiah syndrome refers to those who have come to believe that they are a teacher or savior, simply because they desire to be a figure of prominence. These sometimes are psychopathic pretzels or oversized egomaniacs.

Which brings us to the business of Ego. There is much confusion with the word "Ego." There is a big difference between the implied meaning of "Ego" when Jung uses it, and when Gurdjieff uses it. The Gurdjieff system teaches that there are many "I's," which, by their multiplicity, split up the energy of men and weaken the power that might be spent upon self-development. The system further indicates that these "I's" should be developed or used in such a manner as to lead to a more coordinated being.

The system of Zen, on the other hand, leans more to the esoteric Christian view of the Ego as being the unhealthy part of the self. This Zen interpretation in contrast to the Gurdjieff system, says that there can be only one "I" for a perfectly functioning person. All of the rest must be discovered to be inferior and unimportant in relation to the ultimate destiny of man.

It is almost amusing to witness the attempts by the mind-mechanics to define the word Ego. I maintain that the Ego is false and has no functional value for the essence of man, anymore than an ingrown toenail would. To me the Ego is the aggregate of many urges whose ultimate value is more negative or harmful than good. The modern psychologists dare not quibble with nature, and are obliged to rationalize for anything that is in that nature—that is manifest.

Let us examine Webster. Under "psychology" we find ego to be the self—"the self, whether considered as an organization or system of mental states, or as the consciousness of the individual's distinction from other selves." The dictionary cannot take up too much space with each definition, and it is difficult to incorporate all that modern psychology does not know in a few lines. However, the first line of the above definition might refer to uncertain mental states, or false states, while the second line refers to the opposite—the final observer that is aware of the other "selves." Some psychologists see that there is an incomplete description of the evident phases of consciousness, or the complex conglomeration of thought-origins and mental reaction . . . and so they coined another word, "Id." From Id, Ego and Libido are supposed to emanate.

As long as the "alienists" continue to operate as public utilities, instead of functioning as scientists looking for the Truth, they will manage to keep doors closed that might allow them to understand the mind. Having denounced most mystics as being psychoneurotic, they will hardly dare to approach the understanding of the mind through any of the formulae approved by mystics.

The three horsemen of dark visage and apocalyptic message for mankind are not pestilence, famine, and death. They are: Authoritative Ignorance, Enforced Conditioning of the Individual, and Enforced Conditioning for the Masses. The first horseman is only ignorant. The last two are mad. They are, respectively, Psychology, Psychoanalysis, and Sociology. And we are the unfortunate horses who support them.

The obstacles of Nature are the most subtle opponents to Truth, and the exigencies of everyday living are the most immediate obstacles. However, the most formidable obstacles are contained in the Ego.

The sad part of this business of seeking for the Truth is the fact that man's greatest enemies in the field are his external fellow man, and his internal schizoid nature. There is no doubt that Zen attracted many great minds, because those minds saw the inescapable dangers of the attempts to categorize and scientize a study before all the data is in. The most that we can do by way of a rational study of the definition of the essence of man before all the data is in (which means too long a wait), is to devise systems of study, or to design new tools with which to evaluate the abstract values of the mind-states. Zen, of course, goes to the heart of the matter. It is one also that works with the negation of untruth, or a retreat from error, rather than a proud, frontal assault on ignorance with such primitive wall-scaling devices as concept-building.

So that, even as the churches have become the enemy of Truth by virtue of a downward chain of attitudes, into rationalization resulting from fatigue, into concept-building or dogma, into ritual as a replacement for interior effort, and finally into a domineering and fear-inspiring mundane authoritativeness—likewise the mind-mechanics have aborted their noble cause. Those brash young men of the adolescent mind-sciences are trying to reach suddenly in a couple of decades, a line of corruption which took several hundred years for the church to accomplish.

So it cannot be advised too many times that we should beware of seeking the Truth through modern psychology. Zen, I consider to be the greatest psychoanalysis, but I use the word "psychoanalysis" only to convey the manner in which Zen functions . . . to the best of my ability. Zen works by negating errors and false structures, with the aim at finding our essence.

LIST OF OBSTACLES

Of External Nature:
    Visible, terrestrial life and planetary relationships.
    Invisible, or dimensions beyond our senses.

Of Internal Nature:
    The appetites.
        Sex
        Security
        Food
        Pleasures other than sex
        Curiosity

    The Fears.
        Fear of dying
        Fear of scorn or social harm
        Fear of mental or spiritual harm

The Blocks.
>   The seven deadly sins
>   The six catches
>   Physical limitations
>   Economic exigencies

Forms of Rationalization:

That we will be able to do the thing better at a later date. Procrastination.

That we will ride the tide of humanity into heaven.

That social services or "good works" have spiritual gain.

That the gods have ears. Salvation through prayers.

That the gods have noses and eyes. Incense and displays.

That positive thinking will make gods of us or lead us to liberation.

That the guru will save us.

That faith will save us.

That spiritual paths may be evaluated by their popularity.

That we can "feel" our way alone. Intuition alone.

That we can do it with our omnipotent reason.

That God, (or Mr. X) will take care of everything. This is a variation of the "Knight on the white horse" rationalization.

That our present belief shall be our final evaluation of Truth.

That everything is hopeless or useless.

SIXTH PAPER

The First Steps

Of course, in order to begin a work we must have an objective. And the objective need not be immediately negated by declaring that we do not know that which we expect to find, when we announce our objective to be the Truth. Such a stated objective actually means that we aim to come to a point of no-ignorance and being. Our objective is to find our definition, whatever the finding entails. Our objective is to find our origin and destiny, if we can do so, but these are secondary to self-definition or the finding out of who is doing the seeking.

There is only one time to start and this is now. And we can expect to battle the urge to procrastinate from now on. The place is right where we are now, not in Tibet or some nebulous material land of magic. The manner of searching is to use the tools at hand until better methods are discovered.

Now all of this above advice involves no great arcane secrets, no magical formulae. It could be used in any research laboratory, or by any man building a shelter. The sad part is,—just that which the simple analogy implies,—that man can begin on any level, with any tools, yet he always hangs back, waiting for the electrifying Messiah or the more propitious setting.

The greatest of journeys is started with a single step. It is that simple. While the feet are making a pilgrimage, the mind is reminded and brought back to the problem at hand. Thus, physical exercises of the hatha yoga type may do little more than promote health, but if they are done in conjunction with meditation, or the repetition of the spiritual objective, then the mind is reminded and it, in turn, will evolve more useful exercises and more sensible spiritual objectives.

For those who think only in terms of their own inadequacy and consequent despair, let us outline the simple steps of beginning that lead to more and more organized systems of climbing and seeking.

To begin with, we have at least our bodies and minds.

We also have available, written works or references on the subject.

We have, if we wish to seek them out, co-workers. And so we can sit alone with the body and meditate or do exercises. Or we can pick up the body and go down to the library and read everything we can find on subjects related to transcendental prospecting. Or we can pick up the body and take it to places where we might meet men who have spent their lives searching for the Truth.

We can look at a successful businessman and look at his competitor who failed. While an occasional failure may be attributed to adverse luck, wherein it was impossible by any sort of planning to prepare for the disasters that wiped out the man who failed, we find generally that the losers applied less energy and less consistent attention to their project. And we are reminded of the simple adage, "If you throw enough mud at the ceiling, some of it will stick."

The same thing applies to a man who may have no competition, a man who might be building a shed in which to live. If his mind wanders, or if he procrastinates, he may begin the foundation but never complete any more of the structure. As the years go by he will observe his unfinished work, and each year come to believe that the task is more impossible or beset by some curse. In the meantime, his neighbor, or many of his neighbors, may have completed the task in a few weeks.

What we are coming to here is that man must develop a system of work, and work with persevering dynamism. And the results are manifest everywhere—he will succeed. So, he must observe the proper manner of working, and the best manner of seeking. And this involves the knowledge that man must become a vector and must employ the laws that expedite success.

Even as we study the man who was unable to finish a shed, we may discover that some of his frustration may have resulted from his having too many irons in the fire. And the same factors are involved in the search.

By this we interpret that man needs to be dynamic, if he wishes proportional results. Piddling at a major task will bring less than minor results. If the search for our identity is not the major task, then it is eventually going to be rationalized more and more to the rear of the attention, until it is finally forgotten.

All men are seekers. However, the degree of energy applied is the difference among them,—and we might add that the amount of honest intelligent study of ways and means also marks the difference. The final page of the last paper lists the general obstacles that a person encounters, once the person tries to wake up and tries to search for the sake of Truth itself.

If we examine our lives and the spiritual lives of people around us, we will begin to see how they were blocked by these obstacles at different stages or levels of work. We may be able to see the other fellow's blocks before we see our own, and if this is so, then it is good to ask ourselves, regardless of the level that we might imagine ourselves to be on—whether or not we too might be incomplete—we might be resting on a step that is still far from the top and one that is itself still a creation of many desires and rationalizations.

Let us take the whole of humanity and take a sort of "Gallup" poll. We will find that the majority of the people are more interested in somatic functions than anything else. Between these body functions they have moments of curiosity and some of them may spend an hour in church on Sunday. This group of people occupies the lower strata of the pyramid-form that is representative of all human action. Gurdjieff speaks of this category or strain as being composed of "man number one," or instinctively motivated man.

The second layer (man number two) may be our habitat for a few years or for a lifetime, but most of us have experienced it.

We weary of the outgoing forces of emotion that identify the emotional approach to religion and graduate from the second level. We eventually come around to doubting the autosuggestion that brought us quiescence. We realize that our mind over-intuited, and this came about by our listening to an emotional zealot who, while being self-hypnotized, in turn, transferred to us his rapture. We also realized that our intuition was not infallibly guided by some soul-faculty or guardian angel.

As Ouspensky so well states it, these first two levels are very deeply asleep. And people on those two levels would not even open this book or one similar to it. So we go on to the third level of the pyramid, or man number three. (These layers do not represent clear-cut division of advancement, as there are many layers within each category-number. Nor do I maintain that this is the only method of categorizing the evolvement of man from ignorance. However, Gurdjieff is one of the few philosophers who was in any way meaningful in his outline of the upward struggle. He does not use the pyramid corollary, but my reference to the pyramid should be easy to understand.)

The third level is that of the intellectual man, the man who employs logic and common sense along with his emotional approach. This man is showing more signs of wakening, but if he is predominately intellectual, he will remain trapped. His trap will consist of excessive attachment to the tool which he proudly labels "reason," and with which he thinks he can solve all problems. This man winds up chasing his own tail . . . or an endless tangent.

We have been operating on the third level in the first five sections of this book, in the hope of stimulating the intuition for those approaching the problem with only logic, and in the hope of applying common-sense analyses to movements that have only an intuitional appeal. It may be said that I have been saying things that would be either told to a sleeping person who had some chance of being awakened by the shock of the words, or else I have been talking to people who have already gone through these three stages—were somewhat awake—and would be stimulated to more effort by knowing that they were not alone in this type of thinking.

Those who are getting ready to graduate from the first three levels are not above conceit, and conceit can be a block in itself. We are now able to look back and see the mote in some other people's eyes, but may still have some big blinders on our own vision. So if any of us think that we can gloat over the discovery of a new cult or ism, which we are sure of for salvation purposes, let us be reminded of the salvationists on the emotional level. The fact that we have erred before means that we may be capable of erring again.

The time is not for resting or gloating at any stage of the game. The history of the most eminent sages is one of men who never stopped working, if for no other reason than to amplify their vector by helping others.

It is only when you are at least partially awake that you are able to do anything . . . except as a robot. And so we ask, how will a person know when he is partially awake? He will begin to realize that he has been a sort of a robot, and still is a robot largely, and he will have the advantage of presently being aware of his robot condition.

It may seem that I have further complicated things by first advising the reader to begin in any manner available, and followed this advice by stating that man is largely incapable of doing anything. This is naturally paradoxical, but both are true. Any waking must be gradual at first. It is understandable to reckon that a man partially awake, or largely in a robot condition, would not be aroused to suddenly do great things or undertake disciplines of a complex nature. Nor would he immediately grasp a concept that was not worded with all the gestalts of his robot nature.

We presume now that we have reached the stage where we are eager to do something about defining ourselves. To feel that we are robots is not to know of our total nature, our total potential to operate as an aware person, or of our essence. It may be better to use the word "sleepwalker" instead of the word "robot," because the latter implies an object without any essence beyond that which is visible. A sleepwalker may awaken some day.

The first questions are, "How do I start?" and "How will I know to trust any advice on the subject?" This means that we are looking for yardsticks and human guides. And, of course, we may realize that we must find some means of checking our own thinking to see if it is impersonal, and not the automatic reactions of a conditioned mind.

And knowing all of these things, together with an awareness of all of the obstacles,—all of this will not get us started. We must, if we are not inspired to a singular method, look to our fellowman for his record of experience on this path.

If we are going to build a shed, it is usually advisable to spend a few hours getting some advice from a carpenter. And so, automatically, we gravitate toward men who have a reputation for being seekers after Truth. The blueprints left behind by Christ and Buddha were both threefold directives. "The Way, The Truth, and the Life," (John 14:6) is given as the means of coming to the Father. We find other directives that fit into and explain the threefold message of Christ. We are told to "seek and ye shall find." "The Truth shall make you free." The Way is the particular path of seeking. The Truth is the objective. The truth is also the practice of honesty. There are naturally many opinions as to the exact meaning of these words, but I believe the "Life" refers to the type of life that is led by a seeker, and to the collective spiritual life of a church or brotherhood of souls. It was in his final order, given to his intimate apostles, in which he repeated, "Feed my lambs, feed my sheep," that he spelled out the "life" of His group.

Let us compare the directives of Christ with those of Buddha. The three ways of Buddha were, the Buddha (the Way of Discernment), the Dharma, (the life of Truth and duty), and the Sangha, or brotherhood.

Next, we go to the teachings of Gurdjieff, and we find that he recommended the Way of self-observation, and the School, and the latter may be synonymous with Sangha. It may be said that Gurdjieff was aimed at truth or greater understanding, by virtue of his strenuous efforts to produce reasonable concepts and techniques.

Now this does not by any means say that we have uncovered the only Way to start identifying ourselves. And the three systems just mentioned are working hypotheses . . . until enough results are obtained to bring us to the point of witnessing such systems as worthy. Again, until we know all things, we remain on the unsure ground of relative knowledge. So in order not to remain forever inert, we must begin with some working hypothesis and work with it until it is no longer endurable, or until it is transcended and replaced by a better working hypothesis.

It is not difficult to accept the Truth as an objective, unless we prefer blind dogmas and fairy tales. It is not hard for us to understand the advantages of a brotherhood, sangha, or school (or the Contractor's Law which will be explained in another section), because man has come to realize that nothing much is accomplished by a solitary individual. However, the other directive, which has reference to Path, brings with it some controversy, since Paths are recommended.

And it is this fact of divergence that makes more literature on the subject necessary. Christ admonished his followers to "seek," but he spent many more words and verses in admonishing them to "believe in" Him. Blind belief is somehow contrary to "seeking and finding." And, again, we must retire in confusion unless we interpret his teachings to have an esoteric and an exoteric meaning, and conclude that the esoteric teachings were not printed, since he was killed for the exoteric teachings. My interpretation of his words allocates the admonition for blind belief to the laity, and is thus an exoteric instruction. Other admonitions, such as "Seek and ye shall find, knock, etc.," were meant for those in a position to do so.

So that many a fundamentalist will contradict my interpretation of that which I claim to be Christ's esoteric intention, but I give this because nearly all men who have received a glimpse of enlightenment, whether it came from worshipping Krishna, Zen contemplation, or a Gurdjieffian system,—all wind up with a sense of harmony with other systems and recognize in Christ's system a roadmap which most Christians fail to see.

In any event, I recommend for those not otherwise addicted, to embark upon a threefold path, without the fear of being accused of being a follower of any particular religion. I would explain the mechanism as a sort of troika, the vehicle being the individual, and the three powers that are pulling the vehicle with proportionate pace are the Truth, the Law of the Contractor (brotherhood), and the Life of Search. And this system involves and includes all of the levels and the evolvement of one working-hypothesis to another.

THE SELF

It is expected of us, if we wish for results, that we will not leave a stone unturned. And this means reading and researching until we come to a movement that we wish to join or to a teacher that we need. And in order to properly evaluate these different systems, we must have some type of yardstick. We must find a method to measure movements before we dive into them too deeply.

And in attempting to be objective, we should not begin the search with presuppositions or refuse to listen to a concept because it promises nothing to us, or promises something not to our liking. Vanity is the worst enemy of the seeker. As we have seen in previous pages, man seems unable to contemplate a God that does not have human form, human concepts of justice, plus a human appreciation for our corporal love. We spend so much of our time gloating over our superiority over animals that we neglect to see our own meaninglessness. Yet, we never stop to think that a genuine comparison of ourselves to the Beings that rule our lives may prove to us that there is a more remote relationship to those Beings than there is to the animals that we use.

The conviction,—that all animals were placed here by a humanly sympathetic Creator, so that we could kill for sport, make trinkets of horns and other body parts, make clothing from others, and use some for food,— is no more valid than to entertain the conviction that we are merely planetary food (Gurdjieffian suggestion), or that our protoplasm or ectoplasm is our chief value, and not any undefined soul.

From the very beginning of our search we should realize our insignificance, as regards our present, unproven state. We should take note of the diffusion of our attention among our many "I's" or personalities. And when we add to this the knowledge that we are almost hopelessly buried under a heavy pile of conditioning that may go back many generations in regard to genetic influence, we can realize that we have a task, and the task is not to be taken lightly.

But by the same token, the task also becomes easier if we keep these things in mind. Because now we will not make the mistakes we would make if we were unaware of our limitations.

We can now dispense with movements that would not have been recognized before for what they were, but which were followed because they encouraged our harem or blessed our marriage, or helped our business. We will dispense with those movements that bring us peace of mind but not wisdom. We can dispense with movements that appeal to our weaknesses, excuse our laziness, or soothe our weariness.

We begin to see that certain "religions of wisdom" were nothing more than theological systems of politics. Under the vanity of our "wisdom," we accepted the religion that seemed to answer all our questions, or to be more precise, we accepted the religion that promised everything but proved nothing.

Of course, the Ego intrudes in many still more subtle forms. And we find ourselves clinging to the hope that we are going to take our personality with us beyond the shadow of the grave. Another turn that we take is to try to give all our weight to a concept that will require more time than we can afford. In other words, we know in advance that some movements require endless practice and rubrics that are primarily designed to keep us busy rather than develop us.

We must be on the alert for impediments that are physical as well as mental. We must begin by setting our house in order, and this means the dwelling in which we live, as well as our physical body. This business of putting the domestic situation in order need not be an enormous undertaking, nor a drive for wealth. It simply means that a person cannot think, study, or carry on work with a group or school, if he is beset by domestic irritations and interruptions. And even after the household has been placed in order, as long as we live we must still work to keep it in order, or run the risk of traumatic interruptions.

So that in this work as in a business or any complex type of work, the degree of our success in the big things depends on how many little things we can manage simultaneously.

The process of setting the body in order may be very complex, and it too will demand consistent attention. Sometimes yoga exercises help, but the practitioner must watch for signs of sleepiness and the type of peacefulness that drowns out any desire for exertion.

PROGRESSION

In this section, I would like to deal with the need for cooperation in things spiritual, regardless of the path chosen. There are many paths and we must be patient with honest men, even if we honestly believe that they are on the wrong path. Words and their interpretations form a high barricade between seekers, but even more formidable is the barricade of Babel that results from different intuitional interpretations of concepts dealing with abstract matters and subjective thinking.

And this brings us to that which this book proposes. We can enter the brotherhood of the ignorant and climb and study together. If this makes for us a wide field in which to work, we can find friendship and comfort at least in the large number of people found there, and we can still find the select few among them that can work more dynamically with us by virtue of their nearness to our level.

Not all of those who read this will be instantaneously satisfied with this system, but all should see the need for helping one another in the ultimate friendship. And so, there is much to be done. There are books to be read. There are experiments which many would like to try. There are scientific compilations, cataloguings and syntheses that some of us might feel compelled to build. There are eminent wise men whom we shall certainly desire to meet, even if they are on the other side of the globe. We must amass knowledge and then whittle it down and simplify it.

Can the mystic relax his ego a fraction and take a lesson from the man with the hoe? Too many of us, having heard that we are a part of God, decide that we alone are possessed of divine intuition, and consequently, we sever valuable contacts . . . a valuable contact possibly meaning some kindly soul capable of tapping our inflated ego-balloon if nothing more. Some of us who have been freed from tobacco or alcohol think that we have crashed through the perimeter of outer space.

Like the pioneer, we are pioneers. Possibly, eternally so. Like the pioneer, we must work collectively, yet with a guarantee of our individuality . . . at least as long as we desire to cling to our individuality. The solitary mystic still needs an ashram. Yet, unless his solitude is respected, we must, like the pioneer, invent and employ commerce between fellow-seekers.

We come now to the concept of an Ashram. To differentiate somewhat between "Ashram" and "monastery", the word Ashram is used to define a system that would overcome the inadequacy of monastic life, and the insufficiency of having just random contacts in our field, whether that field be philosophy or religion.

The monastery has a closed door, the Ashram, an open one. The monastery suppresses individuality and doubt, the Ashram must not. While the monastery keeps wisdom in, it also keeps much more wisdom from getting in.

We need a spot on earth upon which to meet. A homing ground, but not an intellectual prison. A library and a clubhouse of philosophers. A place with quiet rooms where a person can be alone if he desires. A clearinghouse of contacts, or a place where a cardfile might be kept with names of those who wish to be contacted. In philosophical research, access to personal contacts is more valuable than any card-index of an esoteric library.

Many people of philosophic drive feel no compulsion to mingle with anyone except their colleagues. But these people must be unaware of future growth possibilities for themselves, and they must be unaware that they must help others in order to grow themselves. This is the Law of the Ladder, which will be discussed later. The Ashram brings the different levels together that are needed for the growth of each member.

It is understandable that if an Ashram were formed by people without teachers or leadership, if that Ashram were managed in a spirit of tolerance and brotherhood, it would either form the matrix that would attract worthwhile teachers, or it would generate and develop them from the membership.

This atmosphere of brotherhood does not mean one of quiet patience alone, but of consideration for the members who might require degrees of anonymity, if they are to function with the Ashram and still carry on professional lives not connected with the Ashram. Some of this protection may be automatic, if the members concentrate their work with people on or near their own level. Procedure for insuring protection can be found and made the custom of the Ashram, and then it should be accepted by all members.

We get into quite a question when we ask for a solution to the problem of protecting members from the human traits of other members. To begin with, we must have a trustworthy person in charge of the gate, in charge of screening those who are admitted to the physical premises. All newcomers should be endorsed by some active member who will vouch for them.

If there are various groups meeting apart from the general gathering, these groups must be protected in the same manner from those admitted to the premises.

There must be this focal point. But there must also be a focus of time for meeting. Not all participants need to be at the point which is the Ashram. The Ashram, where intensity of effort breathes life into the focal point, cannot survive by itself. There must be a much wider association that includes those who are unable to stay in one place, and for those who have not yet decided to enter the work with fuller participation. However, many organizational problems will take care of themsleves if the initial nucleus of founders take sensible precautions in their early planning.

I feel that a sincere seeker who possessed the determination to find the Truth at any cost, suffering, or expenditure of energy, would most certainly find the Truth, if he followed the threefold path with an open mind. The part of that path which is hardest to realize is that dealing with the brotherhood or school. We can begin work upon ourselves with a spiritual discipline, and we can follow the truth in all our words and deeds, but it is quite another thing to be part of a brotherhood. This latter requires compatibility with a group of people and requires that we find a group that is doing something worthwhile.

But, given that group, we begin to experience results according to a process which I will call Progression. This means that evidence of a little of something may automatically imply that more may evolve from a little. If we find some men's minds capable of great knowledge, there must be some capable of greater knowledge. The concept of Progression is related to the Law of the Pyramid. Each layer of capacity in the Pyramid automatically presupposes the existence of another higher layer or level.

The suppression of Galileo, if successful, might have retarded the present explorations of space, but that suppression would never have removed the potentiality of man for spatial exploration. His suppressors presumed even to read the mind of God and imagined that God, as well as Nature, planned for man to remain helpless and ignorant. Progression is opposed by fanaticism and futility.

If there is a recognized pyramid of knowledge, and of effort, then it is possible to have a larger pyramid. If the mind of man is changing and growing in complexity to meet the complexities of its problems, it is possible that that mind might change and adjust to meet the infinite scope of spiritual problems. Only the foolish ones are suppressors. They should know better, because today's suppressors were yesterday's oppressed.

FRIENDSHIP AND THE SEARCH

There generally comes a time for all searchers when an individual becomes significant to us, if we believe him to be capable of being a guide or consultant. There are many little gossamer threads of understanding and decision points in which a good friend with experience would be of value.

In most instances, and on most levels of spiritual work, the friendship of a guide is not of great importance . . . we can listen to words often while not accepting the speaker. However, there are levels in which the personal guide is in a position to do us some damage, if he is not motivated by compassion at least.

We must be fairly sure of those teachers who would have us dedicate our lives to them. We realize that we must experience a change of being, if we are to experience or feel the Absolute in all things. And as we approach this challenge, near the end of our quest, we are eager to be helped by someone who is able to push us over the goal. Our error lies in our haste to leap and embrace any teacher who promises to annihilate our ego. The "ego" that he may annihilate may be the only awareness that we have.

The teacher must show some reason why it is advisable to lose your ego, must try to explain the process, and somehow manifest the loyalty of a friend that would survive any test. We must reject the "Master" who commands us to believe without explanation.

It is true that much of our mind is filled with garbage that clings like barnacles to a stem of make-believe, vanity, or ego. But we need not subsidize a marble palace in Kashmir just to remove those barnacles. The barnacles will start to fall away with meditation, self-analysis, and the encouragement of analysis and criticism from our friends.

In being alert for various tricks, it is good to know a little of the history of trickery, and of the history of movements that are based on the use of "gimmicks." Rom Landau mentions that some Tibetan priests have a trick by which they can hypnotize at a distance. By using such mechanisms, they manage to hold the laity. The African sorcerer has a trick by which he can hypnotize the minds of his victims, to bring their bodies to the point of suffering or death. These tricks do not enhance the soul of the victim.

Some of us will say, "Nothing ventured, nothing gained." But it is also unwise to put everything upon the single roll of the dice, if there is a less risky manner of bringing about the same result. It has been argued that certain wonderful secrets are available to men who may be trusted. In order to prove that trust, the applicant must be made subservient to a point where he will not be strong enough to betray the master. And we wonder why the master should need to fear betrayal. This demanding pose is often encountered in the persons of those who pretend to be able to initiate us into magical rites and powers.

I have the highest respect for Zen as a system, but I cannot convey that same respect to all who claim to be Zen teachers or masters. I have written evidence that one Zen student, a lady, slashed her wrists. Another lady admitted that she was driven to the point of insanity, but still she never reached Satori. She came to the conclusion that her teacher was a sadist of some peculiar type. She studied under him for over twenty years. The lady who slashed her wrists also became an alcoholic. Is all this necessary for spiritual development and the identification of the Self?

The Zen master is a very mysterious character. The mysteriousness is necessary, he tells us. A hypnotist finds that an atmosphere of uncertainty and mystery expedites the hypnotic processes. Hypnotism may have therapeutic value, and in such a case the end might justify the means, if therapy alone resulted. In which case the subject would at least know that therapy was the reason for being hypnotized, and would possibly know the hypnotist long enough to trust him.

We come now to a very important conclusion. *There is no religion greater than human friendship.* Now this conclusion should not be quoted out of text. It does not mean that people are greater than truth. It does not mean that we should worship humanity or individuals. In fact, I strongly oppose getting the idea of love and friendship mixed in deciding the attitude of the student toward the teacher, especially if the student cannot discriminate between physical love and platonic devotion.

Nor does the above mean that we should reject a particular religion, if it interferes with friendship. That which is meant is quite the opposite, in that a religion should not be found acceptable if it holds that human friendship as a principle should be cast aside. Strangely enough, this demand, if made, has to emanate from the mouth of another human, not a divine spirit. It has been a long time since man has received any messages from burning bushes or voices in the sky. So that to our knowledge, our whole spiritual education and help must come from other humans or their books.

We need to trust any man whom we accept as a teacher, because he holds in trust our hopes for salvation or enlightenment, as well as our sanity which, until we make the final jump, is the only true communication with our essence or absolute being.

SEVENTH PAPER

Discernment

Some of the preceding papers have been critical of the lack of orderliness in the outstanding sects and movements. Now this does not mean that I wish to be destructively iconoclastic alone, or that I intend to build a better icon. If I have a system, it is simply a system by which Truth is reached by the continual analysis (not breakage) of various transcendental poses, and by a constant vigil over the many factors within the self. I make this statement because it worked for me, and in my lifetime. The system, is not new, nor mine alone. I only hope to clarify things a bit.

If the Truth is within us, and we do not see it, it can only be that we see through the glass darkly,—at this stage of the game.

This book has been in the writing-process, for about ten years. This time, while it should have given me ample time and opportunity to rewrite and rewrite again, was also spent in studying ways in which to express that which few people ever try to express, once they have reached the experience.

Consequently, I chose to ignore grammatical symmetry, and worked more in fear of not saying enough to describe an abstract goal.

We come at this point to the business of the paradox. Which may have been explained before. However, to point at myself for a moment, you will find that I attack many movements for their lack of common sense. It must follow then, that there must be a way,— using a little more common sense,— to outline a sort of summary of what this book is about. Of course, the ultimate paradox lies in the knowledge by me, or the intuition of mine, that there is not any common sense method of describing that which I presume to be the discovery which might be labelled cosmic consciousness.

However, until such time as when we are wired to this wheel no longer, we must make out the best we can with words. And pray for the proper intuition to speak the best ones, and pray that the reader has an intuition of rapport.

I would like to list the five following premises as a summary to the previous papers:

1. That the majority of the isms that serve as religious and philosophical guidelines for humanity are permeated by inconsistencies, and that in these isms many of the so-called facts are illusions or half-truths, and that most of man's beliefs are the products of fear and wishful thinking rather than an unbiased search for Truth.

2. That the human mind is not infallible in its processes, and that it suffers errors as a result of many factors, such as the conflicting clamor of appetites, intellectual limitation, fatigue, inadequate intuition, inadequate reasoning (or inadequate common sense faculties), difficulties of the dual mind in the solving of abstract or absolute considerations, and the lack of individual control over states of mind.

3. That there is a system of overcoming these errors, and the system is practical, and Truth may be realized.

4. That the rate of realization is directly proportional to the amount of and quality of energy and attention applied to the quest.

5. That illusions are the great obstacles to Truth, and that the dispelling of these illusions involves the improvement of the inadequate factors mentioned in premise 2, and better control over them. This process involves an ever-conscious schooling of the mind, so that it will be an instrument of Truth.

In reference to the message of premise 3 and 4, I have come to the following conclusions:

A. That there is a path to Truth. From ignorance to relative knowledge. From relative knowledge to an awareness of the limitation of such knowledge. And finally we pass from that which we recognize as loosely associated intelligence to a reality of Being.

B. That this Path is not visible even by many who profess to be on a "Path." It is true that there are many paths, and it is also true that most people on those paths are quite convinced that theirs is the only real path. It is not until after they become broad enough to see that their path is at most only equal to many other paths, that they take another step and look about for a path that will lead them still further.

C. That the graduation from the field of many paths to a more selective path among the decreasing choices of paths (as the searcher retreats from incomplete or lesser paths), is a phase of entering the final Path.

D. That the Path does not require years of lesson-taking, and it is not bought with money. By the same token, we should not expect it to be brought to us on a gold server. Money spent should be so used as to hold a particular group together.

E. That if we applied the same amount of energy that is wasted in any of the material pursuits, we would see spiritual results. And as in any material venture, the results of transcendental efforts are also proportional to the efficient interrelation of workers and brothers, whether it be in a study-group, or in some act resulting from mutual convictions.

We go back to premise 2 and add the following notes. A lot can be said about techniques that are relative to our thinking processes, or that help in understanding ourselves. This is a partial list:

1. Progressive elimination of concepts and concept-building by eliminating those not as consistent within themselves, not as inclusive, and those whose scope does not bridge the range of unexplained phenomena as well as some other system of thinking does.
2. Self-observation.
3. Self-remembering. (Looking at our past.)
4. The respectful doubt.
5. Application of the paradox.
6. Development of the Intuition.
7. Retaining the identity of the Real Observer in various states of mind.

I do not wish to give the impression that I am about to embark upon a course that will employ premises with pursuant conclusions, and thus produce facts from a jumble of words. I only wish to list some observations in an orderly manner. If the reader is looking for syllogistic proof, he can quit reading now. If psychology is in its infancy, transcendentalism, its parent, also has its share of confusion. And the application of logic to trancendentalism will, in most cases, increase that confusion.

A lifetime accumulates for us experiences, and the hope that a new slant, and the description of such, will, if nothing else, bring a new type of enquiring mind into the search. The slant is not all new, either. Many of the suggestions found here will be found elsewhere, but not always in this combination.

We come now to laws. Down through the ages, mystics and scientists regarded the finding of laws to be the equivalent of finding milestones of progress. The discovery of natural laws has had a profound effect upon theological convictions. And the observation of laws of nature has caused some theologians to claim them as proof that a central, or singular intelligence was running the universe. The notice of the same laws has caused materialists to proclaim that the universe is running itself.

For an example we refer to the Law of Equilibrium. Everything seems to be in balance. At the same time, everything is changing. The planets are not bumping into one another, but the whole universe is either decaying or growing. So that the Law of Equilibrium is conditional to the Law of Change. And all of this operates in pre-established, particular degrees.

These degrees are gauged by the environment of each entity, over which that entity has no control. We might liken it to the cohesiveness of the water in the ocean. There is a built-in equilibrium system in the sea levels. Water is supposed to flow toward its lowest point, yet we know that the water is humped up in the middle of the ocean to conform to the shape of the earth. The ocean is not flat across, in other words. Supposedly, the centrifugal forces balance with gravity, and the continents are neither flooded, nor is the water flung out into space.

Yet there is something that is not built into this earth-system, such as allowances for catalytical results of other celestial bodies, when those bodies come too close. Thus, when the moon and the earth are in a certain relationship, we have the tides. That cohesiveness-quality diminishes, and a part of the shore is flooded.

The same discrepancy occurs within the human body. There is an equilibrium among the cells of the body, but each cell is dying and being replaced. There is an equilibrium between the bodies or persons of humans, but these same bodies are being replaced. We notice that the stars are floating in what seems to be an eternal pattern, but we have learned that they too, are either changing or dying. Each in its own environment is subject to laws controlling its environment but such laws do not effect the environment which is a degree or more above.

Recent observations in ecology have demonstrated that man can upset the equilibrium of the balanced aquaria of lower forms of life. Perhaps thousands of years of organic growth and soil-balance may be destroyed when the farmer plows in the cold winter, freezing out the grubs, and altering perhaps the whole ferment of life that differentiates soil from clay. At any rate, the grub is certainly deprived of his equilibrium in his dimension. Man can seine the seas empty of fish, and possibly create in a test tube the proteins that have been lost by the forfeiture of our natural food-source. And by the same token, we are expendable. But man is somewhat inhibited from depleting the human population, either by the killing of an individual or the slaughter of an army.

So that equilibrium is a changing thing, and is subject to the eternal paradoxes brought about by incomplete human knowledge of our final resting place, and the final resting place of all things, including the planets and suns. Equilibrium is a changing thing, because the equilibrium that existed among animals and plant life in the days of the dinosaurs is not the same as that which exists today.

And so it is with things spiritual. There is a Law of Equilibrium here too. It is called Karma, the Law of Retribution, or Divine Law. It is viewed as being punitive, while in fact it is only regulatory.

The Law of Equilibrium, or Karma, says, in effect, that a being may kill its inferiors, but not its equals or its superiors. It may offend its inferiors, but not its peers or its superiors. So that we suffer no great consequence if we kill off spirochetes or mice, but we rarely get away with killing another human. I am aware that most Indians define Karma as being a chain of responsibility that ties men to animals in their temporal destiny, and this Indian definition leads me to use the word "equilibrium." Many Christians prefer to use the word Karma because of their abhorrence of the word sin or any word that might imply personal guilt. But they still do not agree with the Indian that man is held responsible for every ant on his path.

It is good to note, that if we follow this neo-karmic line of thinking,—(that of non-responsibility for lesser beings), there is no reason for us to presume that creatures superior to ourselves are restricted to our laws or our concepts of generosity. Different moral and ethical standards may be found in different environments and dimensions. This has been perceived by some transcendentalists, who have taken advantage of the knowledge by first claiming themselves to be superior, and secondly claiming themselves to be above the karmic laws of this environment.

We can see, however, that if entities of a superior degree are not held to our laws, it is rather vain to presume that they operate on our code of justice. We may be either the goodies in their garden, or the grubs.

Man cannot help looking desperately for changelessness,— immortality. It is evident to us that all of nature is a dying process, from the virus to the constellations. The urge to live is as meaningless as the fear of death. We do not really know the reasons for either life or death. It is a fair guess, however, that we are able to point upward, and note that there is a higher degree, using the concept of Progression. We feel like microbes dying on the face of the earth in order to promote something for the well-being of this planet, but we must not hurry to deify the planet. It too, is dying, waxing or waning.

A few of the laws:

The Law of Equilibrium.

The Law of Change. (This negates anything as being constant, outside of the absolute state.)

The Law of Proportional Returns.

The Law of Extra-Proportional Returns.

The Law of Relativity.

The Law of Paradoxical Immanence in All Things Relative.

The Law of Complexity.

The Law of Love.

The Law of Faith.

The Law of the Ladder.

The Law of the Vector.

These are by no means inexorable laws, which, once broken, will damn us to the world of the crustaceans. It is not a complete list, nor would a study of their interrelation give us the final key to the ultimate cause or the final end. The application of them, or the observance of them, will help us understand things not previously understood. They may also save us a few sore spots which are normally incurred by banging our heads against walls that do not move.

In the process of setting up a system of work for achieving Truth or appreciating Truth, these laws have a very important place . . . There are laws which we find expressed in occult works, and I think that they are all worthy of notice if they were not invented to impress the reader. Gurdjieff speaks of the Law of Three and the Law of Seven. There is a certain periodicity and reoccurrence that pervades the physical world, but I consider it tangential at this time to study all of the material laws.

Let us run through some of the Laws and apply them to the Work. The Law of Proportional Returns is another way of saying that you will get that which you give. This is the reversal of retribution. We offer instead of taking, and we find that it works.

The law also implies that we can cause a ripple . . . that we can accomplish something and still not upset the equilibrium of our dimension. We may say that effort is rewarded, as long as it works within the laws of our dimension. We take another step, and say that helping others inspires help. Helping also develops in us a more acceptable attitude, but these social advantages do not measure a law. The mechanism of a law implies an automatic result.

Historically, the Christians were the first to utilize this business of giving and to make it a functional part of their philosophy. They gave of themselves to the point of self-immolation. They practically worked the law to death, along with themselves. Another law should be observed concurrently with the Law of Proportional Returns. It is the Law of the Ladder. The ladder is here used as a symbol to show that there should be a selective giving of goods, energy, or spiritual help. The Law of the Ladder simply says that you should not reach below the rung upon which you stand, except to the first rung below you—in order to help people. If you reach down too low, your efforts will be wasted, and you may be hurt. Or crucified.

The Law of the Ladder also says that you cannot be helped by anyone too far above you, because you are not prepared to work with that person on the same level at which he is working.

The Law of Love is another law which brought trouble to the early Christians. It was discovered that hate only generates hate. Killing invites killing. Love, on the other hand, invites love. I doubt if there is any advantage for a person who loves someone who would like to kill him. Such a union might bring about a homicidal child that might really kill and love the killing. In fact, Christianity bore such a child . . . it was the monstrous acts of the Inquisition.

It has been said of the Sikhs that for generations they were a peaceful people. I do not have the exact figures as to the years involved, but a guru of an Indian sect who was formerly a Sikh, (he may be a Sikh still), told me that there had been quite a long line of peaceful gurus. The Mohammedan invasions repeatedly afflicted the state of Kashmir which is the Sikh home-ground. Holy men were tortured and slain. Finally one day, one of the gurus rose up and told his people that passivity was a mistake. He advised them to defend themselves, and as a result of his advice, we have a very formidable group of people who find the sword to be the partner of the Granth Sahib, the Sikh bible.

The proper application of the Law of Love should be in the direction of the friends upon the path, meaning those on our rung, and the two adjacent rungs. This love can be expressed as friendship of the most unselfish type. For those too many rungs above us we can only offer respectful silence. For those who cannot see us too well, being less fortunate,—we can only afford compassion. Anything other than compassion may verge on self-deifying egotism.

The Law of Extra-Proportional Returns can be effected only with the cooperation of friends. The Law of Proportional Returns tells us that we can count the number of yards that a gallon of gas will take a truck. It adds, that if we put two gallons in, we can expect only to go twice as far. The Law of Extra-Proportional Returns implies an unexpected increment. To draw an analogy, two factors (human) will accomplish more results together, than will either of the two factors in twice as much time.

This is also known as the Contractor's Law. If this law did not exist, no contractor would hire men. The work would all be done by individuals working alone. It was only when Henry Ford progressed to the assembly line production that he really started making money.

The principle works in somewhat the following manner. One man can build a certain type of house in ninety days. Two men working together will be able to build it in forty-two or forty-three days. And five men, each specializing in a particular trade, may build it in fifteen days, or seventy-five man-days. And with more men, the work will be closer to perfection.

We apply the same principle to spiritual work. Since we are

working with inadequate tools, in the hope of doing something more difficult than building a rocket for the moon, it is a good idea to give some of these laws a practical appraisal. Especially in view of the fact that men,—whom we have recognized as being spiritual authorities,—have found the employment of the Law of Extra-Proportional Returns to be expedient in the same way that it is recommended here. We must work in groups, in other words. You can call them brotherhoods or societies, or you can work in groups without a name.

Gurdjieff called it the school. It is very difficult for a man to work alone. He tends to drift. If he does not drift, he may slip off on a tangent, become hallucinated, self-hypnotized, or plainly obsessed. He needs a mirror to watch for his own possible deviations, and he finds such a mirror in the minds of his colleagues, if nothing else. And when he realizes the value of cooperation, the only sensible thing to do is to form a pattern for cooperation, which pattern should allow for new brothers on the path.

Now the Law of the Ladder has more meaning. We do not visualize a single man upon each rung, reaching down, pulling up the man below. We find that the ladder is "A" shaped, pyramid in form, for one thing. There are less people on the higher rungs than on the lower rungs. We will be lucky if we can find one man who can help us, but we should be working with six or more on the rung below. We also find a new meaning for the brotherhood now. The man above may be pulling up the man below,—but they are pushing him a bit, at the same time.

It is good to read books, hold meetings of sundry types, and even join a cult or two to hear that which they have to say, but there is no substitute for the Ashram or School. Forty years of solitary reading will not do for the individual that which would be accomplished by a two year stay at a genuine Ashram. If this were not true, monasteries would not have endured down through the centuries, and monasteries are not always ideal Ashrams.

We come now to the Law of the Reversed Vector. This is first recognized by the student who has become mature enough to define himself as a student and not a god or perfect being with perfect understanding. In spiritual matters, man must become identified as a vector, or force, if he wishes for results. If this vector is aimed in the wrong direction, his life is wasted. Most people do not even bother to make of themselves a vector, even in positive spiritual drives. They announce their objective before they begin to study, and then later announce that they have reached it.

The Law of the Reversed Vector states that you cannot approach the Truth. You must become (a vector), but you cannot *learn* the absolute Truth. Not knowing the Truth in the beginning, nor even the true path, we still wish to move toward the Truth. We find that there is only one way, and that is to first build of ourselves a very determined person,— a vector. We cut off tangential dissipators of energy and ball up this energy for the work ahead. And then like most of the clergy, we make the mistake of putting years of this precious energy into first one blind direction and then another . . . until we learn that we must reverse the vector.

We must back into the Truth by backing away from untruth. We still may gamble a bit, because we will not know those things which are untrue in every case. We must develop a faculty, consequently, for being more aware of the difference between things true and things untrue. And it will not come suddenly. But we must begin with a simple start, and with faith in Progression. All of us can discern between things ridiculously unlikely and things possible. Later we will take the category of things possible, and search it for those things which are more possible, brushing aside the category of things unlikely. And still later we will begin to realize our reasons for making erroneous choices in the early stages of discernment.

Research or study along transcendental lines cannot parallel material or objective scientific research. The laws of physics, as we can see, hold some good, or hold inspiration for psychic research. But when we reach the point that we feel that we must become, rather than learn,—then many things operating as physical laws must be looked at in a new light. We are still relative creatures, in a relative world, trying to find that which may be an absolute value. And those who find it, call it the Absolute. But this word has about as much meaning as the mathematical term "infinity." One divided by zero. In a way it is useless to use the term until we know that which we are discussing. And when we know that which the Absolute is, we may feel that it is useless to discuss it or use the term.

Being relative creatures, we must use words. They are still the language that makes the ladder possible. Words are the cursed cause of nearly all confusion and lack of understanding, but also the means of considerable rapport on abstract ideas not communicable with telepathy.

When we reach the stage at which we decide to become, we have to launch this reverse-vector, and only after it has cleared the last heavy interference from any obstacles listed in the Fifth Paper. And as we launch it, we find ourselves receding away from the relative world and its laws to a point where we find things in a paradoxical state of flux, rather than answering to laws of physics.

Here is not here, and it is not there. Time does not exist apart from space, and yet time is eternal.

We now come to the Law of Paradoxical Immanence for All Things Relative. Very early in the search we get a hint of this. We find at first observations, that the visible world is in a relative state. We identify an interdependence among all things and their definitions. Everything is, for instance relative to the ability for measuring by the eye of the beholder.

We notice a mental dependency upon relationship or association. We cannot think without association, and this form of identification with ourselves, is expressed in the words "Law of Relativity" (which has nothing to do with Einstein). Paradoxically, we are related to all things, even to our hallucinations, illusions and intangible emotions. We are related, but we cannot ever clearly think, until we come to a process of disassociation from the endless tangle of identification. Buddha hinted of this process when he advised, as a third step, that we "think of nothing."

There is another instance of relativity. We find that the cycles of the electrons are similar to the circling orbits of the planets around their stars. We find that the single reproductive cell may be a microcosm of the relatively huge human being or elephant. We find that the size (mass) may be affected by speed.

Then we go a step further and notice that things may often be, or appear to be, the opposite of that which they were originally.

We discover what appears to be an immanent paradox in all of our findings and postulates. This tends to confuse and deter most minds from coming to a positive stand on many matters. And this may be a good thing. Too often the critical mind poses as being infallible in its concept-building.

The paradox, while disquieting, is often for the thinker, the first real hint that there is a transience about the observable, physical world that will always elude his enquiries. There are several paradoxes in physics which have to do with the curvature of space and the nature of time.

The paradox only exists in the relative phases of analysis, or in the observation of laws with this relative viewpoint,—and this includes spiritual laws. The student must keep the application of these laws within the dimension in which they were intended and in which they are operative.

For instance, we may observe the Law of Love. And conclude that love has a power over hate. Then perhaps the student, a bit bravely, or stupidly, launches out to conquer some space with love . . . and finds that he comes under increasing attack. And in another compartment of space, he observes that another human being is conquering quite a bit of space or people with hate. So that, for a while, he thinks that the opposite of the Law of Love may also hold true, or thinks that the Law of Love is spurious, or is mere pollyanna.

In the first place, if the student abided by the Law of Love, he would not have played politics with it, nor tried to change people. And secondly, he would have known that the Law of Love has definite limitations in the natural world. It cannot clash with other laws, and least of all, with the "Law of the Jungle." All of the love in the world will not avert the carnivorous functioning of nature.

The Law of Inertia is likewise paradoxical. The definition of the Law of Inertia reads that things tend to remain inert, or in status quo. Things actually tend to change, to drift into inactivity, and to burst forth into life, as well. Some theorize that the universe is dying, and others theorize that the universe is ever expanding. And still others theorize, with equal reasoning that the entire universe sprang forth from a black hole of inactivity. We witness the death of a planet or a man, or we note the disintegration of an atom, and say that everything tends to die. However, we witness that throughout nature, the process of dying is simultaneous with the process of birth.

And there is an innate essence that goads all forms of life against the inert tendency. Of course there may be some argument as to whether this force is innate or external to the organism. Sometimes it is apparently internal (as the procreative urge), and while it seems to work from within us, it has no long range benefit for us as an individual organism. And thus we may be slow to own an urge that seems to be using us for the benefit of others or other purposes.

This force manifests itself upon us in the form of curiosity and desire. We do not plan to have desire or curiosity. Consequently, while seeming to be motivated from within, we are moved by "implants."

Some parents, such as certain spiders, and caterpillars, are eaten by their mates or by their young. Actually, all parents are, to a degree, eaten by their young. But when we witness the mating instincts of this spider, we must assume that such instincts are powerful indeed, to prompt it to copulate when it must almost immediately die when the act is performed. The same situation applies to the salmon, which literally tear their bodies to pieces to find a remote sanctuary for their eggs.

Unless these urges are exerted upon the salmon, spider, caterpillar and the man, from outside (meaning a possible directive force in his environment not necessarily visible and not yet properly subjected to scrutiny),—they would try to prolong their lives rather than submit to momentary pleasure.

It is reasonable to presume that all forms of life (and even matter) are similarly inspired, or forced.

The Law of Faith is another law that has its limitations. Faith will not move mountains, possibly because of other laws. Too many people believe that the mountain will remain at rest, and not be moved by faith. This is counter-faith. The Law of Faith does have to do with the changing of the apparent status of matter by means of human belief. It has been recognized by some occultists as being the actual method of the creation of the physical universe.

We might say that the limitations spoken of above, concerning the capacity of faith to affect material objects, are dependent upon the mind-quantum factor. This presumes that there is a quantum called faith, which though evidently immeasurable except by result, would signify certain units of faith-power per mind-unit (per person). The size of the miracle would depend upon the intensity of the belief of those minds. Healers are found to be most effective in multitudes, and less effective among people from their home town.

Since the Law of Faith is generally applied for ostentation, and applied to physical bodies, much of its value is overlooked. Some quiet theologians indicate that our very post-mortem existence hinges upon the creation-through-faith of lands to come, by combined faith-acts of all men, or a majority of them.

The Law of Complexity may well be called the Law of Life, since life is found only in very complex structures. Some thinkers take another brash step and announce that life is in fact nothing but complexity. Cybernetics indicates that complexity may be related to responses which might be identified with life.

The Law of Complexity, in application to the Work, has a particular meaning. While the complexity of molecular structures forms a life-matrix, it cannot be denied that such structures are highly unstable. So that protoplasm is forever dying and being replaced.

We also note that any transcendental movement that has allowed itself to become complex, and to sprout all sorts of ramifications is in the same jeopardy as protoplasm. It tends to die.

And the avoidance of this complexity makes the work of members in a brotherhood even more difficult and complex. They must be vigilant for symptoms of any tendency toward becoming a vegetating institution, and must at all times follow the path of simplification rather than that of elaboration and dogmatism.

MILK FROM THORNS

It may be said that the Absolute is a state or essence from which all untruths have been subtracted, leaving behind a region of pure fact. Such a statement as "pure fact" would, of a necessity, mean non-relative fact,—a state undefinable, because all facts, if described, or states, immediately are qualified with colors not intrinsic to the fact-state itself.

I have tried to describe the effects of this coloration upon the mind of man, so that we can expect to suffer its removal. The most treacherous coloring agent for all fact-finding is the self with its emotions and voices. By the self is here meant, not the final, absolute self, but the apparent self,—the self which we accept as "us."

As we run the gamut of many religions, cults or teachers, we discover, (only later), that they were acceptable in the first place because they flattered our self. Rarely are they accepted because of their logical symmetry. And rarely do we try to protect them with logical implementation or common sense, but choose to confound our critics with such protests as divine visitation or intuitional guidance.

If our intuition is not perfected, this maneuver will only serve to bury us deeper. We are only setting up a smoke screen to prevent further questioning. This paper is not designed to muckrake religions that are sincere, nor to bring despair to people who are sincere, but whose capacity will not allow them to probe into clearer waters. I doubt if anyone will experience too great a feeling of despair, because those who cling too tightly to blind belief have a perception apparatus that blinks shut at the mere approach of the next step. They have an automatic control-valve.

I must admit that I have depicted man as being little more than a helpless fish out of water. Gurdjieff depicts man as being asleep, functioning in graded stages of sleep-walking. Van der Leeuw sees man as being the figure in the cave, chained to his ignorance, and beguiled by shadows.

If all this is true, we are at a terrible disadvantage, to say the least. So much so that most men sense this from the beginning, and decide not to try to find reality. Like a drowning man, who is beginning to relax and find peace in giving up the struggle, we weigh the effort that is needed to keep ourselves awake long enough to solve the problem.

A true seeker is a very unique person. Outwardly he will not appear to be different from anyone else. His uniqueness comes from the particular game that he plays. He allows himself to become addicted, or to become a vector,—once the idea of being a vector makes sense to him. He is like an eccentric deep sea diver who has experienced the rapture of the deep. He needs no motive to live, except to live to continue the pursuit that seems to hold the most promise.

The enlightened man has nothing to live for (by most people's standards), and yet he continues to live. Everyone else seems to have something to live for, but they are always ultimately disappointed. The seeker gradually grows indifferent to the objects of his appetites, continues to move, even though those objects are the only motivation for other people.

And with this thought we come to the business of taking advantage from a negative situation, or taking milk from thorns. It has been said previously that the man who begins the search, changes as he goes down (or up) the path. The man who arrives is not the same man who started out.

Many a person has entered a religious life in order to get rich, or to set up a foundation to avoid taxes. Others have gone into occultism with the idea of getting power. Some have entered monasteries because they had homosexual inclinations. Yet many who so began became fascinated by the study of the Truth, and lived to observe the untruthfulness of their initial motives, and also lived to make progress on the path.

These errors are not to be laid at the feet of mankind, but largely at the feet of nature. I have proposed that nature is both waxing and waning. And that in order to prevent all of the visible universe from collapsing into a void of inertness, there are certain "implants" or revitalizing factors that charge the ever-collapsing fountain of protoplasm and planets alike. These implants may be a dynamic catalyst that is not only present in the genes of the chromosomes, but in every atom-nucleus as well.

And I noted that they stir us in the form of curiosity and desire. This power-source is like controlled atomic energy. It is as relentless as death. Why not tap it?

Some of us do. Some of us allow our curiosity to study curiosity. We go along for the ride. Gurdjieff studied the behavior patterns by doing the opposite of expected behavior, so that he could observe the results and possibly be freed by those observations.

It is evident that the purpose of curiosity is to move the being or person from his immediate environment in search of food and a sexual mate. The curiosity-urge thus promotes a healthy species because without it the mating would occur within a sibling circle with consequent degeneration of the species.

When man began to consciously focus his curiosity upon something besides food and sex, the era of science began. And, of course, it looked as though man was on his way to becoming a free agent, or an agent in charge of his environment, at least. But nature managed to move back in, at almost every effort which he made to liberate himself. At this point, we do not need to enumerate the means by which nature brought this about. We can look at the list of obstacles in the Fifth Paper.

Only the relentless study of curiosity itself will give us its meaning, and point to us the worth of applying that curiosity to self-definition, rather than to the creation of mountains of scientific definitions, relative only to the functioning of bodies.

The observation of sex will show that animals build up energy to a point where they are of an age and ability for reproduction. Then they are either allowed to grow weaker because their purpose is attained, or else the process of reproduction triggers a weakening process. We have heard of the death-gene, and it may be that such exists, and if it exists, it must find its cause before or beyond the individual's life-experience.

For centuries mystics have looked upon sex with a seemingly unfavorable eye, and some pledged themselves to a life of celibacy. They did this because some of them thought that sex was an entrapment. But some went a step further, and tried to use sex, or the inhibited sexual energy to build for themselves and of themselves,—a new mental mansion.

The inhibition of the appetites, for a period of time, is conducive to the development of the intuition. Sex, being the appetite with the strongest influence, must be proportionately inhibited.

A variation of this idea is found in a yoga-science devoted to raising the *kundalini*. The illumination of the chakras is supposedly effected in this manner. In the Western world, Percival came up with his book, *Thinking and Destiny,* the keynote of which claims that man is able to raise and transmute his seed-atom and thus bring about immortality.

These concepts should not be called absurd until we know the complete line of thinking. I do not believe that they (the concepts) were created out of whole cloth. I do believe that we certainly will attain a new perspective if the usual sex-flow, or expected sex-flow, is inhibited, or rechannelled. Mystics must have found that celibacy was amenable to the search, or they would have given up after a hundred years or more of the experiment.

Since the sex-act has a definite impact upon the mind, inasmuch as it is able to alter states of mind, or to bring about deceptive states of mind, it is worthwhile to assume that the inhibition or control of the sex-act will somehow inhibit or control a state of mind that is not conducive to our search. I do not presume to identify the complex mechanics of this tool, or lever.

In other words, the sex-instinct that has been implanted, may be used to promote other than its manifest purpose. We can even speculate that the Intelligence that designed this scene (the creation), planned it so that some shrewd and determined beings might find their maker, if they discovered and followed some labyrinth leading from illusion into the sunlight, and thus discover the Truth subtly woven into the fabric of the living-dying drama.

In dwelling on the topic of sublimation, we are talking about the easily understood process of invention. The wonders of invention are brought about by using things in new combinations and in ways, that to all appearances are contrary to the original design.

Out of the horned, paradoxical world of philosophy, and out of the thorny, relative world of pretensive beauty, we must surely draw some studies of worth. Only through the word Satori, will we know of Satori. We may experience it, but each of us will never know but that it was an experience unique unto each one's self, unless someone makes the effort to talk about it.

Like the fakir who stands upon his head to gain new circulation for inverted lobes in need of blood, so the mystic must stand occasionally upon his intellectual head, and look at things from different angles.

Relative words are supposedly used in the form of koans to bring about a wordless state of being. Prolonged observation of sense, leads to an attitude or conviction that it is nonsense. It follows, especially with the koan, that a prolonged observation of nonsense may bring us to a conviction of sense.

We like to think that a system that brings peace of mind is one that has the answers. But we know that peace of mind is mental lassitude, and to be really awake, it may be necessary to find an irritation to galvanize the mind from its "tendency toward inertia."

We like to think that scholarly study will keep us awake, and we rejoice that we have developed an interest that keeps us awake, as we absorb concept after concept. But after a while we discover that study is just the rolling up of a huge ball of yarn of relative world-observations, that can go on forever and never bring us closer to the understanding of the mind.

We come to the conclusion that the finite mind *will never* pierce the infinite. Nor will a cast iron ball soar into the sky by itself. However, the vehicle can change. The mind can become, at least for a short time, less finite, and the balloon can be made of cloth instead of cast iron.

When a sewer is plugged, it can be opened sometimes by forcing water through from the opposite direction. When the human nervous system becomes fouled, we use shock-treatments . . . a sort of clearing of the circuits by changing the current direction or the voltage. These same "reversal" techniques aid in the clarification of the mind in relation to reality,—meaning final reality.

There are two schools of thought about the advantages to be gained by harnessing those which are generally accepted as negative or energy-spending emotions. In dealing with emotions, we find society aware of the danger that results from emotions, and lately we find society trying to rechannel that energy. It is far better if the individual finds a way to identify his violent emotions, and shunt their energy by observation and analysis.

In the child, the mind is not self-conscious enough, so we find children being slapped when their anger reaches a certain point. One school of thought indicates that the "voice" or "particle-self" that boils with anger or hate, should not cause the host to be slapped, suppressed or eliminated. Ouspensky talks of the strengthening of these voices, rather than their elimination. By observing them, we find new faculties, which can be very useful if properly directed.

The other school of thought, which is party to most theologies, holds such voices to be evil, and holds that they should be purged from the system.

We might say that the observation of hate should not be strengthened for us to learn to hate haters, but rather to be unshackled from the whole impulse, and to hold that the impulse is utterly absurd and energy-consuming. Once this energy is loosened, we find more time and vigor to pursue that which takes so much time and effort.

We come now to systems that give credence to the concept of cosmic consciousness, and we will undertake to observe them, looking for a chance to learn, if possible, the mechanism by which such an experience can be brought about.

One of the most lucid books written on the subject is the *Conquest of Illusion,* by J. J. Van der Leeuw. Most authors claim that it is useless to try to talk about Nirvana, Satori, or Cosmic Consciousness, or to try to verbalize phases or findings relative to such.

It is just as foolish not to talk about it. I personally have encountered a few pseudo-mystics, or pseudo-masters who sold their wares under the impudence that showing their proof, or attempting to demonstrate the end-result of their teachings was impossible. They chose to quote a line that is heard in relation to Zen teachings about one who has reached Satori,—"He who talks does not know, and he who knows, does not talk." Armed with this bit of incomplete truth, they manage to get by with a lot of quackery by parrying any pertinent question with the above quotation, and the sly wisdom of silence.

It is true that most people who have reached any such realization are generally reluctant to talk to those who are not close enough to their "rung of the ladder" to understand. It is more a matter of not wishing to waste one's energy, or of avoiding the giving of an impression that might cause bad reactions. After a person has left some listeners with the impression that, as a speaker, he is a sly huckster, or a lunatic,—he will be slow in speaking of his discovery before all levels of minds. I remember recently the aftermath of a meeting with a group of ladies. They remarked, after I left, that I sounded like a communist. This did not result from their exposure to any arcane secrets, but to the simple exhortation to look within themselves for the Truth.

It is good to take a note from this. I did not check out the capacity of the members beforehand. I was invited to speak by a well-meaning lady, and succeeded not one iota in being of any help for them. None of them were prepared to hear anything with which they did not already agree.

To get back to Van der Leeuw, we find that book describes the possibility of an Absolute state. This is a powerful book in that it pioneers the attempt to explain at least, Satori, or Cosmic Consciousness from a viewpoint of common sense. "The mystery of life is not a problem to be solved, it is a reality to be experienced."

This book, however, does not tell you precisely how to reach cosmic consciousness. Because of individual, personal factors, no book can furnish a complete, guaranteed roadmap. The author is very good in listing other authors such as Ouspensky and Plotinus who seemed to know about the subject. Van der Leeuw is also very good in his diagrammatic explanation of the relation of restricted or relative consciousness to absolute consciousness.

We come now to Ouspensky, and his book, *The Fourth Way*. This book as well as *In Search of the Miraculous* is written as a result of his association with Gurdjieff, and is an effort to convey the teachings of Gurdjieff about the liberation of the mind from illusion.

Gurdjieff, via Ouspensky, does go a step further than Van der Leeuw. He comes right down to the individual and shows each of us how we can start to eliminate self-delusion from ourselves. In practical language, Ouspensky gives us techniques for emancipating ourselves from the cave of shadows. And we feel that many of these techniques were used in monasteries for decades before the time of Gurdjieff, but no one ever bothered before to explain them in laymen's terms.

Another author, Rolfe Alexander, has come up with a variation of the Ouspensky system. Mr. Alexander leads the reader to believe that his system will enable the student to control the physical environment. There is a frontspiece in the book, showing the author in the act of dissipating some clouds by concentration. That little picture ordinarily would discourage quite a few from reading the book, if such readers were interested in finding the Absolute. And especially if such readers have an inkling that the physical, relative world is not the object of conquest. No true possessor of Cosmic Consciousness would ever try to change anything but his own erratic view of the world-picture.

And yet, I found the book by Rolfe Alexander (the name of the book I do not have) to be of some value, in that he gives specific exercises for "expanding the consciousness." Alexander brings into use the lever of hypnosis. I have never encountered this means in any other system which purported to lead man to the Absolute.

Naturally, I have not tried his system, and so my comment on its success must be limited. I have explored several systems which told of levers or techniques for shattering the illusion. His is one of them. Having worked with hypnosis, I realize that man is hypnotized nearly all of the time, and there is no better way to demonstrate man's sleepwalking condition than with hypnosis. It may be fair to presume also, that, by using the technique of reversal of negative influences,—it is possible to awaken man by using hypnosis to direct the subject toward being a reverse-vector.

The point to consider about autohypnosis is the qualification we must place on any state of mind that is reached by autohypnosis. When you are hypnotized by another person, a state of mind is imposed upon you also, but you remain more in control over it because an external intelligence has control over it. In other words, a person may become very hysterical, as in the case of a young lady who had come to believe that she was being executed. If this condition had been induced by the lady herself, she may not have been able to extricate herself.

The next thought, or course, is,—can we trust anyone that far? What assurances have we of his expertise, his morality, etc.? Or his ability? Or the outcome of such experimentation?

And, or course, the only answer to these questions is that if we desire such a short cut, we must either take our chances with autohypnosis or with a hypnotist with whom we would trust our very mind.

There is another method, but this alternative has its risks and uncertainties as well. But it is better than doing nothing, and it can be an interim-gamble, while you are waiting to find a better teacher. A group of people can form a work-society and use "sensitivity" techniques to open one another's eyes to some of our thinking techniques, and our errors. It is similar to a psychological group-therapy session. Thus, we may free ourselves by accident, from many illusions, using other people as irritants and critics. Such a system would be especially valuable if each person coupled with it, a subsequent hour of meditation, or if the group managed to adopt a skillful mentor.

To summarize the observations on the different methods of enlightenment, we can conclude that man, in his quest to find himself, has intuited the need for a catalyst. The catalyst takes on different forms, because of the uncertainty of any human mind as to the type of catalyst it thinks it needs. The catalyst, if it is a system, bears the stamp of the originator, because it worked for his type of personality, or was accidently discovered by him.

That which occurs by accident is more reliable (for evidence-value) than that which is born out of an intense desire of faith, because the human mind is the matrix from which many weird things are hatched by faith. We must be careful not to conjure up a preconceived idea of the Absolute.

EIGHTH PAPER

Maximum Reversal Technique

THREE STEPS IN USING
THE MAXIMUM REVERSAL TECHNIQUE

As I noted in the last paper, in the diagramming of the mind, there are two important goads implanted within us from the very beginning of our lives. I also talked of finding reality by focusing on the focus of the projector—looking back through our source, and the source of our light.

The two implants, desire and curiosity,—the catalysts used to force us to keep going in life,—can be used by us by the same simple reversal, to keep us going forward in the pursuit of spiritual life. In fact, this is a primary step, and unless this is done first, we will not have the "desire" to concentrate very long on the projector.

We must use that which uses us. *And when we employ curiosity and desire to search for our definition, we are on the path.* Curiosity and desire are a team of sorts. Without curiosity we would never bother to find the intended objects of our desires. We would not forage for food, and our bodies, the vehicles of desire, would perish. And by the same token, without desire, we would not reproduce, nor produce the energy which occultists believe is used by creatures in other dimensions or other world-views.

We take the energy away from the source (of curiosity), which is identified for want of a better term as "Nature." We pay less and less attention to curiosity for food and sensual pleasure-means. We learn not to try to negate curiosity all at once, but employ gradualism,—even as gradualism was employed against us.

We automatically absorb some of the energy from desire, and turn it in the direction of its source, for the study of and penetration of that source. We encourage a desire for Truth, and for all that might expedite our work in that direction. And at the same time we ignore the desire for pleasure, sensuality and diversion. As Buddha advised, we must first learn to think of "one thing." Again, we do not negate pleasure, but reverse it by means of honest analysis.

We do not eliminate the objectives of desire,—those intended by Nature. We still eat, but eat for the sake of nutrition rather than epicurean pleasure. We still function sexually, but in no way that would enslave our thoughts, tie up our time, or chain us to a personality whose unbridled desires will cause frustrations and conflict.

The Reversal Path is the surest path. There are other means that have been used, and the users claim some success, but other systems are either so slow that nothing is achieved in an entire life, or they are so violent that they form a slow suicide. In this latter category we find people who have tried to blast their way into Reality with the harsh use of drugs or alcohol.

Step-two deals with developing the intuition. The reversal of desire and curiosity, affects the natural, relative vehicle,—the relative mind. And while such a process does lead us to the state of Reality, the process may be slow because of the limitations of the relative perspective. An intuition with some degree of infallibility is needed.

And the intuition is automatically developed, but its development can be accelerated by personal techniques. We must get into the habit of taking this energy which is projected into us, and channelling it into exercises that consist of looking into pertinent things for their consistency or lack of it, which exercises are the first steps, or are meditational techniques that lead to becoming. Finally, this habit develops a sense,—an automatic computerization of greater and greater accuracy. This is needed to abridge the massive libraries on transcendental writings, and to quickly scan the many paths or pseudo-paths. And concurrent with the developing of this sense, should be the developing of a system of checking. We must find a way to periodically check our intuition to see if it is straying into hallucination or an egotistical belief in its own infallibility.

The third step involves a conscious effort to retraverse our projected ray. It does not involve the reversal of the projection from the Absolute, because it is impossible to reverse that which IS, or is the final Reality. We can only reverse the forces of Nature, because Nature is part of the relative world-view,—which being relative, automatically possesses negative characteristics. I have used the picture of peering back into the focus of the projector, as the final step of being one with the Absolute. Actually, we go back in one sense, and at the same time we find that we were back there all the time.

Some transcendentalists have described the Absolute or Brahman as having tentacles or rays that touched upon, and were one with, every particle of moving matter in the universe. We can understand this possibility only when we travel back along that particular ray which is aimed at our relative mind. It does no good to describe Brahman, unless we describe the means to witness that which we describe.

Buddha supposedly advised three steps, of which the second step was to think of all things. This seems to be a vague directive, until we are able to project ourselves back into the Manifested Mind. I am quite sure that he did not mean for us to study all relative science and statistics, but rather to see that we are both a mental experience, and a mental inhabitant of the mind-dimension which is the matrix from which all things are launched into (illusory) existence.

Likewise, his third step,—to learn to think of nothing,—does not imply unconsciousness, but implies the acquisition of thinking techniques which will bring the mind to a stop. I think that many students have come to think that Satori or enlightenment is the experience of a reality of nothingness. It might rather be called the experience of everythingness.

As we project ourselves back through the mind-ray, we naturally come to the universal, or Unmanifested Mind-Matrix. Specialized mind is the result of absolute mind-stuff. And here, it is true, we do experience the truth of our own insignificance, or nothingness in relation to values once assumed by the Individual Mind. Thus, we are still observing with traces of the Individual Mind. This viewing with the Unmanifested Mind is often mistaken for Satori. It is, in fact, the "mountain experience" which we often hear described. Often it is quite depressing, depending on how much we remember of our relative selves.

It is only when we completely forget our relative selves that we transcend the Unmanifested Mind, and enter the Absolute. And when we do, it shall only be a glimpse. However, the glimpse will be enough to carry the Individual Mind in unshakable conviction for the rest of its relative sojourn.

MORE ATTEMPTS AT VERBALIZATION

That which follows must be read with some intuition. Seven bundles of relative words have now been passed. Their purpose is to illustrate the treacherousness of words and the instability of the reasoning faculty. The mob looks at everything with two billion eyes. No two people see the observations the same. But they agree to accept things or rules, and suffer the foolishness of such rules, to avoid physical mayhem. And having sunk into the habit of accepting rules and laws, they become the victims of pattern-thinking, or convention. And egotistically, they begin to think that the mob can make things right by simple legislation.

We pass over the sciences, since they are very adequate for measuring a relative dimension, only. We pass over religion with sadness. It is born in the fears of children,—who were inspired to fear by a ruthless, venal, priest-craft. It is at best, motivated by curiosity, and if it served that purpose truly, it would admit that motive and place no limits on the solution of the unknown. We must not neglect to admit our motives, nor should we anticipate that which we expect to find, nor should we rationalize our position at any time along the path.

Let us for a moment, review our motivations, such as curiosity or desire. We can do so without harm to our altered objectives. In fact, the admission will clarify the mist between us and the objective. In other words, we begin life as a justifiable coward, quaking at the observation of the corpses of our friends. We visualize that we too, will become corpses. It may well be that Nature has instilled that fear into the animal-being in order to maintain animal life. If animals had no fear, the herbivores would be quickly eaten, and the result would be the end of all carnivores. Evolution, or the drama of life, would be in retrogression because of the removal of the fear-instinct.

So man, at length, comes to the point where he neither wishes to be digested by other animals, nor by Nature. Nature seems to have the animal programmed to survive long enough to reproduce. In most animals, the fear instinct is neutralized by another instinct when the babies are threatened. This implies that only the new seed is important, not the old individual, nor any individual. The cycle of the moth ends with the laying of the eggs. Some parent-insects are devoured by their offspring, or their female mates.

Likewise, when the animal has passed the peak of reproductive ability, the fear of death wanes. The organism, in its decline and weariness, changes its views and looks apathetically upon death. From this pattern of nature we can learn two things. First, we can decide to use the survival urge placed in our beings by nature, to carry survival-anxieties beyond the natural purpose of those fears. Secondly, we must employ that fear while young. The man who has not begun to seek before senility sets in, will naturally view the search with apathy and rationalization.

The young man who observes the foolishness of man in relation to his function as soil-fertilizer, will turn his back on nature. And he does so at considerable risk. There seems to be an awareness on the part of nature to any force that might try to change the direction or mechanism of any part of nature. There seems to be more evidence for this type of awareness and Nature-control than there is for any supervision by a personal God not associated with nature or earth-progress.

It is possible that we have been taking the wrong meaning from some of our scriptures. The story of the Garden of Eden is an example. We have an account of two unfortunate wretches, punished for wishing to be like "the gods." What happened there? What is the relation between eating, knowing good and evil, and death? Today we see nothing wrong with wanting to be like God. We are puzzled by God's behavior in this story of contradictions. Pious fundamentalists have filled the Bibles with footnotes, attempting to apologize for God, and in so doing have only succeeded in exhibiting egoes whose pretence would make them superior to That for which they apologized.

Do we have a God that plants trees, and makes men out of mud, or is the whole thing allegorical? There are many explanations when we take the interpretations of symbolism, and we can build symbolism until it becomes as unwieldy as the tower of Babel, and as useless. Why do not the theological giants speak more plainly? Is it because they fear that the Lord will hear that they are plotting to get at that tree that stands in the middle of the garden? The story of the tower of Babel is another example. Can we picture to ourselves a God becoming furious because people wasted their time piling up rocks? I am more inclined to believe that nature has a way of confounding those who build an open effort to understand nature. It is more understandable to me, that the tower of Babel represented the scientific beginnings of man, or the early use of symbols to disguise those beginnings, or represented the confusion that automatically resulted from mountains of those symbols.

It is not advisable for us to worry about the symbolism of the Bible, or any other work. We need to know only ourselves to see the conflict between nature and the survival-urge of man. In the writings of philosophers we find many books that bear out the cognizance of learned men of this conflict, and show their intuition that primitive men are beguiled about concepts of a personal God. Frazer goes to great historical lengths to show the evolution of the "corn-god." The intuitions of primitive men were not originally confused with complex rationalizations, such as that which created God in the image of man. They saw God simply as the being that favored the growth of life, and their prayers were for food and existence, not for immortality. They may have had more sense than their civilized progeny. The story of Christ is one of a man who was physically punished for encouraging the pursuit of immortality. He is spoken of as a sacrifice, and yet the writers do not make it clear as to the need for the sacrifice, nor do they say who was the recipient of that sacrifice. I can only conclude that the mechanism of nature, using the fickle emotions of the local mob that denounced him,—was operating automatically if not sentiently against a contrary principle. Not only did Jesus fail to reproduce, but He encouraged others to abandon their families in the pursuit of Truth.

Mystics have decided that desire is the cause of suffering. This is another way of saying that nature implants in the animal an irritation of magnitude so intense that the release from it brings joy or ecstasy, depending upon the degree of suffering. Nature also implants in the body of man and animal a capacity for nervous titillation, or mucous-membrane sensitivity. The implanted curiosity helps to locate the membranes whose titillation will lead to the reproduction of the species. What the average man does not realize, is that the same curiosity,—that may later spur us to look for immortality,—discovers the titillation, and the titillation brings on more irritation. The offspring are a result of that irritation.

Now man's computer occasionally takes the position of observer of this process of the reproducing slave. Yet, for some reason, nature confounds the computer. Frantically, the man tries to block the irritation, inhibit his sex, and focus his attention upon the "Path," or upon anything that might negate sex or other chains. He tries to meditate and he falls asleep. He tries celibacy and fouls the gears of his body, or imagines the joy of the temporary liberation from sex to be indicative that he is on the right path, or that God is smiling at him. The irritation eventually returns. He tries exercises, prayers or pills. He may even turn to alcohol.

By now we have a middle-aged man or woman. Still driven by sex, but now ulcered by anguish, and pickled in some cases by alcohol. He has lost some of his ego, like an old goat about to die. But he manages to still hold on to the egotistical pose that he is a philosopher of sorts, and that he has been able to see some of the nonsense of nature and life, by simply being buffeted and used. He sees time getting shorter, however. He finds his vehicle less elastic and less and less able to cope with the demands of the competitive organic existence. He is still trying to carry a young man's load of emotional involvements. His children are tugging at his emotions, and his mate is testing his mettle. He runs like a rat in the maze to first one voice, and then another . . . until some of his ego breaks down and he lets go of things.

He or she will never let go completely, because until death occurs, we must all work to eat. But our friend breaks down under the pressure of all of the irritations. He runs to the confessional, or to the psychiatrist. He has a nervous breakdown, or enters into shock. And for a few hours or days, he is free. His joy, or peaceful release, becomes a sort of milestone. He loses his taste for alcohol, and for his mate as well. He relegates his children and property to their destiny.

The burden is lifted. The alcoholic thinks that he is cured. He looks at the sky and imagines that God is smiling at him again. He thinks that he sees the pattern of creation because he is no longer fighting nature. The unity that he feels is the intense rapport with nature at work in all its magnitude and marvellous complexity. . . . . in the interdependency of beings. He will tell his friends that he has really found God this time. But we notice a blatant difference in testimony of the many people who have similarly witnessed this release. Their description seems to be altered in proportion to the severity and manner of irritations which preceded the surrender.

We come to the word surrender again, and to the word joy. Surrender may bring joy, but this is no guarantee of a spiritual value nor is it a symptom of Truth. I do not wish to deprecate the mystical experience just described. To be free, in any degree, is desirable. The point I wish to make is that we are not completely aware of the nature of our own essence because of the joyful experience. Joy is still the tool of Nature. The Absolute has neither joy nor sorrow.

Our aim is not to sink back into irritation and despair again. The joy that is followed by anguish cannot be said to be real joy even, for it then becomes the root of anguish. We must always bear in mind that when the load is lifted from the weary beast of burden, the beast experiences that which is known as joy. If the burden is taken away for any long period of time, the beast will instinctively go about looking for another burden, in hopes of experiencing joy again.

This is the difficulty of the mystic. They speak of the dark nights of the soul. Each time that the burden is lifted, it requires that the burden be heavier, and be carried longer the next time, in order to bring about proportional peace or release. So that the patterns of both physical (or sexual) release, and the joy of the mystics, are tied up in the relative world of pain and necessity. It is for this reason that female or feminine male-mystics enter into rapture more quickly with the contemplation of a male God. The ecstasies described by some of the female saints may have been intensities resulting from prolonged sublimation and from pious fetishism.

The mystic is both blessed and pitied. He must go back time after time, wearily bearing his burden for a few moments of relief, until one day he sobers himself, and casts the discipline in question away forever. The fact that the mystic must return from joy to suffering again, indicates that he is lacking in a sound appreciation of his state of mind (and being) at both times or experiences. He does not have the final answer. If he has really found God, he should be happy forever . . . if finding God brings to people the feeling of divine acceptance.

The mystic *is* blessed, however. He should not be condemned even though,—to all human standards,—he is psychotic. He is a pioneer and a heroic casualty. He has dared to stand alone against nature. He has torn from his being the egotistical drives that beget children and enslave mates. He has struggled against the instincts of gregariousness and has ignored the customs and mores of his age. He has compounded his irritations, and so has stimulated his computer. He has gambled everything with the expectation of "nothing for certain," but prefers gambling to the game of desire and reward. He has fasted, sublimated and meditated to sharpen his intuition. He should be able, therefore, to sense the sensible when it is advanced to him.

Thus, if we can catch the mystic at the moment of his exaltation, he may be disillusioned enough to be thrown off his pleasant tangent,—and he may be brought to the door of the Absolute. The mystic must pause, and know, deep in his being, that joy and sorrow are emotional reactions, and are polarities in feeling, in relative experience. He should sense that he must never try to identify the Absolute according to relative values or measurements of appreciation. He calls for joy, and he receives joy. He unconsciously does this, because his nature misses the physical joys.

That man should look for peace, is another thing. But man must realize that man expects a reward sometimes for a particular discipline. The rewarder is man, in all cases. And man as a rewarder, can only give that which he already has.

When a mystic tells you that he has found God, he does not realize his own facetiousness. In the first place, his meditations on the subject of God or gods, will make him aware of the misuse of the word "God" and of the myriad different interpretations of the word that have rendered it meaningless and useless in describing the Real Essence, or the Real Experience. It has been abused to such an extent,—by traffickers in theology,—that it has no sound meaning, relative or absolute. The mystic should also know, from his long and arduous life of mental struggle, that hardly anyone will understand that of which he talks, if he were only to describe his mystical experiences as such. And he is actually doing the field of mysticism a bit of damage if he leaves himself open to the pointed finger of psychiatry because of his inability to get his point across accurately.

When I speak of Nature, I refer to any part of our environment that affects us or controls us, regardless of the nature of such forces or factors. Nature, I believe to be a coordinated pattern of control, or a coordinated pattern of intelligence or laws that bring about such control.

The human keeps bees. When Winter is long, and the human overlord has taken too much honey, he may return a little sugar. The same human is lord over the cattle. He kills the nonproductive steers, and keeps the heifers for breeding. This analogy between the farmer and Nature is strained because we cannot visualize Nature as being used in turn by a higher force unless we are to turn to the concept of Kal. We can understand, however, that bees or cattle might take a reverent attitude toward their human lord, if they came to a clear understanding of his intentions.

Our destiny in Nature is uncertain. This uncertainty causes us to be circumspect in making a final appraisal of our relation to Nature, or of any duty to Nature. It takes no intellectual giant to see the balanced aquarium of life, and humbly take note of our place. We sense that we are under some kind of law. Nature has evidently set up a fantastically complex coordinating and governing system. Man has tried to guess about it. Those who guessed that the tower of Babel was a sign of man's limitations and restrictions, may have to take another guess, now that rockets are piercing the blue. Or it may be that rockets are part of Nature's plan as well. There may be a swarming of the bees for another hive . . . one of these days.

It is idle and foolish to guess that Nature is aware of each of us individually, or that Nature is a computer-operator, aware of each of the two billion units or factors that comprise our computer. The operator alone, would be interested in the answer and results. Yet the computer may well have a mechanism for automatically sifting the sands of humanity.

We need not be concerned with the chemistry of planetary functioning. It matters not if the earth has a spirit. It matters whether or not the human unit has an individual spirit, or whether or not the human can find for itself an extension of its being which is beyond the dominating power of Nature.

We contemplate the possibility of eternal life, and at times, grow weary at the thought of it. Any proof of such endlessness is not likely to come with a feeling of joy, unless there is evidence of a state of being that would patently be adaptable to such endlessness. We may find joy in the assurance that we will not die, but that is not describing the state of being after death. We may have sorrow in the observing of the difference between the state of the finite man and that of the absolute man,—but that sorrow is not hell, nor is it a true characteristic of our state of being in the Absolute.

There is an account of an experience, appended to this Paper. It was written over twenty years ago. The experience described,—had all the symptoms of sorrow and despair, which changed as I progressed in the experience. I tried then to convey the unusual conviction that settled upon me, and do not think that it can ever be said better with any other words, by me.

It happened when I was thirty-two years of age. I had reached a sort of culmination of physical desire and spiritual frustration. My spiritual objectives were still hounded by my intellectual ego. and to compound the foolishness, I was indulging a few other personality-voices. That which I am trying to say here may not be clear enough (about my personal life), but one need not advance into morbidity to describe a dead horse.

I was playing the drama of life with one face, and was looking eagerly to heaven with the other. I came apart at the seams. Very quickly. It was almost as though a chemical catalyst had been dropped into my mind. At the time, I was sure that I was going insane. I should pause here to acknowledge the many psychiatric fingers pointing in my direction . . . at that admission. You may even say that I was preparing for this admission when I attacked psychiatry in my previous writings. Perhaps I was. But, if I have been *there and back,* I should know a little more than the mechanic who has had a more limited confusion of the mental type,—because of his protected vegetable existence. And I should be more reliable than any ink-blot specialist who may have "been there too," but whose professional pose prevents him from admitting it.

I did not do anything rash. I had no reason to. I had no reason to do anything. While the ego is being melted, there is no joy. Sorrow permeated my whole being . . . sorrow for myself and for humanity. The distress became almost unbearable, and it came upon me from the field of my mind, not from emotion. Emotion may have triggered it. Or a brick in the pavement may have caused it, or my emotional experiments may have triggered it. However, once the catalyst started the change of mind, absolutely nothing mattered. I had no attachments beyond myself . . . once I became . . . more deeply.

The initial attachment for myself became the prime source of my sorrow. I met myself face-to-face, and the division shocked me. Everything upon which I looked had a different meaning and aspect from previous comprehension, and was impossible to convey in language. Things in their essence are tangible only to mind-essence, and not tangible to the mind of everyday cognition. Somewhere in the being of man there is an eye that must open. We open it by closing all other eyes or egoes.

Many things might qualify a deliberate attempt to arrive at such an experience. This is where a brotherhood or sangha becomes useful. It is like walking a tightrope in the dark. A friend to guide each step saves many a fall or loss of time. The friend needs to have walked the tightrope himself, before, to know what it is all about.

The term "tightrope" is used to signify the precariousness of the position of the mind which adventures into intangibles. This acrobat must be balanced by intuition and common sense. He must be eager, but his eagerness without some skill may cause much spinning of the wheels. He must keep his attention on the search for Truth for years, and decades, if need be. If he is young, he must look forward to a relentless struggle with no guarantee of immediate success. I remember that when I was twenty years of age, I decided to make this search my life's work. I decided then that I would try to change my being (I thought that it was that simple) within a couple of years. However, I was determined that if it took my entire life, and if at the end of that life I had still failed to pierce the veil,—I would be nevertheless more satisfied than if I had never tried.

I thought that I had a powerful mind in those days. I mistook a healthy body for a dynamic mind. I found myself able to decide on plans and carry them out. I made a few predictions that came true, and I thought that I had a superior computer. It helped a bit, but I was living in a glass house. Now and then emotion would settle on me like a stifling fog, and it would interrupt my meditations or studies. Irritation set in and the respites from it were brief periods of mystical peace or joy. I found yoga to be a wonderful sedative. I thought at the time that I was dialing heaven. Years went by, and with the years, my conceit began to shred away. When I reached thirty years of age, I decided that I had been kidding myself. My intense hunger for Truth was waning. I was not sure of anything except that which I could see in the mirror, and that image was not faring too well at the hands of time. Then came the accident, or the event which is referred to as cosmic consciousness. It is important to remember that this was an accident. I had never met anyone previously who had that type of experience. My previous preconceptions about spiritual awakening were the result of readings of lives of mystics, and their glowing personal accounts. These readings brought me to the expectation that enlightenment was coincidental with overwhelming joy.

The fact that I experienced almost the opposite of that which I expected, convinces me that wish was not a father to the result. In other words, the state spontaneously evolved.

I was on the Pacific coast at the time. I hurriedly left for Cleveland. I had a friend there. I did not wish to go home in my stunned condition. I remained relatively stunned for several weeks. The world was still a very strange place. The people moved about like robots, but gradually they became people again. Then I found a kind of gentle amusement in the apparent foolishness of their aimless scrambling.

I took a job in Alliance, Ohio, and rented a room there. My friend had moved there from Cleveland, and he managed to get me a job with the company that employed him. I do not think that his recommendation of me added any to his prestige with the company. I did not care for the future of the company, and that is not an attitude conducive to social harmony in a research-laboratory. My objective then, was to write a poetic book. The physical world had now become very beautiful to me. It was as if I had died, and had come back to life, to a drama with new meaning. Actually, I was losing contact with the motionless condition imposed on me by my momentarily beoming a part of motionlessness. Motion was once more enchanting. A rose was once more a rose. I came home from work each day and propped myself up in front of a typewriter. I thought that I had a message of joy and beauty for the world.

Then one day I began to write my feelings about the strange experience. Previously I had avoided writing anything down because I felt that there was no use in trying to describe it or account for it. I am still not too sure about the value of efforts to convey it. I used an emotional medium to describe that which ultimately was without emotion,—that which gave way to nothingness. I called this writing, *The Three Books of the Absolute.*

They were written automatically. They were not composed. I just began writing, and my thoughts flowed through the typewriter. I did not realize completely at the time that my experience came under any mystical category, or had any label known to the general public. I read the *Three Books of the Absolute* to my friend, and he was impressed by them. But then he was impressionable, or so I thought.

I filed them away because I did not encounter many people who were interested in the apparently temporary derangement. Between five and ten years later, while working with a psychic-research group in Steubenville, Ohio, a thoughtful lady gave me a book called, *Cosmic Consciousness,* by Bucke. As I read it, I learned for the first time the extent to which it was possible for laymen to experience the same thing that I had. By laymen, I mean, people with no religious affiliation or mystical discipline. The layman, in fact, may be better able to encounter the experiences needed to bring about the grand experience more so than a cloistered monk. And so I became convinced that it was not impossible to communicate the idea to others, if I took enough pains, perhaps.

A writing of this type was planned over ten years ago. I realized that man's thinking apparatus was almost hopelessly programmed to give out rationalization and wishful errors. I realized that man was not only a prisoner of space and time, but also a prisoner cast in an unreal world,—completely out of touch with his unidentifiable brothers. All of humanity are hopeless robots, even though their egoes are as eminent as their skyscrapers. Occasionally and accidentally, a robot puts to his own computer a question and comes up with an answer about himself, which tells him that he is a robot. And, thus he becomes less of a robot.

And so now, I am trying to contact the other robots . . . especially the robots who have progressed to that accidental computerization that makes them aware of their robot state. I have seen this theme portrayed in science fiction stories, and marvelled at the hint of truth in them,—and wondered about the authors of some of those stories. Could they too, be trying to give the robots a hint?

The Three Books of the Absolute

BOOK I

Out of the valley of the river came a wanderer. Peace was in his eye and his soul was wrapped in Nirvana. Peace to the wanderer.

O Eternal Essence, I was that Wanderer. I it was who left the gardens of tranquility that I might labor for Truth.

I sought Thee, O Eternal Essence, in the grottoes and in the tabernacles. I called out thy name to the stone ears of statues. And Thou answered not.

I sought Thee in the voice of nature. I looked for Thee in the footprints of animals, in the habits of birds. I listened for a revelation in the murmuring of waters and in the soft moaning of the forests. I laid my ear against the roaring cataracts and bared my head to the tempests. But Thou answered not.

I have sought Thee, O Eternal Essence, within my self. I have sought Thee in my mind with my mind until I was cursed with confusion. And I saw Thee not.

Then, O Eternal Essence, I sought Thee whence I came. I sought Thee in my womb. As the wild beast flees from the elements into his cavern where his wild dam littered him, so I fled the darkness of my clay. And naught did I find save the turbulence of my imagination. There in chaotic pattern did I find the seeds of all confusion that pretended to be wisdom. Where man was born was also born his gods. Where man was born was also born his demons. And where in glorious pain, man first raised his foetal head, there too in ignominious joy was he devoured.

My eyes are extinguished although I see the earth beneath me. And my ears are destroyed and my mouth speaks no words for my feet carry me through a realm that needs no language. And my mind is silent and humble in its dismay, and all within that House there is not one thought. And within that House is heard the painful tolling of a tiny silver bell, and within that dome is felt the surge of mighty roaring tides that will not be stopped.

For the keeper of the House is gone, and all that remains testifies that he never was. Exploding thunder shakes its walls, and heaven and hell are within its region. For All is within that House, swelling it to burst its comprehension. All joy is here, and all of joy is pain, torturing the House that cannot contain it.

All of joy is tears, and the world will not contain the reaving sorrow of this House. All this House is fire, straining to burst forth until these walls stand no longer.

O lamentation of lamentations, has thy agony no tongue? O sorrower in the spaces of desolation, who shall hear thy anguish, and unless it be heard, how shall the pain be stopped?

I, O Eternal Essence, beseech Thee,—where within Thee have I dissolved myself?

Where are prisoned those who follow love? Where have I left my I-ness, and now having left it, who is it that cries out to Thee? Where is the dirge of sorrow that is all that remains of me? Who feels this pain that burns and consumes, yet is felt not by I-who-am-no-more? Who is it that looks from the windows of my mansion like a strange prowler? Who is it that hears and hears not, that yearns for life and lives not, that seeks out death and dies not . . . . ?

O Ever-Allness, what is Thy pleasure in my sorrow? Thou hast damned me to thoughtlessness, and yet I cannot leave off thinking, and still my thoughts are not words. Thou hast robbed me of my soul and mind, and my body laments for all ages, for my body dies not nor yet walks among men. Thou hast delivered me from my Ego, and what is there that remains? O Ever-Allness, forever insensate, pitiless to entreaty, speechless to my prayers,—weep Thou with me, for I am of Thee ... . . and all that remains of me is Thee.

What is the magnitude of Thy nothingness! O what are the limits of Thy plenitude! . . . . What is the thunder of Thy silence! . . . . . . How quiet are thy cataclysms! Thus shall I sing the praises of myself.

Peace to the wanderer!

BOOK II

Who shall hear of Moses, Gotama, or Amenhotep, if hearing is not? Although Jesus weep, and Socrates drown, who shall hear their anguish if there is not hearing?

Who shall know of love and godliness, of peace and serenity, if knowledge is not?

Who shall not perish in the heavy seas of forgetfulness if knowledge is not . . . . Though his convulsions and agony for life be mountainous,—shall he not perish . . . . ?

Though the worlds scream from their vertiginous orbits, how can they cast themselves up or down while knowing is not . . . . Though the stars roar in anguish at their distances, who shall know of their roaring?

How can the atom know of the sea . . . . How shall the atom know of the universe . . . . ?

How shall the spaces know of their nothingness . . . . How shall nothingness hear the agony of nature that cries out against it . . . . ?

Where, where is where . . . . ? Why, why is why? Where O wise among wise, is When . . . . ? In what drifting sandheaps are its footprints . . . . in what continuum is etched its lightning rate like music etched on ice?

Who, who is who . . . . ? Can the sage, more the fool, say that which is being . . . . and among beings, who are what? Is the spark an entity, or is it merely part of flame, and is flame only illusory heat . . . . or does it live?

Is not man a question asking questions, frustrated by the unanswered, laboring to answer himself . . . . and creating a mountain of questions in the answer . . . . yet who shall know?

Who shall know the circle that has no radius, and who shall know the point that is a line of infinity . . . . ?

Where is maya . . . . If all is maya, who, knowing, sees this illusion? Is not his knowing also maya . . . . ?

In what pitiful hells are the wise. . . . . In what blackest abysses are the oblivious ignorant . . . . ?

How shrill is the hunger of inertia,—how maddening the stupor of extinction that comes from action?

O wise and foolish, look about you in your joys. Where are the joys of yesterday . . . . and being gone, did they ever live? Did you enjoy, or was it another's lips that drained thy cup?

Hear the voice of shadows . . . . Look about you into the invisible memories of the ether. Where are they?

What matters it if the infant starves,—if the angel is raped,— or if the saint burns upon the spit? Are they not gone . . . . is not the sorrow gone? And who shall remember . . . . since knowing is not . . . . Who can hear their anguish?

Where are the beautiful . . . . Where is their beauty washed by the years . . . . where are the years drowned in the ocean of the Unknowing?

Think ye on the folly of light. Does it not perish when the eyes are closed? But the power over us by light is feared by man. He sleeps and dreams of darkness, and wakens, screaming into it . . . . .

Relax ye and die and live the darkness, and enter the impassive pool of the Unknowing . . . .

Who shall extol the memory of man that leaves him often before his life . . . . Who remembers after life? If man forgets his infancy before his manhood is upon him,—what shall he remember hence . . . . shall he remember nothingness? Desist and enter the pool of the Unknowing.

What is time, O mind . . . . ? Is it the number of steps in a day,—the number of thoughts in a step . . . . ? Then of the thoughts in a day, how many years of days would it take to know all that is known, and then how long,—to know the magnitude of the Unknowing . . . . and how many steps will take thee from here to there? Who shall anoint thy limbs?

Though he who forgets more seems greater than he who strived not and died in ignorance . . . . who shall know . . . . who shall know? Mourn ye for the hour when the cloud of the Unknowing passes and the falseness of light dazzles the eye. For the light is a liar unto the Light, and the light is the darkness of the mind. Yet who shall know . . . . ?

I is dead. Death is dead and life has no living . . . . All that remains is All.

I of the cloudier corpus is slain. It is slain that the "I" of the mind might live.

"I" of the mind is slain, for the "I" of the spirit to live.

"I" of the spirit is slain that the spirit may come into its glory.

"I" of the spirit shrinks from the vanity of life. Space is upon it. Space towers above it, silently mocking its absence, and the spirit takes its leave like a thought . . . . like the vapors and like the solitary sound that is heard not . . . .

Eternity wanders through infinity like a blind minnow in an empty ocean whose bounds are limitless . . . . Yet who can see its boundlessness?

Eternity probes itself like a blind idiot for it knows not its immensity, and it roars and rages in its madness because it cannot find its edges. Yet who can hear its roaring . . . . ?

And the candles of time are lit, and their wax congeals in cold spheres . . . . but they burn so long and die so quickly that no man knows if they burn.

Eternity convulses in its pralaya, seeking for definition.

Death agonizes silently for motion . . . . And all that remains is All.
O who shall hear of this anguish, for all that remains is All.

BOOK III

O Dream of Dreams, tell me, where is the dreamer?
O Dream of Dreams of Dreams, tell me, where is the dreamer?
O Dreamer, speak unto me,—in which of these dreams wilt thou be found?
O Dreamer, speak unto me, art thou the dreamer in the Dream, or the dreamer of the Dream?
O Dreamer, answer me,—if thou speakest unto thyself, and hear the sound of thy voice and reply unto it,—are there then two people speaking, or is it but one?
O Dreamer, answer me,—how many people are dreaming thy dream?

O eternal spaces, art thou black or white . . . . Is thy form clothed in light or darkness?
Reply unto me
Who walketh in wakefulness,
Knowing not if wakefulness be but an illusion of wakefulness,
Or if sleep be the door of the Absolute . . . .
Or if sleep be the dreamer awake . . . .

Speak unto me
Not in the ringing of my ears
That know not if such stridency be the dawning of new perception,—
Or the damnation of all that was real.

O world, where are thou, that but a second past, clung to my feet?
Where in space am I caught?
O love, where are thy children,—the friends of my youth?
Who has frozen them in the eternal ice until they stand in transient memory, seeming as statues . . . . ?
Who has placed the halter of time upon their necks, to swing them in the listless abysses of silence . . . . ?
O never-never-forever . . . . why art Thou?

O tender I-ness forgive me . . . . O lovable I-ness forgive me . . . . for my hand has shattered the mirror, and I can see thee not.

O hunger that begets creation, O wistful memory of myself, O transient I-ness, forgive me . . . . for the probing finger has shattered the veil of illusion.

I have shattered the chimera of all Knowing . . . . and all that I know is naught.

Time did I seize in the fingers of my mind, and that which seemed to move as a phantom did I hold in my fingers . . . .

The peoples of the earth did I see, all that had lived or will live, and their thoughts were upon their faces.

Beneath my feet did I seize space, and that which seemed afar was near, and beneath my feet I suppressed the mountains . . . . and yet did the cool oceans rise harmlessly to my nostrils.

And in all this land there was not one sound, for my fingers held all time, and in time are the fields of motion. So that no atom stirred, nor did one audible wave afflict the ether.

For the blood of the Serpent is coagulated, and in its mind all thoughts are one.

And I saw the voices of men . . . . and I saw the beautiful patterns of motion . . . . but the world was as still as death.

And I saw beauty as it liveth . . . . yet no color was upon the eye.

The rose upon the bush was only a pale weed, yet Red and Pink shook the shimmering twilight with their loveliness . . . . and the soft perfume of memory tinted the void with its essence.

I saw the flight of the swallow, rolling across dimension like a silent surf.

And as I looked, I saw the emerald dye of the deep, drawn from the ocean's waves . . . . and even the whiteness melted before the snow upon the mountaintop.

Plain was the picture. Plain was the picture for I had concentrated upon color and motion . . . . and now they were no more.

Strange was the land for I concentrated upon dimension until it waxed and waned, and that which seemed small was as great as that which seemed great.

The nightingale sang in the gloaming . . . . but his beak is now silent . . . . and yet his song liveth forever.

O friend of my childhood, O lovable I-ness, what have I done to my world? For I have turned my eye upon it and delivered it unto chaos!

And now I look upon the looker . . . . Twice I see myself. Twice I see myself, and then I see myself no more.

I see myself as a suppressor of mountainous space and a conqueror of time. Mighty are my sinews, as I stand upon the mountain.

Then I see myself as an infinitesimal man in the infinitude of humanity . . . . caught in the congealed blood of life.

I see this tiny man, happy, living, responding to illusions of color and motion and dimension, and happy in his response, knowing not the illusion of his indulgence in non-existent happiness.

And looking upon the tiny man, I see his joys leave him, for joy is a thing apart.

And looking upon him I see his response leave him because motion is a thing apart.

And seeing these things, my heart burns with love for existence.

Yes, I on the mountain, conqueror of illusion, now weep for the beauty of illusion.

And looking back into the panorama below, I, the mountained man,—I the consciousness absolute, see that the tiny man now no longer liveth . . . . for life is a thing apart.

And since he no longer liveth, he cannot see me as I see him, nor can he see himself as I see him, nor can he ever know of his joys that are things apart . . . . or know of his love which is now a thing apart.

And knowing his love and his longing for the pattern, I on the mountain bewail and sorrow in his loss.

Great is my anguish in his silence, great is my agony in his loss.

And feeling my agony, I on the mountain, know that I am the tiny man in the endless cavalcade.

And soon I see, looking ahead, that all my joys are not, that all my love is not, that all my being is not.

And I see that all Knowing is not. And the eminent I-ness melts into the embraces of oblivion.

It melts into the embraces of oblivion like a charmed lover, fighting the spell and languishing into it.

And now I breathe Space and walk in Emptiness. My soul freezes in the void and my thoughts melt into an indestructible blackness.

My consciousness struggles voiceless to articulate and it screams into the abysses of itself. Yet there is no echo.

All that remains is All.

My spark of life falls through the canyons of the universe, and my soul cannot weep for its loss . . . . for lamentation and sorrow are things apart.

All that remains is All.

The universes pass like a fitful vision.
The darkness and the void are part of the Unknowing . . . .
Death shall exist forever . . . .
Silence is forgotten . . . .
All that remains is All.

About The Author

By Michael Treanor

Richard Rose wrote the <u>Albigen Papers</u> to fulfill his commitment—a commitment he made to the living and to the unborn who, like himself, have already, or will eventually become weary of the "pictureshow," the "dynasty of fear in a playhouse of desire." The book was his last hope for sharing what he had found during his life of search and struggle, all other casts of the net having been fruitless. Few people, in the twenty years between the experience described in the "Three Books of the Absolute" and the writing of the <u>Albigen Papers</u>, were willing to listen to a short, stocky chemist, popcorn vendor, physicist, waiter, contractor inform them of the possibility for each of them to know, beyond any haze of ignorance, what he **IS**, ultimately—take away name, take away body, take away birth, life, and death; take away mind. Fewer, still, were able to accept that the knowing comes, not only from subordinating all other desires to the desire for Truth, but from laboring under the long, painfully slow process of exposing, rooting out, and dropping the many contradictory concepts, binding gestalts, and false self-images that impair perception—the myriad grains of sand in the inner eye that is single. So Rose, in 1971, removed the dust cover from his typewriter and pecked out his message-in-a-bottle, his note to those lost at sea.

The finished work, originally intended as a series of papers, lifesavers, to be sent to those who responded to Rose's ad in an esoteric magazine, was first published in 1973. It is a history of Rose's battle for spiritual understanding and survival, a philosophical autobiography. Every direction that Rose suggests, or warns against in the book, he has either tried himself, or has witnessed the trying of, firsthand. The hypothetical examples he uses are factual cases, divested of names and dates.

When Rose speaks of churches and monasteries, he draws upon his years in the Capuchin seminary at Herman, Pennsylvania. When he speaks of the illusions and entanglements of love and sex, he recalls his attempted suicide over a young love, his seven years as a celibate observer of the mating drama, and his twenty-five years of marriage and family life. When he speaks of the confusion and charlatanism in the various cults, religions, and systems, he opens the files from his foot-slogging, door-knocking, library-raking investigation of every teaching and technique that offered hope for diminishing man's ignorance of his true nature. When he speaks of the mind, he relates observations won in forty years of studying his own mind—in the tone of one who has viewed it from an indefinable vantage, from the point of no-thought, no-memory, no-feeling, no-perception. No mind.

Spiritual history began early for Rose. As a young boy, he had wanted to find God. So, at the age of twelve, he entered St. Fidelis seminary. He believed that to succeed in the search, he must go to those who had dedicated their lives to God, where he would come in contact with people who knew Him. But in 1934, after five years, he realized that the priests, though they may have been devotional men who were well versed in the scriptures and Canon Law, knew no more about God than he did himself; at seventeen he left the seminary and sought Truth elsewhere. He looked into spiritualism and the occult, and he read what books on psychology he could find. He went to college and became a chemist, hoping to intellectually solve the problem he began to call "self-definition"; and he juggled symbols and concepts until he realized that wisdom is vanity. At twenty-one he began his study of yoga, seeking to change his state of being, rather than accumulate knowledge. For seven years he practiced hatha and raja yoga, vegetarianism, and celibacy. And for seven years he languished in bliss, free from life's irritations, convinced he was "dialing heaven."

But at twenty-eight Rose awoke from his serenity. The face he saw in the mirror was aging, hair and teeth were beginning to go. He realized, for all his tranquility, that he still did not know what he was, Essentially, and he feared that he had botched up his life. In mounting despair, he let go his disciplines and entered the mainstream of existence—the pictureshow. But he still read his books, and he meditated. Half of him wanted to give up the spiritual goose chase; the other half clung desperately to the drive. At thirty-two, the contrary forces finally ripped him apart, and the dominoes of his personality, the egoes, the urges, the many aspects of himself began to topple over, one after the other. He experienced death. He was torn from his body and brought to an intuitive mountain peak where he saw the world, the universe, as illusion, a cosmic hypnosis. From there his stark I-ness slipped into oblivion, and then into the ineffable experience yogis call **Sahaja Nirvikalpa Samadhi**—what Zen writings refer to as Enlightenment.

Rose returned from the experience, a state of being he terms the "Absolute," and descended again into the world of illusion and relativity, a world inhabited by sleepwalkers and robots, to discover that he had no means of communicating what he knew. He was unable to convince people that they were not that which they assumed themselves to be, and that the reality of their nature was indeed attainable, however small the eye of the needle, however immense the haystack. He could not speak of the unspeakable, though he sensed, he knew, that he must. For two decades, then, he weathered the gales of unsociable stares and indiscreet pointing of fingers, only to acquiesce in the end, and jot down a few pointers to whom it may concern. And it was while writing the Papers, while "leaving a few tracks," that his voice was finally heard.

People started to show up at his farm near Wheeling, West Virginia, local people at first, people who had heard stories of this peculiarly wise man, this unshakable, determined man. He was asked to give talks at the Theosophical Society in Pittsburgh, then at the University of Pittsburgh, and at Kent State University in Ohio. And from these talks came college students, people who, on LSD, had tasted dimensions other than this arm-pinching "real" one, had opened unconscious, psychic doors, and had begun to wonder about themselves, about death, and about illusion; people who, with or without the hazardous influence of drugs, had delved into the sundry methods of God, or Truth seeking, and were frustrated by the towering, complex babel of systems and religions and sciences and philosophies at odds with each other, at odds with themselves, at odds with intuition and common sense. A group formed, "ignoramuses anonymous" Rose calls it, a small group of individuals who came together to take advantage of the Contractor's Law—the Law of Extra-proportional Returns—and to get help and advice from someone who has "been down the trail," a teacher who is more of a psychic mirror and a catalyst in times of spiritual crises than a figurehead, a dogmatist, or a preacher. Richard Rose has fulfilled his commitment, yet he works on, standing by those who wish to make the same bold commitment.